THE BATTLE-WEARY EXECUTIVE

EXECUTIVE
A BLUEPRINT FOR NEW BEGINNINGS

Lawrence W. Tuller

This publication is designed to provide accurate and
authoritative information in regard to the subject matter
covered. It is sold with the understanding that neither the
author nor the publisher is engaged in rendering legal, accounting,
or other professional service. If legal advice or other expert
assistance is required, the services of a competent
professional person should be sought.

*From a Declaration of Principles jointly adopted by a Committee
of the American Bar Association and a Committee of Publishers.*

Sponsoring editor: Jim Childs
Project editor: Joan A. Hopkins
Production manager: Diane Palmer
Jacket design: Michael S. Finkelman
Compositor: Caliber Design Planning, Inc.
Typeface: 11/13 Century Schoolbook
Printer: Arcata Graphics/Kingsport

Library of Congress Cataloging-in-Publication Data

Tuller, Lawrence W.
    The battle-weary executive : a blueprint for new beginnings /
Lawrence W. Tuller.
        p.   cm.
    Includes bibliographical references.
    ISBN 1-55623-246-2
    1. Career changes. 2. Executives. I. Title.
    HF5384.T85   1990
    650.14′024658—dc20   89–71411
                                                              CIP

Printed in the United States of America

1 2 3 4 5 6 7 8 9 0 K 7 6 5 4 3 2 1 0

*To Ginny O'Connor, who was the light at the end of the tunnel
that showed me the way and opened my heart
to a new beginning.*

PREFACE

"SmithKline to Lay Off 500 Supervisors," "GE to Close Plant Employing 325," "20,000 Lose Jobs at Eastern," "CEO of Stock Exchange Giant Found Guilty of Cheating," "Porhit Accused of Shore Dumping," "Farmers Dump Grain as Millions Starve in Africa," "4,000 Cases of S & L Corruption Pending Trial." Every week such headlines appearing on newsstands across the country characterize the radical changes transforming the corporate world. Giant corporations acquired by other giants close or sell off facilities to retire debt. Traditionally secure businesses lose ground to foreign competitors. Corporate raiders bankrupt once prosperous companies. Moral ethics are replaced by selfish greed. Companies deliberately contaminate our environment. Special interest groups appear unconcerned for the welfare of others. Bankers are caught with their hands in the till.

A frightening philosophical aberration is occurring in corporate offices across the country. Leaders of once paternal, socially responsible financial institutions and corporations that were traditionally dependent on valued employees, loyal customers, and public confidence to sustain profitable growth have abdicated responsibility and moral values for ever increasing power and accumulated wealth. The era of moral commitment has been replaced by one of uncertainty and confusion. Executives in every industry—laid off, forced to retire, or shuffled to different jobs—have become the losers. These battle-weary stalwarts, sacrificed in the race for power, feel betrayed by the very corporations they have supported for years.

Whether on the street or struggling to cope with a dissatisfying job, executives of all ranks experience frustration, confusion, anger, and disenchantment with unfulfilled corporate promises. And they are searching for options—new careers, new jobs, new life-styles—to pick up the pieces and go on with their lives.

The words *corporate* and *corporation* as used in this book are not restricted to large public companies. The designation is catholic and applies to small and mid-sized companies as well as large conglomerates and not-for-profit organizations.

The term *executive* applies to any employee or member of an organization of any size—although in the context of this book it is most relevant to management personnel in larger organizations and owners, partners, or principals of smaller companies.

The book is divided into four segments. The first three chapters identify the source of and reason for anger, fear, self-doubt, and other bad feelings common to the disenchanted executive and propose a workable recovery program as the mechanism to regenerate and rediscover our true selves and regain our sanity. For those executives opting to remain with their existing company, Chapters 4 and 5 offer tools, methods, and suggested standards to cope with these feelings. Chapters 6 through 11 propose new life-styles and careers for those leaving the corporate umbrella, including:

1. Unique techniques for changing jobs to another company.
2. Nonbusiness careers in the professions, government, education, and social services organizations.
3. Starting a management consulting practice.
4. Starting a business from scratch, including a franchise.
5. Buying a going business.
6. Income-producing activities in retirement.

The final chapter offers a way out for private business owners afflicted with the same emotional upheaval as their corporate counterparts.

No proposed solutions to human suffering are infallible. Changes in behavior patterns do not always meet with the approval of family members or bosses. A new life-style sometimes results in as much frustration and unhappiness as the one abandoned. Expected financial recovery might turn to financial disaster. The risk of venturing into untested waters can be enormous. The majority of those who have risked the road to recovery have been successful, but there is always the chance for failure. I do not presume to have universal answers. But the majority of those who have followed this program are living happier, more personally fulfilling lives than before they took the gamble.

The true-life stories from over 75 people who willingly shared their successes and failures with me form the foundation for this book. Some have graciously allowed the use of their real names. Most, however, for personal reasons, prefer to remain anonymous. I have respected their wishes and used either first names or no names to describe their stories. In a few instances, locations and names of companies have been changed or omitted to protect individual privacy, but their stories remain essentially as they were related to me.

Some who have taken the road to recovery have failed, but the majority have succeeded in building new lives based on moral virtues and a new personal code of ethics. Their successes prove that we have the solutions to emotional turmoil and dissatisfied lives within ourselves. Only we can make the changes. Only we, as a group of caring individuals can take a stand, rejuvenate our disrupted culture, and rediscover true loving relationships with each other.

This is a book of hope and joy. By facing the dichotomy of corporate behavior head-on and striving toward moral community, the business man or woman will recognize that there is a better way to live, that life can and does have significant meaning, that happiness can be achieved in concert with production of income, and that anyone can begin living a life of fulfilled dreams, love, and goodwill. Not next year, not tomorrow, but right now!

Lawrence W. Tuller

ACKNOWLEDGMENTS

A debt of profound gratitude goes out to the more than 75 people who were not afraid to share their successes and failures with me. Most wish to remain anonymous for obvious reasons. They all know who they are, however, and know that without the willingness to open their hearts and risk vulnerability, their stories could never be told and this book would not have been written.

A very special and heartfelt appreciation goes to all my friends from St. Croix who have helped me to understand the inherent goodness in people, to experience first-hand their genuine desire to help others pass through the spiritual wasteland, and to recognize how necessary the acceptance of a Higher Power really is to survival. Once again, there are far too many to list. But I would be remiss without thanking those extraordinary friends who led the way: Louisa Holloway, Jean Mahadeo, Bea McArdle, Alida Krind, Jack James, Peter Des Jardins, Susan O'Quinn, Judy White, Joe Johnston, Nini Cohn, Dana Davis, Jenny Sternstein, Virginia Wilder, and of course Ginny.

Dr. Douglas G. Sprague, PhD, noted psychologist, psychotherapist, and career counselor provided invaluable guidance and critique for the technical sections of the manuscript. Without Dr. Sprague's support, the authenticity of psychological interpretations of addictive behavior would be, at best, dubious.

Sharing vulnerability with my St. Croix friends and experiencing a true spiritual awakening, I knew this book had to be written. But it would never have reached the publisher without the courageous encouragement, creative recommendations, and dogged determination of my agent, Michael Snell. He believed that by sharing these experiences, enough people could be helped to make publication worthwhile.

My editor, Jim Childs, has been of enormous assistance in helping to structure the book in readable form. Though the temptation was great to pontificate pious revelations, Jim continually brought me down to earth. Without Jim's guidance, it is doubtful anyone would be reading this book today.

CONTENTS

CHAPTER 1

THE CORPORATE WEB: LIFE AND DEATH IN THE BUSINESS WORLD

"Damn doctors, they're all alike," I bitched to my wife when she picked me up at the doctor's office. "Take your money but don't do anything to help. Doc Bolster said my blood pressure tested too high and I'm 40 pounds overweight; but so what! He still can't find anything to explain this insufferable depression."

A typical middle-aged executive with a multinational American Stock Exchange corporation, I suffered from nightmares, depression, and obsessive eating and drinking. I was almost constantly fighting with someone—my wife, the kids, my friends, and peers and subordinates at work—anyone who expressed an opinion different from mine, about anything. Frustrated and angry with the world, afraid to be alone, and obsessed with controlling people and events, I developed all the symptoms of a breakdown.

When I was younger, the daily combats and hurdles at work were fun and something to look forward to. In middle age, when my possessions included a large house, a company car, and a fat bank account, the 10-hour days as division general manager became an unbearable grind. The best years of my life had been devoted to the company, but now the wasteful meetings, ineffective policies, political infighting, and empty promises created a feeling of futility. I was disenchanted with the entire corporate culture and what it had done to my life. Cheated and betrayed, I was fed up.

But what could I do? Over 20 years of dependence on the corporation had robbed me of self-confidence. Doubting my ability to manage a change, I was afraid to try anything new. I felt sorry for myself. The corporate web was still too secure.

Marjorie also experienced disenchantment with the bureaucratic life style. After 20 years as a public school art teacher; 8 years of night school earning her master's degree in education; and untallied political battles with school boards, state education bureaucrats, and school administrators, Marjorie finally achieved the position of principal in an Ohio secondary school. Now 50, with her doctoral dissertation almost complete, Marjorie began to have second thoughts. Were the uncaring pupils, incompetent school board, and modest salary really worth all the aggravations and sacrifices she had made over the years? What did she have to look forward to except more of the same? Would she ever have time to become the one thing she had always wanted to be—an accomplished artist? The deeper she looked within herself the more she came to realize that to live an entire life without accomplishing the one thing that mattered most was a travesty. But she was trapped. Her teaching profession provided a lucrative retirement program, plenty of time off, and a salary she needed desperately.

Marjorie didn't dare disclose such traitorous thoughts to the school board. What if they fired her? She had no other income and, knowing that the world was full of starving artists, she couldn't bring herself to make a change. Her emotional control continued to disintegrate. Crying spells, fits of depression, angry outbursts for no tangible reason, and an unrelenting fear of an early death forced Marjorie to seek assistance. Meetings with her minister accomplished nothing. Her husband was sympathetic but unhelpful. Friends listened but offered little hope. Finally, distraught, confused, and frustrated she sought solace in a local support group.

Two days after driving off the road in a drunken stupor and nearly killing himself and two passengers, Dale entered an alcohol abuse treatment center. He was a confirmed alcoholic and finally admitted it to himself. But how he had arrived at such a state was a mystery, at least to Dale. A successful certified public accountant (CPA) after 20 years of practice in his own firm, Dale felt the need to do more. He had accomplished everything he had set out to do: earned a CPA certificate; established his own practice, which prospered and grew beyond his wildest dreams; married a lovely woman and raised two children who were now doing very well in college; owned a large house in the Minneapolis suburbs; drove a Lincoln Continental; and had enough money stashed away in investments to provide for retirement whenever he wanted it. But he wasn't happy. He still wanted more.

After selling his CPA practice, Dale took a job as division controller with Honeywell Corporation. In three years his boss was so pleased with Dale's performance that he recommended Dale for a promotion to a larger division as Vice President-Finance. But the corporate office decided someone else could handle the job better and the promotion never occurred. For the first time in his life, Dale was rejected. He didn't know why. He was certainly qualified. He had played the corporate political game to perfection. Nevertheless, he lost the promotion. Dejected, and frustrated with his present position—once again having accomplished everything he wanted to do in this job—Dale grew angry and depressed. His self-confidence was shaken. Repressed feelings of self-doubt and failure combined to shatter his expectations of increased power and prestige. Driven to the brink of despair, he was emotionally devastated. To drown his sorrows, Dale turned to alcohol. Within six months he was a confirmed alcoholic and two months later drove off the road.

I had not met Marjorie and Dale at the time, but looking back it's clear we all had one thing in common: suffering what we felt was a betrayal by our employer. Each of us recognized that life should hold more promise than what we were experiencing in our current vocations, and each of us was disillusioned with what we perceived as dead-end careers. Our lives were empty, yet we couldn't see a way out. We felt trapped.

We each blamed our employers for our failure. We refused to acknowledge that both the reasons for the betrayal and the ultimate cure for our maladies rested within ourselves. It was easier to blame someone else. We were caught in the corporate web of dependence and blinded by our own greed, fears, and false goals. In the end, each of us did find a solution—but not without sacrifice, changes in moral standards, and a complete restructuring of our lives.

In Marjorie's case, with the help of caring and compassionate members of the support group, she worked through her problems, left public education, and opened a small gallery near Philadelphia. Unfortunately, her husband rejected the move and sued for divorce. Today Marjorie has a new life-style, a new career, much less money, no husband, and an entirely new personality. She is happy for the first time in years—perhaps ever.

Dale completed the rehabilitation program. Recognizing the danger of reentering the corporate world, he volunteered his time to help other addicted executives cope with their internal hells. To make ends meet, he also took a part-time job doing bookkeeping and preparing tax returns with a small accounting firm. Helping others, Dale realized for the first time that his life meant something, and he achieved the peace of mind that no amount of money, power, or prestige could ever bring.

Eventually, after several tries at recovery, I also learned to cope with my morose feelings of inadequacy, depression, frustration, and confusion. Recognizing that the corporate life-style was not the only way of life, I began to learn how to deal with my emotions and feelings in a constructive and healthy way. This recovery required a total change in moral values, career objectives, and in the end, a completely new way of living. The corporate web was finally broken as I moved into a new, satisfying life-style controlled by me—not by an impersonal corporate leviathan.

If Marjorie, Dale, and I could win our personal wars, so can others. The starting point, however, must come from the recognition that disenchantment with corporate life is a result of an internal distortion of personal values. It's easy to blame an employer or "the system" for problems. Certainly, many corporations have earned a deserved reputation as destroyers of personal lives and distorters of social values; we'll see how and why this happens later on. But without willing participants, no organization can inflict hardship, pain, and suffering on its members over the long run. Greed, self-aggrandizement, overindulgence, and self-gratification are human traits. Desire for more money and power are self-proclaimed goals. Needing recognition, praise, and prestige are self-imposed objectives. The uncaring, impersonal corporate system would collapse if it weren't supported by an army of willing employees.

Yet the fact remains that in many corporate offices, care and concern for the welfare of individual employees goes unsounded. Caught up in the ever increasing spiral of demands from the investing public for growth in earnings; from the federal government for handouts; from unions for higher wages; from boards of directors for an expanded power base; and from corporate leaders themselves for bigger, better, and longer lasting compensation packages, corporate empires have become breeding grounds for discontented employees.

There is no deliberate attempt on the part of corporations or corporate leaders to hurt people. In most cases, harm is caused when companies are ignorant of employee needs, or bosses are too busy to pay attention to their people, or turmoil in executive ranks causes the welfare of the individual to get lost in the melee of trying to stay afloat. There are even some corporations genuinely trying to pay attention to individuals and put a high priority on their needs and welfare—although these are usually small, private organizations.

But this book is not about corporations. It's about people and what the executive, the manager, or other employees can do to alleviate feelings of discontent and disenchantment with the corporate life-style. It's about steps that can be taken to change a person's own set of values to find a solution to his own dilemma. It's about the need to change moral criteria and standards to form a new foundation for a more prosperous and satisfied society—and in the process changing some of the practices of corporate America currently inflicting pain and suffering on thousands of employees.

Many people don't come to grips with their emotional discontent until after they leave the corporate environment, either by resigning or getting fired. Their choices for a new, satisfying life-style are unlimited—ranging from finding employment with another company to starting a business themselves to retirement. Chapters 6 through 11 explore several available options. Others become cognizant of their disenchantment while still waging war on the corporate battleground. Rather than changing careers or finding new employment, they choose to remain with their existing corporation. In that case, changes can be effected within the framework of this work environment to achieve the same peace of mind. Chapters 4 and 5 deal with steps to take in this arena.

THE CORPORATE SAFE HOUSE

Whether you are currently employed, actively considering a job in another company or other organization, or even examining a completely new career, a major questions is: How can you spot an emotionally safe working environment? In most cases the following characteristics will be evident:

1. Communication both up to the boss and back down again is nearly always verbal rather than written.
2. Internal bickering between peers is minimal with little internal competition to get credit for an event or decision.
3. There is no secrecy between employees and their bosses or between departments. All matters are open for discussion and no one has anything to hide from each other or from the public.
4. The corporation does not waver from its stated mission. If its mission is to design, produce, and sell semiconductors, it doesn't expand by acquiring a magazine publisher or a casino. If its mission is to maximize dividends to shareholders, its leaders don't take on active roles in the federal government.
5. If something goes wrong or a mistake is made, the responsible person acknowledges his error and doesn't pass the buck. This is especially applicable to the CEO and his staff of vice presidents, but also to department managers.
6. Corporate leaders are open and honest with all employees.
7. If problems exist, corporate leadership does not deny their existence.
8. The real goals of the corporation are long-term, not monthly, quarterly, or annual.

If an organization exhibits these characteristics it's probably not too bad a place to work. Emotional problems occurring in this environment usually result from conflicts at home or within the individual psyche and are within the power of the individual to cure. On the other hand, many, if not most, large corporations and other bureaucracies fail in one or more of these criteria. In that event, they contribute heavily toward individual emotional disorder. Before disclosing methods to cope with the corporate system, however, several steps to resolve inner conflicts and value systems must be addressed.

A corporate executive or other employee, psychologically disoriented by corporate philosophies and behavior, and dissatisfied with the life-style mandated by the company, can and should disengage himself from corporate "enslavement." He can obtain peace of mind and achieve financial security, whether remaining with the corporation or seeking a new career elsewhere. The road leads to radical changes in moral criteria affecting value systems, relations with other people, and his total way of life. Personal values and standards establish the environment for corporate dependency to flourish, so it is only through changes in personal ethics that freedom can be achieved.

Before we can determine *what* can be done, however, we need to understand *why* today's corporate executive faces such a severe psychological dilemma and how corporate dependency is a product of his own desires.

THE IMITATION FAMILY

Throughout recorded history, the family unit has been the mainstay of healthy relationships. Man, as a social animal, requires constant support, assurance, and acceptance from other people. Everyone needs to be accepted as a human being and reassured from time to time that his actions and behavior meet with the approval of others. "No man is an island" applies more than ever in today's world. With the constant threat of a nuclear holocaust, potential financial ruin for our great nation, drugs and alcohol that destroy the very fiber of our existence, and a suicide rate that is escalating to near catastrophic proportions, no wonder individuals often reach the brink of mental, emotional or nervous breakdowns. They need others to confirm that, though not perfect, they are attractive, their actions are acceptable and their lives are OK, even when the world seems to crumble around them.

When matters become overbearing, a person invariably seeks solace and comfort from the closest support group—usually his family. His spouse, parents, children, brothers and sisters, and other relatives are ready to step in and give reassurance. He feels safe with them. It matters not that family members bicker, argue, and at times become violent with each other. The family is still the family. When the chips are down, a person inherently knows that he can trust family members and get comfort and support from them. "The family is a Safe House. A person can find love and security in the family when the rest of the world forsakes him."[1]

But something has happened to the traditional family unit, at least as it applies to the corporate executive. Working 10-hour days and most weekends, worrying about job security, traveling around the globe for extended periods of time on company business, and entertaining customers and corporate dignitaries during precious leisure hours leaves little time or energy for developing or nurturing family relationships. The executive's spouse learns to be emotionally independent and children learn to do without the love and teaching of their absentee parent. The corporate executive, severed from the traditional family unit, turns to the only other source of support he knows: the corporation.

The corporation and its leaders welcome him into their family fold with open arms. In fact, at many of the larger corporate conglomerates acceptance of this imitation family becomes a mandatory, if unwritten, requirement for continued employment.

As in a real family, the corporation has a defined structure, with a role for each employee—some as leaders, more as followers. The household leader (board of directors, CEO, or department manager) establishes rules of conduct. If the employee adheres to these rules, the corporation provides most of his basic needs—security, support, challenge—just as his real family did in the past.

Many companies proclaim policies designed to protect, nurture, and develop the personal growth of employees. Pension programs ensure retirement income. Stock options, high salaries, and bonus programs guarantee financial security. Company paid schooling and seminars stimulate the executive's intellect. Company picnics, golf tournaments, bowling leagues, fishing and hunting trips, and paid vacations camouflaged as business trips provide recreational and leisure activities. Expense accounts, company cars, country clubs, and other special fringes tempt employees into believing that the corporation really does have their best interests at heart.

The corporation insidiously strives to make this family bond so strong that the executive's cooperation and support will be assured for whatever economic and social programs corporate leaders advocate. The executive learns to depend upon the corporation for social acceptance, moral guidance, and financial security. The corporation dictates what is right and what is wrong. It accepts the executive as a "true blue" employee and implies that this means acceptance as a valuable individual. When he is sick, the corporation provides medical care. Paid vacations and holidays offer rest and relaxation. To provide moral rejuvenation and psychological uplift, the corporation sponsors weekend retreats and seminars conducted by religious leaders, organization consultants, and psychologists. By providing these human needs, the corporation weaves an insidious web of dependence around the executive and, in effect, controls his actions, thoughts, and even personal growth. No longer free to choose, he belongs to the corporation and, for accepting this role, pays a high price.

According to Anne Wilson Schaef and Diane Fassel in their marvelous book, *The Addictive Organization*, the corporation and its leaders, in exercising total control over the individual and demanding absolute obedience have, in fact, become addicts of the process. They exhibit the same addictive behavior as drug addicts or alcoholics. An addictive process is ". . . a series of activities or interactions that 'hook' a person, or on which a person becomes dependent."[2] Addictive processes such as gambling, religion, sex, or overwork are well-known, but any process which shields an individual's actions from his true feelings becomes addictive.

Promises from this addictive imitation family demand compliance and uniform thinking and hook the executive by rewarding his unswerving obedience with money, prestige, and power.

The addictive corporate family thwarts his natural feelings and beliefs and thus fosters ever greater dependence.

RULES OF THE GAME

In a real family there are certain rules of social behavior required to maintain peace and harmony and to optimize interpersonal relationships of family members. Many of these rules are implicit and learned over time: don't track dirt into the house, be courteous when others speak, attend meals at specific times. Others are more explicit: the children must be home by 10 P.M., the new car may be driven only by the parents, family members can have privacy when in their own rooms.

The imitation family also has a set of rules to be followed as the price paid for belonging. Although policies and procedures controlling behavior vary with each organization, certain rules are mandatory in most addictive corporate environments. I call these the *Rules of the Game*.

Rule 1: The Executive Must Be Dedicated to the Corporate Goals

Every corporation has its own goals. Sometimes these goals are not announced and are learned by osmosis. Most of the time they are formal goals, widely circulated throughout the company. Everyone knows them and understands what they mean. Harold Geneen set a very clear and simple goal for ITT Corporation: a fixed annual growth in earnings per share. He said, "Because most measurements of performance are in terms of improvement, I set my goal at ITT at a 10 percent annual increase in earnings per share. That was my 'bottom line.'"[3]

A number of implicit goals also existed at ITT and every executive understood that they reflected the personal beliefs of either Mr. Geneen or other top management personnel. For example:

- Never retrench, always find a way to grow.
- Always support recommended actions with financial facts.

- Obtain approval from the Corporate Office for all except routine decisions.

ITT, as with many corporations, expected executives to comply with corporate goals without questions. They were sacrosanct and if executives wanted to keep their jobs they had to find a way to meet them. Those not willing to comply with both explicit and implicit goals should look elsewhere for employment—and fast—because they wouldn't be around very long.

Rule 2: The Executive Must Be Committed to the Boss's Objectives

In any organization, the boss, whether a department manager or a corporate president, maintains a personal set of objectives and agenda for survival. He mandates compliance by subordinates to create a personal safe house. It makes no difference whether these objectives and criteria are irrational or hurt others. Family membership demands that the executive follow them.

Rule 3: The Executive Must Be a Team Player

Team players are crucial to the survival of the addictive corporation or the addictive boss. Individual needs and wants must be subjugated to the collective goals of the group. Change cannot be tolerated. When the individual becomes too creative and tries to improve a given activity or function, a reprimand can be expected for not considering the impact of such an action on the group's goals. The primary objective, to support the group, must be adhered to. Individuality and creativity are sublimated; enhancing the group image is the name of the game.

Rule 4: The Executive Must Compete with Bosses, Peers, and Subordinates

All employees want to achieve the highest post—or so we are led to believe. Predominant corporate theories advocate that those who play the game best will reach their goals, while others falter. This philosophy promotes nonproductive competition between employees and produces the now infamous brand of back-stabbing corporate politics. But infamous or not, the requirement to compete will continue to foster political maneuvering as a way of life. Individual feelings are ignored. Hurts inflicted on others are insignificant in the overall game plan. Winning the competitive battle is all that matters.

HOW THE CORPORATION CONTROLS

By acknowledging the need for an imitation family and accepting the Rules of the Game as required behavior, a person abdicates control of his life to the corporation. Once he renounces personal responsibility, he further acknowledges the role of the corporation as the center of the power universe. Complete power over what he does, how he does it, his standards, and his values rests with the corporation. His real family may plead for attention, favors, time, or effort, but the executive, now caught in the corporate power trap, no longer has the freedom of choice to determine when or how he will direct his energies. The corporation demands, and gets, his undivided attention.

The power of the corporation and its leaders is staggering. Chapter 2 reveals how corporate leaders become power addicts and in turn cause employees to become addicted. Psychologically, by subjugating all of his personal feelings and beliefs to the corporate family, the individual can no longer think or act for himself. Subconsciously, his thought processes are continually directed toward the corporation and the job. If his real family, or some other external stimulus, causes him to begin thinking or acting contrary to the corporate rules, he experiences overpowering guilt. This dependency dictates that he *should* dedicate his life to the corporation; that he *should* spend all available time and effort for the benefit of the company; that he *should* place everything else secondary to the good of the organization.

Some call this brainwashing, and indeed it is. Corporate leaders know full well that to protect the corporate image (and thus enhance their own welfare), the individual must be made totally dependent on the corporation. In most cases they succeed. In an increasing number of cases, however, they fail. And therein lies the psychological dilemma for the executive. When he begins to question the wisdom and the value of this dependency, the house of cards begins to tumble and he becomes confused, frustrated, and frightened. However, the corporation doesn't give up easily. It has many tools at its command to squelch the rebellious executive. Four of the most widely used are: greed, fear, failure, and promises.

Control Through Greed

The free enterprise system—founded on the principle that ever greater amounts of power and money are the measure of success—became the breeding ground of greed. Corporate leaders know this well. After all, if management personnel at ITT didn't constantly strive for more power and money, Harold Geneen's goal of continually increasing earnings per share could never be met. The recent wave of mergers and acquisitions by major corporations would be stifled without rapacious maneuvering in corporate board rooms. Greed is no strange bedfellow to the corporation's leaders. Over many years they have perfected the art of utilizing greed to achieve continued mastery and dominance of the individual.

No wonder so many executives fall prey to corporate tentacles. Dependent on an addictive corporation, they find it nearly impossible to resist the carrot of more power and more money. Few, if any, would say no to an offer of increased compensation, more staff assistance, or a key to the executive washroom. Carefully nurtured in the philosophy of greed, they believe that the acquisition of more wealth and greater control over others can be beneficial. In fact, led by greed, many executives continue to put up with addictive corporate behavior long after they recognize the harm to themselves. A corporate employee, inducted into the corporate family and imbued with corporate rules, receives ever increasing amounts of power and money. His increasing hunger for these gifts results in increasing dependency, and so the cycle continues.

Greed is insidious. At first glance it appears to be a very natural phenomenon. In the Adam and Eve chronicle, greed caused Adam to taste the forbidden fruit. Greed triggered the industrial revolution, and greed spawned the great California gold rush. Greed is the very foundation of the free enterprise system. What could possibly be more universal? So why shouldn't corporate executives respond to more power and more money? They would be foolish not to. In fact, in the business world, greed is so inbred as a way of life most people hardly ever recognize it.

Because many corporate leaders are so well-versed in the insidious nature of greed, they are able to use this deceitful addiction as an effective control mechanism. The corporation can't lose. Not only has the executive been inculcated with corporate goals and rules, but the capitalistic philosophy—upon which all of us were weaned—teaches that more power and more money equate with good. Of course the executive will respond. That is why greed is one of the most effective control tools at the disposal of the addictive corporation—and it almost always works. On the other hand, if in the unlikely event an executive can resist the temptations of greed, there are other ways to control him.

Control Through Fear

Fear can be as powerful as greed. Fear has been used for centuries to control people. The Church effectively uses the fear of Satan and Hell to gather the flock to its doors. Hitler utilized fear to subdue an entire populace. The criminal justice system threatens imprisonment or even death to deter future criminals. The American system of taxation threatens fines or jail terms if tax returns are not filed accurately and on time. Fear is a powerful tool that can coerce individuals or entire nations into believing and acting in a specified manner. Powerful leaders have long recognized the awesomeness of this control mechanism. As Franklin Delano Roosevelt is quoted as saying, "We have nothing to fear but fear itself."

The use of fear to control the executive isn't quite as dramatic as these examples, but its subtle use may be just as effective. There are three ways corporate leaders control through fear: (1) Fear of reprisal, (2) Fear of failure, and (3) Fear of termination.

Reprisal
Fear of reprisal occurs when the corporation threatens to withhold additional power or money as punishment for deviant behav-

ior. If an executive believes that by taking a certain course of action or by proposing a concept foreign to corporate goals he will be deprived of additional benefits, position, or stature, the odds are high that he will remain silent.

The threat of reprisal need not be explicitly stated. Indeed, in most corporations it is implicit. In crossing the boss or taking action contrary to avowed or perceived goals the executive assumes he will lose something—a promotion, stature in the eyes of peers and subordinates, or favors from superiors. The fear of reprisal immobilizes initiative. It encourages the executive to play by the rules and not rock the boat. His personal feelings must be subdued. His needs and wants must be made subservient to the perceived or stated wishes of the boss and the corporation. And his creativity and individuality must be subjugated to the will of the group.

Failure

Potential failure is another extremely effective tool for controlling executive actions. Our public education system uses the fear of failure to perfection. Classroom teachers continually imbue our children with the ignominy of not obtaining a passing grade on a test or of not performing as well as expected. Failure means chastisement, not only by the teacher, but also by the child's peer group and parents.

Fear of failure permeates the entire sports network, professional and amateur. Coaches, the media, student bodies, and the athletes themselves use this tool to control the participants in athletic events. To win by any means is paramount; to lose is considered failure, and therefore, bad.

Failure to gain promotions and keep pace with peers, failure to achieve earnings levels comparable to friends and associates, and failure to make the Million Dollar Club are all benchmarks of not succeeding in business. The executive's fear of not achieving these socially acceptable measures of success is a powerful tool in the hands of corporate bosses.

But failure includes more than just losing a game, not passing a test, or not getting a promotion. In our society, quitting equates with failure. A quitter and a loser are synonymous. Quitting is verboten! From childhood to adulthood we have been taught by parents, teachers, coaches, and bosses that to quit any endeavor valued by society amounts to failure. To quit school, to leave an athletic team, or to resign from a job are all considered personal failures. Even a good reason for quitting meets with disapproval. Maybe if the reason is good enough, by society's standards, we will be acquitted—but even then we must continually explain the justification for our actions, over and over and over again.

Termination

The ultimate failure in our adult world is losing a job. How good or bad, satisfying or disappointing, beneficial or detrimental the job may be makes no difference. Society automatically assumes that when a person losses a job, he somehow failed at something and deserved to be fired. With the threat of termination comes blinding fear. As Carole Hyatt and Linda Gottlieb point out in their work, *When Smart People Fail*:

> No matter how many times people tell you that in the long run you will be stronger, in the short run there are few things worse than feeling you have failed. You feel pummeled, destroyed, violated, betrayed, terrified, angry, guilty, depressed, vengeful, lethargic, impotent—and occasionally relieved and resolute. Your defenses have been shattered. Armies of warring emotions now seem to be trampling over what was once an intact you. Your mood swings wildly from hope to despair. It is a time of great confusion.[4]

The threat of losing a job carries with it two unthinkable conditions. First, it means the loss of income and benefits. This in itself can be enough to dissuade a person from expressing his feelings. Because an executive is dependent upon the corporation for his livelihood, to be deprived of income is catastrophic. Without a substantial salary, company benefits, and a year-end bonus, how can he pay the bills and take that long European vacation?

The threat of losing support from his imitation family frightens the executive even more. Bad enough to lose income, but the subconscious fear of losing the entire support mechanism of the corporate family—upon which he depends for most of his needs—becomes unthinkable. The psychological impact of such a potential disaster can, and does, leave many floundering in an abyss of depression. Without the self-confidence and inner

strength to weather such a storm they can become totally debili-
tated by the fear of such a potential loss—whether or not it ever
happens.

No wonder the corporation regards the threat of termination as its ultimate weapon. Few, if any, executives can face the
possibility of losing their jobs without experiencing cold chills.
In many respects corporate America uses the fear of termination even more effectively than greed as a control mechanism.
And the higher a person climbs the corporate ladder, the more
susceptible he becomes. No matter how bad circumstances may
be, most people will do anything to avoid being terminated or
coerced into quitting. Many will find ways of coping with an
unpleasant and dissatisfying job even though they recognize the
harm it brings to themselves and to their real family. Anything
beats the ultimate failure.

However, many corporations have consciously tried to
mitigate the hurt of terminations resulting from retrenching or
cost-cutting programs by utilizing popular outplacement services. On occasion, some are willing to absorb short-term financial
losses rather than enforce large-scale layoffs. A few enlightened
small and mid-sized corporations have progressed to the point of
rating employee welfare as a top priority.

Nevertheless, when you come home that first night and tell
the family you have lost your job, or when a neighbor sees you cut-
ting the grass in the middle of the week, failure is assumed.
Failure, with all its bad connotations. Failure—to be deficient or
negligent, to be unsuccessful, to be replaced by someone else.
Failure—the worst of all possible conditions.

Control Through Promises for a Better Tomorrow

As the song from the Broadway show *Annie* states, "Tomorrow,
tomorrow, there's always tomorrow, it's only a day away." We all
like to dream. America was built on dreams and without the hope
for a brighter tomorrow, many people see no reason for continuing
the struggle for survival. Tomorrow must be better than today.
Nothing could be as disheartening as the arms buildup, high
crime rates, addictive behavior, and the near death of moral
values. The future must be brighter. And it's only a day away.

As a division Controller with TRW, Inc., I learned the technique of using false promises for a brighter tomorrow to soothe the internal conflict of disenchantment. Every week we prepared a new plan for the next week, the next month, or the next year. We spent little time managing the daily turmoil of the business but a great deal of time and effort forecasting tomorrow. Planning for tomorrow kept the disappointments and frustrations of dealing with today out of sight and mind. It provided intellectual stimulation when the routine of management became oppressive. Not surprisingly, these forecasts always showed improvements. Promises of a brighter tomorrow kept us drugged to the realities of daily corporate conflict.

Not only TRW but also many other corporations utilize the promise of better things to come as an effective tool in controlling employees: the next raise or promotion, future retirement benefits, options granted in anticipation of market surges, a promised promotion when someone down the hall retires next year, and on and on. Hope springs eternal. The if–then scenario encourages optimism. If Joe retires next year, then you'll get his job. If profits are up, then you'll get a year-end bonus. If the boss likes your report, then you'll be showered with praise.

An executive may be dissatisfied with the way things are going now, but corporate leaders make sure he knows that tomorrow will be better. Just keep following instructions, don't rock the boat, be a good corporation man and tomorrow you will be rewarded. This is a very appealing scenario, even for the disillusioned executive. Unfortunately, for many people tomorrow never comes; there are just more todays.

HOW THE INDIVIDUAL REACTS

Many executives eventually find the role of being an obedient corporate family member, following the rules of the game under the watchful eye and control of Big Brother, too much to cope with. At some point, the executive realizes the fallacy of delegating responsibility without authority. He learns that although the corporate panacea for planning may be stimulating, tomorrow never comes. He becomes dissatisfied with the impersonal, material priorities set by corporate leaders. Eventually, much to his chagrin, he learns that in the corporation, nothing succeeds as readily as incompetence—or so it seems. And he recognizes that somehow, somewhere, there must be a better way to live.

Jack Russ was an active participant in the corporate culture for many years but recently felt stagnated. The implicit goals and politically motivated unwritten rules were so conflicting that his authority in the corporation became blurred. He seemed to be going in circles. Confusion and frustration set in. Going to his office each morning became drudgery rather than fun, as it once had been. Worse, he actually began to question the wisdom of many of his boss's decisions and even of corporate policies.

Jack knew that psychologically something was happening to change his outlook. He was seldom happy any more. His wife complained that he never joked at the dinner table—in fact he was seldom at the dinner table. His kids grumbled that he rarely attended their school events. The few nights he was home he was grouchy. Something was definitely wrong, and Jack began to worry. But he didn't have the foggiest notion what to do about it. He couldn't even define the problem.

Edward Freeze lost his job as Vice President-Marketing at a division of 3M Corporation. One Friday afternoon he received word that his marketing function would be handled by a new, recently formed division and that his position was redundant. The representative from the personnel department was polite and even offered Ed a new assignment in a small division in Texas—at a reduction in salary. Ed declined the offer, packed his brief case, cleaned off his desk, and stormed out of the building. So much for 3M. He'd show them. Or would he? When he explained the situation to his wife, she responded sarcastically, "Terrific, how do we pay the bills now?"—and panic set in.

What do Jack and Ed have in common? They both realized, in their own ways, that the security and well-being promoted by the corporation for so many years, were in fact nonexistent. The corporation had hoodwinked them into believing they would be taken care of forever. "Once a company man always a company man" was a grand slogan, but it didn't work that way. The life-style founded upon job security with the corporate family was nothing but an empty lie.

One was worried, one was angry. One still had a job, one was on the street. But psychologically, they both faced the same dilemma: How could they cope with the realization that what seemed to be a truism, was nothing but a lie? How could they accept that the culture and life-style they had believed in all their working lives consisted of false ideals and broken promises? How could they deal with the disappointment of betrayal? What could they do to find a more meaningful life-style and rebuild their lives?

Anger and Rebellion

The immediate reaction to betrayal is overwhelming anger. For some this means shouting, swearing, and blowing up. For others, the reaction is to direct this anger inward. Blaming oneself for getting angry results in strong feelings of guilt and withdrawal from other people. As Harry Levinson states in his book *Executive Stress*:

> When they feel guilty about their anger, particularly if it mounts and they have strong impulses to punish the other person, executives will not talk about their feelings of anger with those at whom they are angry. They act as if the anger will go away if they do not discuss it with the person. Sometimes it does. But much of the time it continues to fester. The executive finds himself avoiding the other person or pretending joviality, or quibbling about minor matters. He or she continues to be irritated.[5]

Feeling guilty about being angry represses the expression of anger. Even if one wanted to let it out, blaming oneself for the feeling automatically bars the door. If left to fester, this bottled-up hostility eventually explodes in the wrong direction. Instead of addressing the true culprit, the angry person tends to take it out on the nearest available victim. The need to strike out at something or somebody becomes overpowering. One experiences a towering exigency to hit back, to vent one's wrath, to rebel against those committing the wrong, to fight back and show the culprits they can't get away with it, and to stand up and flail away at the perpetrator of the hurt.

For the disenchanted executive, this perpetrator of broken dreams is the corporation, that impersonal, nonhuman, legal entity without feelings or physical being—an invisible ghost. In an addictive organization, it isn't the fault of any one person that things have gone wrong. No individual can be blamed when a job is eliminated, or a merger occurs, or a reorganization takes place. Such events are dictated by the need for growth and survival of the corporation. It is all the fault of the phantom corporation.

The executive's natural inclination is to fight the system from within rather than quit and risk the label of failure. This rebellion often takes the form of covert action. He begins to create rumors about his boss or the company. He either intentionally or inadvertently creates antagonisms between other employees as the divide-and-conquer process becomes second nature. Criticisms of the corporation and its policies creep out in casual conversations with employees and others outside the company. In more severe cases, this rebellious critique becomes the focus of small group meetings at the lunch table, water cooler, or rest room. Gossip and rumors permeate the work place and others begin to wonder if they're next.

Such undercover tactics can only create fear and uncertainly in others and continued frustrations for the individual. The corporation remains impervious to pain. Although rumors and gossip can disrupt work flow, in the end no amount of individual anger will influence corporate decisions or policies. After all, the corporation is merely an apparition.

When, on the other hand, an executive loses his job, and cannot foist recriminations onto the corporation or its leaders, he tends to direct his anger toward innocent victims outside the corporation: his spouse, friends, business acquaintances, or even his children. He tries to find some way to strike out. The psyche demands satisfaction for its hurt. It needs to be cleansed, to be redeemed. As Harry Levinson points out, a person deprived of vengeance against the real perpetrator lashes out at innocent, often anonymous victims. Knowing he will never again meet the police officer on the corner, the driver on the expressway, or the ball player on the field, he chooses verbal chastisement against these nameless persons to take the place of measured response to the originator of the hurt:

> Like animals who develop a pecking order among themselves, executives find easily available targets who are less powerful than they are, or who must, for some reason, take their hostility, or from whom they cannot easily escape. Thus store clerks, public officials, waiters, housemaids, children, or subordinates are frequent victims.[6]

Guilt often goes hand in hand with anger at betrayal. Was it something I did to lose the promotion? Could I have done a better job and not been fired? If I had paid closer attention to political maneuvering, could I have weathered the storm? Whether anger results from fear of losing something or comes from damaged pride, to relieve guilt feelings by blaming either yourself or innocent people is nonproductive. There must be some way to release the anger without damage. Chapter 2 offers some suggestions from others who have met the same problem head-on and won.

Executive Stress

The second reaction usually occurs after a cooling-off period, when the intense anger and guilt feelings begin to disperse. One then realizes that it is really the pressures of job demands and work environment that create the unbearable psychological burden. Demands from the corporation for the achievement of false ideals conflict with one's emotional and moral values and eventually cause additional pressure on the psyche. He recognizes that his anger reflects an inordinate buildup of stress created by the corporate life-style. He knew all along that the Rules of the Game were biased toward the corporation. Now he recognizes that playing by these rules only exacerbates an already stressful condition. Even though he recognizes stress as the culprit, he probably doesn't know how to deal with it.

> Often the person himself is not aware of the feelings which have been aroused. One may only know that one is tense, worried, restless, physically upset, excessively fatigued, irritable, or otherwise uncomfortable. Sometimes one may level off in performance—hit a

plateau or slump. This is frequently a form of flight. One may, on the other hand, fight—attacking one's environment by becoming increasingly competitive or burying oneself in one's work.[7]

There must be a relief valve or these pressures will cause an explosion; but the corporation teaches that showing emotions such as anger, disappointment, or frustration is unacceptable behavior and plugs this relief valve with fear of reprisal, failure, or termination. If an employee feels unjustly threatened, senses that his family or livelihood is at risk, or recognizes that his long-standing beliefs are betrayed, his defenses go up. The subconscious takes over and begins playing psychological games. Role reversal, denials, excuses, and blocking out the real reasons for the betrayal all merge to form defenses to ward off further hurt. Executive stress creates a psychological tug-of-war, the corporation pulling one way and the conscience pulling the other. If emotional strength holds, the individual always wins, and winning this first round affords him the opportunity to begin to regain his sanity.

The inability to release stress eventually causes real physical and mental harm. An escape must be engineered. To remain with the company might require requesting reassignment to a job with less responsibilities, or a transfer to a different location. As a last resort, the executive may quit the corporation and face the ignominy of failure.

For executives who resign or are terminated, these stresses may be dealt with more directly. They can laugh, cry, exercise, or perhaps take a long vacation. Free of the corporation, they can react to a much broader spectrum of alternatives. Just getting away from the pressures helps.

Emotional Breakdown

Everyone has heard of nervous breakdowns, but what about emotional breakdowns? A person suffering a severe emotional breakdown is called a manic depressive, experiencing periods of extreme emotional highs followed by just as extreme lows. He feels on top of the world one day and ready to throw in the towel the next because everything seems hopeless. Recent medical studies indicate that a person suffering from this mental illness may be experiencing a physiological chemical imbalance. Such severe emotional breakdown is not a subject to be dealt with in this book and, clearly, anyone with such an illness should immediately seek professional help.

The type of emotional breakdown often experienced by battle-weary executives, however, is much milder than manic depression, yet uncontrolled emotional swings still persist. When emotions are out of control, despair, mental fatigue, and feelings of hopelessness and helplessness tend to alternate with enthusiasm, optimism, and periods of exuberant happiness.

At one time or another, we all experience bad feelings—anger, fear, self-doubt, self-pity, and even hatred—that seem to tear us apart. And we all know how good feelings—joy, serenity, self-confidence, and love—build us back up again. But someone suffering an emotional breakdown has difficulty differentiating between good feelings and bad. He feels joy one minute and depression the next, for no apparent reason. Tears of happiness and tears of sadness alternate indiscriminately. He loves a person today and despises the same person tomorrow. In other words, his emotions are out of control and he can no longer regulate his feelings.

In more extreme cases, physical deterioration begins. From mild cases of headaches and backaches to severe cases of cancer, the body reacts strongly to mental aberrations. As Dr. Bernie S. Siegel explains, the link between emotional disorders and physical ailments has been recognized for centuries in medical annals and only comparatively recently have Western cultures appeared to have forgotten this correlation:

> Until the nineteenth century, medical writers rarely failed to note the influence of grief, despair, or discouragement on the onset and outcome of illness, nor did they ignore the healing effects of faith, confidence, and peace of mind. Contentment used to be considered a prerequisite for health.[8]

Disillusioned with the corporate promise of happiness, a person might be able to withhold his feelings of anger and fear for a time and sublimate his reactions to betrayal and executive stress. After all, the corporation taught him for many years that these feelings are unimportant and therefore should not be allowed to surface. In the long run, however, psychological pressures become too traumatic to be withheld any longer. When that happens, and he continues to try to be cheerful, optimistic and forceful, ready to play the corporate game, an emotional breakdown is on the horizon. Such a breakdown causes mental and physical incapacity. A person's thinking process becomes blurred, his ability to handle the most simple problems may be impaired, and he won't be any good to anyone– including himself.

A way to let these emotions go must be uncovered. It's crucial to express those pent-up feelings openly. Open expression can prevent an emotional breakdown. Still, some people just can't let go. When an executive either quits or is terminated, he experiences the deep-seated fear of failure. This self-doubt creates a loss of self-respect and self-confidence. Fear of the future, leading to self-pity, can result in severe depression. Financial stress quickly becomes overburdening. Carried to the extreme, psychosomatic physical illness may be completely debilitating, and an emotional breakdown is imminent.

Somehow a person must escape from this morass of despair. Some find temporary escape in alcohol or drugs. Some take an extended vacation in the mountains or by the sea. Faced with a severe case of psychological trauma, some people disappear completely for extended periods of time, and some take new identities in faraway places and never go back to their families and friends. Not a very promising picture. But there is a way out–a sure way out. And it does not require the expensive and soul-wrenching experience of a psychiatrist's probing. It is difficult and it is time consuming, but it does work. I know. I did it.

ENDNOTES

1. Reginald P. Smythe, *Where Is The Family Now?* (a talk presented in London, England, September, 1982.)
2. Anne Wilson Schaef and Diane Fassel, *The Addictive Organization* (San Francisco: Harper & Row, 1988), p. 58.
3. Harold Geneen, with Alvin Moscow, *Managing* (New York: Avon Books, 1984), p. 44.

4. Carole Hyatt and Linda Gottlieb, *When Smart People Fail* (New York: Simon & Schuster, 1987), p. 39.
5. Harry Levinson, *Executive Stress* (New York: New American Library, 1975), p. 54.
6. *Ibid.*, p. 54.
7. *Ibid.*, p. 44.
8. Bernie S. Siegel, *Love, Medicine & Miracles* (New York: Harper & Row, 1988), p. 65.

CHAPTER 2

LIGHT AT THE END OF THE TUNNEL: TRANSITION TO RECOVERY

Emotional dysfunction is the inability to control one's feelings. Anger, fear, frustration, sadness, pleasure, serenity, elation, depression, hatred, self-doubt, and self-confidence are feelings experienced in everyday living. An emotionally healthy person deals—almost unconsciously—with each as it occurs and continues a normal living pattern. Brief periods of sadness and frustration pass nearly unnoticed as a person addresses the cause and dispels any long-term effect. Openly expressed, fear and anger go away without becoming bothersome. After a good night's sleep, serenity and self-confidence replace brief feelings of depression or despair from the day before. When one hears from an old friend, momentary elation and pleasure soften the day's turmoil. We all experience emotions continually throughout our days, dealing with them as they occur, never giving them much thought, and easily distinguishing between good feelings and bad.

Emotional dysfunction occurs when any one or combination of emotions distorts rational behavior; when we become unable to differentiate good from bad feelings; when we feel anger, fear, depression or other emotions without knowing what has caused them or why they occurred; and when we continually blame another person or event for how we feel rather than taking responsibility ourselves. When emotions begin to control us rather than the other way around, they are dysfunctional.

The spectrum of emotional dysfunction ranges from disenchantment, frustration, confusion, or disillusionment on one end—mild, but strong enough to affect our daily living patterns—to a complete lack of control over our lives, on the other end. The latter describes an emotional breakdown, as described in the previous chapter.

Noted authorities in psychology, psychiatry, and other mental health fields study the workings of the mind from a detached intellectual perspective. Theologians, sociologists, and public welfare officials spend their lives researching and analyzing the workings of the heart and interactions between people. They are all concerned with resolving the age-old questions of human behavior. Treatises coining catchwords to describe emotional dysfunction abound by the score and are only outnumbered by those expounding theoretical, clinical solutions.

Having been a businessman all my life, I can offer none of the expert opinions of an intellectually trained, independent observer. The analyses and solutions offered in this book might not reach the pinnacle of intellectual sophistication; however, they do represent actual, real-life confrontations and achievements of over 75 businesspeople. These hardy souls have confronted the bad feelings of confusion, frustration, and self-doubt engineered by the American business community and discovered that solutions are within the grasp of the individual. Each of their stories offers the perspective of someone looking from within rather than a professional coming at the problem from without.

Executives dissatisfied with the corporate life-style, frustrated with unworthy motives of their company or boss, and feeling betrayed by corporate teachings, policies, and actions experience emotional dysfunction. Most cases are mild; others may be severe. Recovery from each requires the same sequence of steps. The milder the case, the less time it takes and the easier the road to recovery. The more severe the case, the greater the sacrifice and effort required. In all cases, changes in living patterns are required. These changes must emanate from within the individual. No one can prescribe a formula to follow with guaranteed results, yet help from the outside can be beneficial and in many cases a necessary adjunct.

As described in Chapter 1, Marjorie recognized the need for change early in her emotional perturbation and sought help from her church and her husband before finding the strength she needed from an organized support group. Through the group she discovered a new set of values, reoriented her personal priorities, accepted the inevitable sacrifices, and finally achieved emotional peace.

Dale, approaching an emotional breakdown, tried to find solace in alcohol as an escape from his inner turmoil—and failed. It wasn't until he accepted his own addiction and become cognizant of the path to recovery through the rehabilitation center that he was able to see the way out. For him, a complete change in moral values and personal goals led to a new career in social service.

My personal struggle required my hitting bottom before coming to the full realization that my affliction was an emotional breakdown. At the time I did not understand severe emotional dysfunction as a sickness in the same light as alcoholism or drug abuse, nor was I aware of the correlation between this mental disorder and corporate domination and codependency.

Although neither Marjorie, Dale, nor myself consciously defined it as such, the road to recovery for each of us took the same direction. The first phase was what I now call the *Four Steps to Survival*: (1) admission, (2) recognition, (3) identification, and (4) redefinition. The second phase required radical changes in behavior patterns and relationships. The third stage, new beginnings, dictated defining and then implementing a new life-style.

The Four Steps to Survival are transitional. They are a sorting-out process, a cleansing activity, an admission of blame, a recognition of the strong forces acting upon our psyches. This first phase requires an understanding of personal strengths and weaknesses, and an overt search for assistance. It involves the identification and dispelling of bad feelings that get in the way of restructuring personal philosophies and values as well as a rediscovery of the role of moral ethics in everyday living.

The Four Steps begin with the admission that feelings of disappointment, frustration, and disenchantment with the corporate life-style result from the distortion of one's own beliefs and moral values. It is one's own confused system of beliefs and standards that fertilizes acceptance of a psychologically harmful code of ethics prescribed by the corporation—not the corporation itself, for it is merely a legal entity; not bosses or other corporate leaders, for they are just following their own agendas; and surely not the free enterprise system, which provides the framework for freedom of choice and action. Instead, blame must lie with the executive himself for allowing corporate bosses and others to control his actions. By agreeing to dependency through following the Rules of the Game he willingly accepts the corporate value system and all the frustrations and disillusionment that go with it. An admission of his own fallibility and lack of control over the corporation is mandatory to begin recovery.

There's a war going on in the business world between you (the individual) and the corporate leaders trying to protect their own positions. To wage a winning battle, one must understand the strategy of the opponent. This requires a recognition of the characteristics of the corporation and its leaders that cause their intense need to maintain control and dependency. It also demands the recognition of your personal goals, beliefs, and standards that led to emotional dysfunction in the first place.

Once a person acknowledges both his role and that of the corporation in the struggle for survival, he can identify opportunities to free himself from corporate dominance. An understanding of his own strengths and weaknesses helps to identify corrective measures to protect his flanks while arming himself with the tools and weapons necessary to overcome seemingly unbeatable odds. This involves the identification of detrimental emotions, which must be dispelled in order to open the heart and mind for a new code of ethics. Admission, recognition, and identification lead to the adoption of a set of conditions and criteria that, when taken as a whole, form the foundation for personal changes.

The fourth step to survival requires redefining a code of personal ethics upon which to base changes in behavioral patterns. To be effective in the recovery process, this new code of ethics must be founded on moral virtues. The recovering executive will find that a rediscovery of moral values leads to (1) radical changes in one's behavioral patterns, (2) a new outlook toward family members, (3) strengthened relationships with other people, (4) exciting, new personal goals, and (5) changes in life-style and possibly vocation.

This chapter deals with the first, or transitional, phase to recovery and how a person can effect a rebirth of personal honesty, integrity, and moral concern. Chapter 3 covers the second phase of recovery and elaborates on changes in personal behavior and goals influencing daily living patterns. The remaining chapters cover the third stage by providing ideas and suggestions for a new personal code of ethics, a new outlook toward the corporation, and a complete realignment of the executive's own life to cope with and resolve emotional dysfunction.

Far from theoretical this recovery process actually works. Many executives, including myself, have followed this path and been successful in discovering a new and satisfying life-style. It is difficult and demands sacrifice, but if you have perseverance and moral fortitude it is a surefire, safe way to dig yourself out of the black hole of corporate dependency.

SIGNPOSTS OF DANGER

In Chapter 1, we saw how corporations and other bureaucratic organizations promote addictive behavior as the cornerstone of control and how this addictive behavior translates to the executive as an acceptable condition of continued employment. To fully understand the conditions affecting personal standards and values, the executive must come to grips with symptoms of addiction conditioning his or her behavior as a codependent of the addictive system. But what do the terms *addiction* and *codependency* really mean?

The Addictive Corporation

Before going on, it might be helpful to define precisely what is meant by an addictive corporation. A corporation is a system, a legal entity with rules, definitions, a hierarchy of roles, and ways of doing things unique to itself. Therefore an addictive corporation is an addictive system. Anne Wilson Schaef and Diane Fassel give the following definition of an addictive system:

> An addictive system is first of all a closed system. It is closed because it presents very few options to the individual in terms of roles and behaviors, or even the thinking and perceptions a person

can recognize and pursue. Basically, an addictive system calls for addictive behaviors. It invited the person into the processes of addiction and addictive thinking patterns. Even if we ourselves are not addicted to a substance or a process (which is unusual in this society), since the addictive system exists as the norm for the society its processes are always available to be tapped into by anyone at any time.[1]

A corporation, as a defined system, exhibits characteristics and traits all its own. Its life extends beyond that of any individual, so when the CEO, vice presidents, or other employees come and go, the corporation remains. Once a corporation is imbued with addictive characteristics, the condition perpetuates itself until its policies, rules, and procedures are changed. A corporation, however, cannot inflict damage to an individual, even though its policies are addictive. Only people have behavior traits. Only people can enforce addictive behavior on the individual. The corporation itself is an entity without desire, feelings, or methodology. It is the leaders of this entity who mandate the continuance of addictive conditions.

Corporate Leaders as Addicts

Power leads to addiction. Many people possessing the power to control others become addicted to that power, which creates a sense of godlike omnipotence. It is ego building to cause other people to do what we tell them, when we tell them, and how we tell them to do it. When people obey our orders we feel exhilarated, commanding, and powerful. Eventually, with our increasing success in controlling others, this power becomes so pervasive we cannot do without it. We become addicted to power. We feel we cannot survive without this godlike power any more than we could live without food or sleep. We cannot conceive of losing this power for any reason—it is too enjoyable! It begins to control our every thought and action, until it permeates our very existence. We become power addicts.

Throughout the centuries, military leaders have controlled their troops with unlimited power. In the eyes of the common foot soldier his commander is a god whose orders are carried out without hesitation. Commanders, who in civilian life may have been ordinary followers, eagerly assume the role of absolute dictator when supported by military law and regulations. They are handed absolute control over the lives of hundreds of other people, and they become addicted. Corporate leaders behave in the same way. The primary personal goal of typical CEOs (or company presidents) is to protect the enormous power granted them by virtue of their positions. They cannot exist without this power and, just as alcoholics will do anything to protect the source of their liquor, the addicted CEO will go to any lengths to ensure continuance of his control. This usually results in demands for ever greater growth and profitability of the corporation and ever increasing dependence of the corporate employees. However, it is unnatural for a human being to exercise godlike power. The CEO's desire to protect his power becomes obsessive. Stress and anxieties mount and soon other addictions—to alcohol, drugs, food, or sex—creep in to relieve him of the constant pressures.

As division comptroller for a giant conglomerate, I saw how power addiction and substance addiction can easily go hand in hand. Nate held the position of division president for many years. He governed his domain with an iron hand, quick to reprimand anyone who did not obey his orders. Pressures from his corporate boss to produce ever greater division profits conflicted with equally strong pressures from subordinates to loosen up and allow personal initiative to flower. It wasn't long before Nate turned to alcohol to support his power addiction. His addiction to power was so strong that rather than reduce his control over people—which he knew was the right solution—he turned to another addiction to buttress his conscience against any guilt feelings. His corporate boss knew exactly what had happened and why but protected Nate and his addictions because the division's stellar profit performance protected the boss's position. This was more important to the boss than curing Nate's addictions: Better to sacrifice the man than lose his own power base.

Although addicts may have a variety of definable characteristics, the following are most common to corporate power addicts:

1. They are controlling; their mannerisms and actions are directed toward controlling other people and events.

2. They are perfectionists. Subordinates must perform to their standards. Everything must be done their way and be letter perfect. There is no room for individual creativity.
3. They are self-centered. Their main concern is how actions and events will affect them personally.
4. They are dishonest. They lie to protect their own positions. They firmly believe that their way is best for the corporation and that the ends justify the means.
5. They suffer from loss of memory. When confronted with conflicting previous orders they can't remember what they said or did. If it's convenient to them, they ignore prior commitments and directions. They claim they didn't say or do what others remember. It's more convenient to forget the past.
6. They deny anything is wrong. If something doesn't go right they deny it's their fault. They will not admit they could make a mistake. They refuse to acknowledge that their actions or directions could be wrong.

The power of an addicted key person in a corporate organization is the power to bring the company to the very brink of destruction—and very often over the brink. So, if your boss has two or more of these traits, look out: he probably suffers from power addiction as well as other addictive behavior.

How does the corporate leader feed his addiction? Through the "power circle": Greed leads to the desire for more power, which leads to fear of losing power, which leads to other addictions, which leads to greed to feed these addictions, which leads to the desire for more power. The circle feeds itself in a never ending quest for more power and more addictions.

Over the long run, many CEOs, presidents, and other corporate leaders become so enmeshed in this circular web that they act irrationally, compulsively, and detrimentally to the well-being of the corporation. Such a leader will implement new policies and procedures to protect his power base. The infectious nature of power addiction transfers addictive behavior from a single addicted leader to other corporate bosses. They learn the necessity to protect their own interests and enact an ever greater number of irrational procedures and practices. Soon the corporation assumes the same addictive characteristics as its leaders, and addictive corporations are born. But this book is not about corporations or corporate leaders—it is about the people affected by these addicts.

The Executive as an Addict/Codependent

Working for or in the shadow of a power addict, fills the executive with the same feelings of grandeur and omnipotence as the boss. He sees the power the boss wields and wants some of that power for himself. By virtue of his position of authority, he has access to some of the same control mechanisms as the boss and becomes infected with the same desires. He becomes a power addict just like his boss. Often an executive not only becomes addicted to his own habits but also becomes a codependent of addicted bosses or organizations, dependent on the boss's addiction to feed his own illness. As a codependent he becomes addicted to the addiction of another addict.

The term *codependent* has a variety of meanings. Although a number of definitions have been advanced by noted authorities since the inception of the concept 10 years ago, all tend to be fuzzy with mixed metaphors. The clearest and easiest to understand in the context of the corporate executive seems to be that advanced by Melody Beattie in her book, *Codependent No More*. Ms. Beattie states, "A codependent person is one who has let another person's behavior affect him or her, and who is obsessed with controlling that person's behavior."[2] In the case of a spouse of an alcoholic, the spouse allows the addict's behavior to affect his or her own behavior patterns and becomes obsessed with controlling the alcoholic's conduct for the alcoholic's benefit as well as for a defense against such an inordinate influence.

In terms of the business environment the same thing happens, although quite often the recognition of another's addictive behavior is subliminal rather than conscious. In Chapter 1 we saw how the executive, by becoming part of the corporate imitation family, allows company goals and Rules of the Game to determine his life-style. The higher he climbs in the corporate hierarchy, the more obsessed he becomes with personally affecting the rules and policies (behavior) of the corporation. He becomes hooked on trying to control the boss's actions or the corporation's policies. Mr. Geneen exhibited such characteristics when he set his personal goals as the primary goals of the corporation.

Compulsive disorders of the codependent parallel compulsive disorders of the corporation. The addictive corporation tends to create addictive executives, and vice versa. Workaholism is one example of a serious addiction fostered through this continuous cycle and has been identified by many as the most prevalent addiction in the business community. Alcohol and drug addictions are also serious problems but thought to be second to workaholism in terms of the number of people affected.

Characteristics of a Codependent

How do you know if you are a codependent? What are some of the characteristics of this disorder? Although not all codependents exhibit all of the same characteristics, the following are definable traits common to many in the corporate ranks:

1. *Need to Control.* Codependents have an overpowering need to control other people and events. They will use any possible means to control the situation including threats, coercion, helplessness, persuasion, or domination. If they can't control events or people they become depressed and angry.

2. *Denial.* A codependent ignores problems and pretends they aren't happening. He maintains a cheerful disposition when it is obvious he should be sad, frightened, or frustrated. He often becomes depressed and confused. He tends to overeat and overdrink when things get too much to handle but denies this is happening.

3. *Dependency.* Codependents must rely on others for approval and acceptance. They are dependent on others to give them direction and to make things happen. They have a strong need to be liked by others and will often be self-deprecating or self-critical just to be well-liked. They must have other people for support because they cannot function on their own.

4. *Low Self-Esteem.* A codependent does not feel good about himself or his abilities to do anything. He is extremely defensive about everything he does and afraid of making a mistake. He

becomes a workaholic to cover up his own inadequacies. He gets self-righteous and defensive when criticized or challenged. At the extreme, he feels he can't do anything right.

5. *Distrust and Dishonesty.* Codependents don't trust anyone. They don't even trust their own judgment but will never admit it. They tell lies to cover up their own inadequacies. They also lie to themselves.

6. *Obsession.* Codependents are obsessed with getting the job done, controlling the actions of others, meeting schedules, and keeping the boss happy. They tend to worry about getting things done and spend time worrying about how they can get others to get their jobs done. They frequently try to catch someone else doing something wrong.

7. *Repression.* A codependent represses good feelings such as joy and satisfaction as well as bad feelings like anger and fear. He feels guilty about things he has done or not done and blames himself for mistakes of others. This guilt causes fear for loss of job or position, which in turn results in repression of other feelings. He appears tight and rigid in his demeanor. He is frequently angry with himself and others but tries not to show it publicly. He frequently turns to drugs, alcohol, or casual sex to drown repressed feelings.

8. *Feeling Responsible.* Codependents feel that others depend on them for guidance and direction. They feel responsible for others' actions. When others make a mistake, codependents believe it is their fault. They live from crisis to crisis, never satisfied if there isn't some new crisis brewing and very often intentionally create one in order to be responsible for solving it.

9. *Confused Communications.* A codependent seldom says what he really means—and often doesn't mean what he says. He talks too much and is frequently critical of others. He will try anything to get what he wants—including lies, threats, or coercion. Sometimes he tries to get what he wants by being self-deprecating and apologizing for bothering others. Seldom putting anything in writing, he would rather pick up the phone or give verbal directions so at a later date he can deny ever having given the direction. This way he can take the credit if something goes right but deny responsibility if anything goes wrong. Usually his directions are vague and difficult to follow.

If you have several of these traits then you are most likely a codependent. This isn't surprising since many authorities in the field believe that over 85 percent of the American population have some degree of codependency. You are not alone. But that doesn't mean the disorder can be ignored. The mere fact that codependency is a disorder indicates the need for cure. Most executives who come from addictive corporations are codependents. So the next step in the transition back to normalcy is to acknowledge your codependency frankly, recognize it as an illness, and begin the recovery process of change.

By now, you may be saying, "All this theory is fine for someone else, but it doesn't apply to me." Maybe not. Maybe you are one of the 15 percent of people who are not codependent. That's terrific and I am very happy for you—but then there is no need to continue reading this book. The odds are high, however, that some or all of the codependency characteristics fit.

As a codependent you have two choices: retain the same addictive behavior that causes you to feel so lousy, or change to a new life-style and leave codependency in the dust. If you are still not willing to take the cure you might as well put this book away and go on to something else. For those still with me, however, let's take a look at how the recovery process works.

LEARN TO KNOW YOURSELF

Before a person can begin to cure an illness he must admit he has the symptoms. One certainly wouldn't think of beginning chemotherapy without acknowledging a cancerous infection. The same approach holds true with addictive behavior. If you can't freely admit such behavior reflects your actions and thoughts, and if you continue to blame the corporation for the bad feelings instead of taking responsibility for your own life, there is nothing more to be done. On the other hand, if some place in the back of your mind there is a nagging suspicion that maybe these characteristics do apply, the self-evaluation form presented here should help clarify your intuition. Self-evaluation can either be a wasteful game or a crucial first step in solving emotional dysfunction. Self-honesty determines which. Honest answers make the tech-

Self Evaluation of Personal Traits

	Always	Frequently	Seldom	Never
I am a strong leader.				
I get people to do what I want:				
by gentle persuasion				
by coercion and threats				
by intimidation				
by promises of rewards				
by making them feel sorry for me.				
It's very important to get and keep the upper hand.				
I give a positive outlook to others regardless of how I really feel.				
If discouraged or sad, I pretend everything is OK.				
I get depressed at the office.				
My home life is not satisfactory.				
I get easily confused and have a hard time thinking clearly.				
I eat too much.				
I drink too much.				

	Always	Frequently	Seldom	Never
It's important to get approval from others.				
I like to be well liked.				
I am to blame when something goes wrong at work.				
I make a lot of mistakes in my work.				
I am not as qualified as a lot of other people.				
I don't like to be criticized.				
I usually work more than 40 hours per week.				
I feel I must finish any job or project given to me on schedule even though I must work weekends and overtime to do it.				
I have a hard time pleasing my boss.				
I think most people lie a lot.				
Lying is all right if you can ge away with it.				
I am really very qualified but nobody appreciates my abilities.				

	Always	Frequently	Seldom	Never
I feel I must get the task completed on schedule or ahead of time.				
I must keep my boss happy to get the next promotion.				
If other people would do their jobs right, I could get mine done.				
Most people are unqualified to do their job and I love to catch them making a mistake.				
It is wrong to show anger at work.				
It is just as wrong to be bouncy and enthusiastic.				
It is best to appear calm and in control of things.				
Occasionally I have sex with someone at the office or someone other than my spouse— particularly when I feel down or depressed.				
If it weren't for me, other people would not be able to do their work.				

	Always	Frequently	Seldom	Never
Others depend on me for help and guidance.				
When I take the blame for something gone wrong, others like me better.				
A smooth-running office bores me.				
I function best under high pressure or in a crisis.				
People accuse me of not being clear in my orders.				
I like to talk a lot.				
I don't like to write memos or letters.				
I like to give verbal orders rather than written.				
I have been trapped by my boss when putting my thoughts or directions in written form.				

nique a lively experience; dishonesty makes it a sham. Since nobody else will see or know about it, why not be honest? After all, if you can't face the facts now, the future looks bleak indeed.

Out of the 44 statements, if honest answers yield 35 or more in the "Seldom" or "Never" categories, chances are high that you are not afflicted with addictive behavior patterns and that your feelings of disenchantment and dissatisfaction are caused by something other than the work environment. In that case, professional psychological assistance is probably warranted to ferret out the reasons. Most of us, however, if we are honest, will check at least half of the statements as "Always" or "Frequently"–and this indicates addictive behavior.

After completing this self-evaluation, save the results. It will be worthwhile reviewing the answers from time to time to see how your behavior has changed. Self-evaluation is a continuing process and, in fact, becomes a part of the Nine-Step Program presented later in this chapter. It also helps to define which weaknesses must be overcome along the road to recovery.

The third of the Four Steps to Survival is to identify those bad feelings resulting from disenchantment and betrayal that must be dealt with quickly. By defining and attaching names to feelings you can determine what to do to alleviate built-up internal pressures and stresses caused by them.

Anger and Fear

In Chapter 1, we saw that anger and fear are the first emotional reactions to corporate betrayal. Anger that the boss or the corporation–or somebody–has seen fit to deny you a promotion, deprive you of well-earned recognition, or even terminate your employment can lead to irrational behavior. As Dr. Willard Gaylin–noted psychiatrist, psychoanalyst, and cofounder and president of The Hastings Center (which researches ethical issues in the life sciences)–describes these emotions, "Fear and anger are generally viewed as the two basic emotions to support our behavior in emergencies. They are part of the biological response mechanisms built into each human animal to enhance survival. They are the servants of security."[3] To begin clearing the air, the executive must dispense with this anger and take appropriate steps to reduce or eliminate the corollary, overpowering fear.

Anger can be dealt with if its cause can be identified. If an action by a peer or subordinate has made you angry, talk to that person. Tell him or her how you feel–that such and such an action makes you angry. It's OK to say, "That makes me mad. Please don't do it again." Just saying you are angry can often make the anger go away. If it's a situation in which a confrontation may be inappropriate or impossible, try to get away for a while. A change of scenery, a long walk, a new project, or a run around the block may suffice to release the anger.

In most cases letting anger out is healthier than keeping it bottled up. Anger is energy. Energy must be used or released. To keep angry energy repressed can only lead to increased bad feelings and eventual explosion. In fact, if not dissipated, anger can easily turn to hate, which is far more difficult to deal with. But the expression of anger must be controlled. Uncontrolled actions can be detrimental to yourself and to others. Controlled release of anger, directed through constructive channels, frees built-up energy and enables you to go on to something else. "Anger is a normal emotion if it is expressed when it is felt. If it isn't it develops into resentment or even hatred, which can be very destructive."[4] So talk to the person or get away from the event that caused your anger. Cry if you feel like it—there's nothing wrong with that. Exercise, take a long weekend in the country, fix the car, paint the house—anything to release the pent-up energy.

Another way you may release anger is to be friendly and considerate toward the very person causing the hurt. Certain experiments pointed out by Carol Tavris in her book *Anger: The Misunderstood Emotion* show that the effectiveness of the form of release depends on a person's upbringing and training.[5] Many women, for example, and some men have been taught that friendliness can disarm and still an adversary better than dramatic methods of aggression. Regardless of the method, however, release must be found—and the sooner, the better.

Fear is also a normal feeling and can be dealt with as long as you recognize the source and take corrective action to eliminate it. Find out why you are afraid. Is it a decision? Then face the decision. Is it an encounter? Then have the meeting and be done with it. Is it financial insecurity? Then make appropriate moves to create a stream of income. Is it the way you appear to others? Then change your appearance: lose weight or gain weight, grow a beard or shave it off, change your hairstyle, buy some new clothes or get rid of the old ones. If you can identify the reason for your fear, you can cope with the reason. Fear itself can be handled; fear of fear must be overcome through moral strength.

Repression of any emotion is unhealthy. Like anger, all feelings are energy and repressed feelings block the release of energy and causes pain. This can lead to headaches, stomach disorders, backaches, and a whole host of similar physical ailments. Repressed emotions during the recovery stage can also lead to all kinds of other addictive problems, such as overeating, alcohol and drug abuse, compulsive sexual behavior, and erratic sleep disorders. A harbinger of evil, repression must not be allowed to linger. As Ms. Beattie states, "The big reason for not repressing feelings is that emotional withdrawal causes us to lose our positive feelings. We lose the ability to feel."[6] Then you're right back where you were as the obedient corporate executive.

Let your emotions go. Don't repress them. Even if it's embarrassing to show an emotion at a particular time or place, better embarrassment than repression.

Hard Feelings

But some emotions and feelings are difficult, if not impossible, to express openly. Hard feelings lead to severe cases of mental illness and must be dealt with as soon as recognized. Many cancerous growths can be eliminated if diagnosed in time. It's the same thing with harsh emotions and feelings. They must be met head-on, acknowledged, and resolved. They cannot be tolerated because they weaken your resolve to recover and cause an even deeper slide into the morass of darkness. Depression, obsession, and self-doubt are three of the worst.

Depression causes us to give up. It saps the very life blood out of our minds and bodies. Depression insidiously begins under many different guises and interacts with other feelings. Freud argued that depression is anger turned inward. In other words, when we feel angry but either cannot or will not resolve the issue with its cause, and since anger is energy which must be released, we direct our rage at ourselves. This in turn increases guilt feelings, and depression results.

Depression creates a feeling of hopelessness: I can't do anything right; nobody likes me; I'm no good to myself or anyone else, and there is nothing I can do to change things; I hate myself; my job is hopeless, my family life offers no salvation, and life itself, is beyond repair. This kind of depression, or extreme hopelessness, can lead to serious mental disorder. As Dr. Siegel points out, carried to an extreme, depression can trigger violent reaction, physical infirmity, and even suicide:

> Depression as defined by psychologists generally involves quitting or giving up. Feeling that present conditions and future possibilities are intolerable, the depressed person "goes on strike" from life, doing less and less, and losing interest in people, work, hobbies, and so on. Such depression is strongly linked with cancer.[7]

There are various degrees of depression from the very mild just-feeling-bad type to psychotic despair. Not trained in psychiatry or psychology, I am certainly not qualified to offer advice on curing severe states of depressive mental illness. Anyone suffering such a malady should quickly contact a professional for assistance. Fortunately, however, most disenchanted executives never get that far. Mild depression merely inhibits rational thought and encourages irritable behavior and withdrawal from social contacts. This can be serious enough, however, and must be dealt with openly as soon as it is recognized.

Most of the time feeling depressed is just a bad case of the blues. When it comes, start doing something enjoyable. Force yourself to be happy. Associate with people. Find a change of scene. Talk, talk, talk. There is no easy way out, but it seems that nothing cures a case of the blues faster than talking with other people—unless it's helping others. I have found that the quickest, surest way to dispel such depressive feelings is to find a way to help someone else. Everyone has problems, and making an overt effort to help another person cope with disappointment or frustration almost always results in cleansing one's own psyche.

A codependent has an obsessive need to control other people. A recovering codependent, however, doesn't dare let this happen. Recovery mandates that you get rid of obsessive feelings quickly. Allowing obsessive control to creep into your life during the recovery stage will be extremely detrimental. When you feel the need to control coming on stop, step back, question your motives for doing the act or saying the words. If you find yourself trying to control someone else, turn and walk away.

Little needs to be said about self-doubt. There is only one sure way of building self-confidence and that's to try to do whatever you feel doubtful about. If you don't think you can swim, jump in a pool and try it. If you don't think you can drive a car, find a friend to show you how. If you don't believe you can make a sale, try it anyway. Even if you fail, the mere act of trying builds confidence. Without confronting self-doubt—and any bad feeling for that matter—you merely feed the weakness that contributed to your emotional mess in the beginning. Even if you are not really sure you can do it, tell yourself you can. And keep saying it over and over again. Pretty soon whatever it was you didn't think you could do will be done.

These are the primary emotions and feelings to be dealt with right in the beginning. Be constantly aware of what is happening in your head. Identify these emotions in their early stages and take corrective action. At first, it's difficult, but with a little practice, all of us can deal with our emotions and in so doing get to know ourselves. If you need outside assistance, there are many sources available. But the impetus must come from within.

Identifying and naming bad emotions and learning how to handle them gives us the strength to begin redefining our code of ethics. A new code of ethics built on moral virtues directs us toward a rediscovery of an inner strength and a belief in our own sense of worth. With this comes the ability to begin to cope with feelings of betrayal and disenchantment.

REEVALUATING MORAL VALUES

A code of ethics is a set of principles defining what we believe is important in leading our own lives as well as interacting with others. To be effective in the recovery process, these principles must be founded on the set of moral values we all know. Moral values are those standards of belief and behavior that reflect the intellectual unconscious. They are directed from the heart rather than the mind. They are a paradigm of standards founded on moral criteria of right and wrong, and come from the need to preserve rather than destroy, to support and encourage rather than degrade and dissuade, to help instead of hurt others. At the core is a belief in the human dignity and sanctity of man. Such ethical beliefs produce a value system recognizing the need for growth in community rather than individual aggrandizement. When I speak of moral growth, I am referring to the development and refinement of this value system.

Each of us has an indefinable strength that enables us to overcome obstacles and solve personal problems through means inexplicable by rational or scientific argument. Each of us has a hidden strength to be called up in time of severe distress to guide us out of darkness and turmoil. Compliance with this subconscious system of moral criteria forms the foundation of the recovery process. Without moral growth, it is difficult, if not impossible, to muster the strength and determination to pull ourselves up by our bootstraps and make the requisite changes in our living process. With adherence to a redefined moral code of ethics a person can survive the turmoil of depression, fear, and anger resulting from betrayal of his trust and beliefs.

Emotional survival requires a personal transformation, replacing old life-styles, possessions, and habits with a new living pattern and value system. We must exchange what we have and what we are for something new. External changes might be reflected in a new car, a new house, or a new job. Internal changes will be shaped by a new code of personal ethics forming the foundation for new personal values, behavior patterns, and a new approach to life. Survival demands a new understanding of one's strengths, weaknesses, needs, desires, and moral convictions— and the willingness to make whatever changes may be necessary to make a new start.

To find a new understanding and meaning of life, some people seek advice from trained experts—psychiatrists, psychologists, or professional counselors—well-versed in the clinically therapeutic treatment of psychic disorders (referred to as psychotherapy). Robert Bellah offers a meaningful layman's definition of the process:

> Psychotherapy in twentieth-century America comes in a great variety of forms, some derived from medicine, some from religion, and some from popular psychology. But what most of the forms consist in, whatever theory may be involved, is a relationship between a patient (or client) and a professional therapist.[8]

But you certainly don't have to use professionals to gain the benefits of therapy in the context of the recovery process. The essence of the therapeutic process as it relates to recovering codependents is a close relationship between the patient and someone else. The someone else may be a religious leader, a support group, or a friend, as long as he or she is caring and safe—someone who has nothing to gain or lose by hearing your story. A complete stranger might very well be the best choice as a safe someone else, because you will probably never meet again. The most obvious someone else would seem to be a spouse, but this hardly ever works. A husband or wife is too close. He or she may have something very real to lose—such as financial support—should you elect to leave your job as part of the recovery process.

The recovery program advocated through the Nine-Step Program presented at the end of this chapter utilizes psychotherapy in a nonclinical sense. It is a process of admission and purification rather than clinical treatment. It holds that by opening up all emotions, by expressing all feelings frankly and completely, and by becoming emotionally vulnerable, you will experience a cleansing effect. Just as shouting, pounding a desk, or running around the block will help relieve anger, so will becoming totally vulnerable in the presence of someone else cleanse the heart of ill will and allow love to enter. Not love in the romantic sense, but love in the sense of caring for the welfare of yourself and other people.

Admitted vulnerability becomes the catalyst to effect this cleansing of the heart. It has a way of freeing pent-up emotions to allow new light to enter. Some people claim it brings an acute sense of awareness, a revelation of inner feelings, a realization that they really are OK just as they are, and that they will survive. This stirring results in a phenomenon whereby love transcends hatred, enthusiasm and joy eclipse sadness and depression, light shines where there once was darkness, hope rises where there once was despair, and an overt loving of self occurs where there was once only numbness or even self-hatred.

Although such a dramatic outcome doesn't happen to everyone during the therapy process, don't be surprised if it does occur. There is a saying that goes: "When the student is ready, the teacher appears"—and strange and wonderful things happen. But it's the cleansing effect of becoming vulnerable that causes you to realize you are important just because you are who you are. The rediscovery of moral standards through the act of vulnerability provides the strength and courage needed to overcome the sickness of emotional dysfunction. When you open your heart during the therapy process, love replaces evil feelings and enables you to begin to cope with a seemingly endless array of hurts and disappointments. It permits clear thinking unencumbered by the pains and sorrows of perceived failure and betrayal.

SUPPORT GROUPS

Organized, anonymous support groups are also available as "safe houses" for therapeutic benefits. Although most executives may be leery of attending one of these groups—or in most cases haven't progressed far enough in their disenchantment to even need them— they are available and useful. I have found one called Emotions Anonymous (P.O. Box 4245, St. Paul, MN, (612) 647-9712) helpful in dealing with emotional dysfunction.

The function of these groups is to serve as a safe someone else in the psychotherapy process, permitting the addict or codependent to become vulnerable and cleanse his heart and mind without revealing his identity. They offer an invaluable service to seriously afflicted addicts or codependents who truly wish to begin the road to recovery.

Before getting into the Nine-Step Program to recovery, let's summarize where the first phase has brought us. In the Four Steps to Survival—admission, recognition, identification, and redefinition—we've seen how addictive behavior patterns emanate from the corporate framework, how these addictions create codependency, and how executives can judge their own behavior characteristics through self-evaluation. We've seen how admitting addiction and codependency, and dispelling bad emotions open the door to the first change in the process: the redefining of a personal code of ethics based on moral criteria. And we've explored how psychotherapy and support groups provide a mechanism for a person to begin the recovery process.

Now it's time to lay out the road map for the rest of the journey: the Nine-Step Program. Similar to the Twelve-Step Programs advocated by most organized support groups and the amalgam of programs presented by Melody Beattie in *Codependent No More*, this Nine-Step Program forms the nucleus of the recovery program from codependency and corporate addiction. It will be the foundation upon which to base all future judgments and decisions in changing your behavior patterns, life-style, and vocation.

The Nine-Step Program

As a corporate codependent, I:

1. Admit that my emotional dysfunction is a result of my own acquiescence to corporate control and dependence, and that because I am powerless to change the corporation I must change my own set of moral values.
2. Have the inner strength to make whatever changes are necessary to regain my sanity.
3. Will follow my conscience to temper intellectual decisions with moral determination.
4. Have made a thorough and honest inventory of my strengths, weaknesses, beliefs, and standards.
5. Have admitted my defects openly to another person.
6. Have made a list of all persons whom I can remember harming in my corporate life, in my family, and in my social life and will try to make amends to them all except where such amends would harm them further.
7. Will continue to take a personal inventory of myself and where I find wrongs, I will promptly admit them and try to correct them.
8. Will tell people about my progress and help them in any way I can.
9. Will try to practice what I have learned every day.

Whether you are still employed by the corporation or suffering from termination blues the active and continuous adherence to the Nine-Step Program will get you started and keep you on the road to recovery from corporate codependency. The starting point is to bare your soul to another person. In so doing you must completely acknowledge that you are *not* invincible, do *not* have godlike powers, and that you need help in controlling your emotions. In essence, you acknowledge the deep-seated need to interact with others and to give and receive love. Although revealing your vulnerability to another person can be a frightening experience, the sensation will be unbelievably cleansing.

One warning, however. To be effective, the Nine-Step Program must become a way of life—not a one-shot exercise. It will continue forever because one never fully recovers from addictive codependency; you will always be in the recovering mode.

BEGINNING THE JOURNEY

The first phase is the most difficult part of recovery. Presumably, by this time you have begun to get a grip on your emotions. If that is so, let's begin the long journey on the road back to normalcy. The second phase in the recovery process is to determine what behavior patterns must be changed and how family, friends, a community of peers, and a broadened horizon of interests can assist in making these changes. New behavior patterns will then lead to a new set of goals that form a foundation for the third phase of recovery—new beginnings.

Discovering a new life-style is fun. It is truly a new beginning. There are many options available. The journey in selecting and then accomplishing the right one will be a real adventure.

ENDNOTES

1. Anne Wilson Schaef and Diane Fassel, *The Addictive Organization* (San Francisco: Harper & Row, 1988), p. 61.
2. Melody Beattie, *Codependent No More* (New York: Harper & Row, 1987), p. 31.
3. Willard Gaylin, *Feelings* (New York: Harper & Row, 1988), p. 19.
4. Bernie S. Siegel, *Love, Medicine & Miracles* (New York: Harper & Row, 1988), p. 76.
5. Carol Tavris, *Anger: The Misunderstood Emotion* (New York: Simon & Schuster, 1984), p. 124.
6. Beattie, *Op. Cit.*, p. 133.
7. Siegel, *Op. Cit.*, p. 78.
8. Robert Bellah, et al, *Habits of the Heart* (New York: Harper & Row, 1986), p. 121

CHAPTER 3

OUT OF THE FIRE:
THE ROAD BACK TO SANITY

Recovering from corporate codependency is much like riding a roller coaster: Starting from a dead stop, you begin the long trek up the first incline. Gathering speed down the first slope you bottom out, begin the hard climb up the second incline, and then descend the second slope with ever increasing speed, and on, and on. Each incline becomes progressively easier to climb as momentum builds, and the descent down each slope becomes faster as its length increases.

Mustering enough courage to buy the ticket in the first place is the hardest part. Entering the turnstile, with your heart pounding, you doubt your ability to withstand the extreme pressure and fear and wish you could back out. But, resolute, in you go, the journey begins, and it's too late to get out now. The roller coaster is full of other executives, all with the same frightened look, all going on the same ride. Your courage builds: If others can do it, so can you. The time has come to settle back, get a strong grip on your feelings, and conquer the monster.

But conquering the monster means taking risks. Under the umbrella of corporate dominance an executive risks failure, with the ultimate risk of losing his job. Traversing the road to recovery entails even greater risks. As each chapter unfolds and for each change to your life-style or relationships there is the risk of rejection. Perhaps when you try to change relationships with your family they won't want you any more. Or maybe you try to renew old friendships but friends find it difficult to forgive and forget. The risk of rejection can be formidable and many who begin drop by the wayside rather than taking it.

The most frightening risk, however, occurring at the very first step in the journey is getting to know yourself. The recovering codependent must risk the unthinkable and heartrending possibility that when he directs his intellect inward what he finds will be impossible to live with. Have you ever awoken in the morning with a bad hangover, looked in the mirror, shuddered, and muttered, "That can't be me?" Madge looked in the mirror of her heart and suffered a much worse experience.

As vice president of sales with an international real estate developer responsible for properties in Florida and the eastern Caribbean, Madge was aggressive, intelligent, ambitious, and an ardent supporter of her employer's policies and practices. Selling international real estate is a cutthroat business where only the ruthless survive–and Madge was a survivor. In 12 years she had worked her way up the corporate ladder. Wheeling and dealing with high-roller bureaucrats and foreign millionaires, lying and cheating when necessary to close a deal, mercilessly controlling her subordinates to her perfectionist demands, protecting her flanks from corporate political sniping, Madge made sure that she was the winner in every battle, no matter what it took or who got hurt. And her $200,000-a-year salary plus commissions bore witness to her success–or did it?

Madge was an addict. Not only was she addicted to the tremendous power entrusted to her by the corporation, but also she couldn't stay away from her white powder and little green pills. In the international circuit, access to whatever she wanted was assured, and Madge sunk deeper and deeper into the black hole of drug addiction.

One morning she awoke from a particularly bad night after trying to close a deal in Grenada. Her conscience was telling her to get out while she still had a chance. That still, small voice from within became louder, and before the day was out, Madge decided to listen to her heart for a change. Arriving back in Miami, she enrolled in a drug rehabilitation program with every intention of kicking the habit. She also joined the local chapter of Narcotics Anonymous. The recovery program began smoothly enough, but the more Madge learned about herself, the less she liked what she saw. She realized how many people she had hurt over the years, what she had done to her own body and mind, how devoid of any moral conscience she really was, and what a thoroughly despicable person she had become.

The shock was too much. Madge had a complete emotional breakdown compounded by a severe case of psychotic depression. The risk Madge took in getting to know her true self shattered her fragile psyche. She entered intensive psychiatric therapy where she remains today.

I don't relate this case history to frighten anyone away from the road to recovery from corporate codependency but to highlight the seriousness of the task at hand. Fortunately, most executives are not as far down the road to power or substance addiction as Madge, and the outcome of taking the risk won't be as great. Nevertheless, discovering one's true self can be the greatest risk a person will ever take. Yet it must be taken, for only by looking within can a person change his ethical values and achieve moral growth. As we saw in Chapter 2, this is a prerequisite to changing the balance of your personal value system.

IT'S TIME TO CHANGE

As you work from a new moral code of ethics, the next phase on the road back is to change behavior standards from those that fostered codependency, and hence disenchantment and betrayal, to a new pattern for living founded on moral consciousness. Redefined standards and personal attitudes will then enable you to structure a new, consistent set of goals. With new goals you can begin the third stage: investigating vocational options leading to a more meaningful way of life.

Fortunately, there is a safety net available during this process. Recognizing the new person emerging like the phoenix, other people will willingly encourage your recovery effort. Demonstrating a desire to become more humane will garner support from family, friends, and, if you desire, a true community of peers.

But others can't actually make the changes for you. They can offer support and encouragement, but only you can change your own behavior, as I pointed out to Roy, a good friend who asked for my assistance. At the time, Roy was a power-addicted vice president of marketing for a major corporation and had mustered the courage to take the journey to recovery. He pleaded with me over his second martini, "I can make it back. I know I can. If you will only help me."

"I can't help this time, Roy. As a corporate codependent you must do it by yourself. I can, and will, give you support—but I can't make the changes for you. That you must do for yourself." I advised Roy to listen to his conscience and practice vulnerability. I also offered to be available, day or night, by phone or in person, to listen, counsel, and support him in his efforts. But I couldn't make the changes for him.

Roy accepted my offer, found the inner strength in his new code of ethics, and within a year had firmed up his rocky marriage, progressed to a new job with the same corporation, and reached out to other disillusioned executives in his company with the same kind of support and compassionate understanding. Today, Roy is a new man, with moral and emotional strength he never imagined possible—and he did it on his own.

Before it's possible to cope with changes to his work environment, a person must rid himself of the five major characteristics of a codependent that allowed the corporation to take over in the first place: dishonesty, denial, obsessive control, perfectionism, and self-centeredness. Then he must replace them with new attitudes based on moral consciousness. In achieving this he will come to grips with those ethical values that provide the strength to move forward. These new ethical values will reflect a deeper belief in the goodness of himself and other people. Personal recovery to sanity will become the prime requisite to a new life-style. He must get control of himself before taking steps to change his environment. When he does, dependency on the corporation will vanish like dust in the wind.

Dishonesty is probably the easiest to stop. Your inward monitor, constantly differentiating between right and wrong, separating lies from truth, tells you what is honest and what is dishonest, every time. All you have to do is listen. With moral growth, that inner voice becomes clearer and louder, and it becomes easier and easier to listen. All you have to do is follow your own advice and dishonest actions can be obliterated. And remember, little white lies are as harmful as gross dishonesty both to yourself and to others.

When Roy started examining himself, he quickly realized that every time he attempted to make a sale he lied to the potential customer. By guaranteeing delivery against an impossibly tight schedule, assuring the customer of quality products every time, promising price discounts beyond his authority, he was in effect being dishonest. Changing his sales pitch to, "I'll do the best I can to get you the shipment when you need it. I'll try to get my boss to increase the discount. I'll make an effort to ensure the highest possible quality for your products," rather than making promises he couldn't keep, lightened his load. And he learned that customers would rather have these assurances than guarantees they knew he couldn't possibly keep.

Denial, the favorite trick of all corporate codependents, means you never admit making mistakes. In effect, this means you refuse to take responsibility for your own actions. When was the last time you told your subordinates, "My judgment was wrong. My orders (or directives) were in error. I am to blame for the mistake. And I am truly sorry—I apologize." Denying that a problem exists, refusing personal responsibility, and avoiding the consequences of your own deeds leads to more lies and dishonesty. It's easy enough to stop denying. Just admit you were wrong—both to yourself and to another person. This has the same cleansing affect as psychotherapy. In fact, it is a form of therapy. And what a great feeling to have the courage to stand up and admit you were wrong. Surprisingly, people will forgive and forget very quickly and you can go on to other matters.

Roy was faced with a different form of denial. For each of the past nine months customer orders had been either flat or declining. His boss, the company president and CEO gave a speech before a group of Wall Street financial analysts; when asked about the order rate he steadfastly refused to acknowledge any problem. His published statements told investors that his company continued to experience strong customer demand for its products. He also cautioned Roy to maintain the same posture with customers, denying that trouble was on the horizon. Trying to cope with his own emotional dysfunction, Roy was damned if he was honest and damned if he followed his boss's orders. Finally, determined to be true to his own conscience, he wrote the president a long report outlining the reasons for the order decline and asking permission to alert his customers to stock their warehouses now before the plant cut back on its production schedule. Caught in his own denial lie, the CEO reluctantly acquiesced.

The biggest lie and the most harmful denial, of course, is denying that there is anything wrong—that anger, fear, depression, and distrust are the fault of the company and not your own weaknesses; that emotional dysfunction will go away; and that everything is normal and satisfactory even though you do feel terrible. By coming this far in the journey, however, I assume you are over this hurdle.

Obsessive attempts to control other people is a behavior recovering corporate codependents must dispel with vigor. Obsessive control results in power addiction. A codependent can never progress toward recovery while being addicted to anything—especially power. So when you feel the urge to control either people or events step back, recognize the obsession for what it is, and let things happen in their natural course.

Obsessive control seems to go hand in hand with the desire for perfection. Stop trying to structure meetings to come out the way you want. Avoid directing others to do your bidding through coercion, begging, pleading, or bargaining with them. This desire to control others to perfect your own agenda must be replaced with the will to control yourself. Many people find this attitude the most difficult of all to change. The power to control others is such a great feeling the temptation is to leave it alone. And what's wrong with perfection? Isn't it logical to do something right the first time? Wrong. Obsessive demands for perfection preclude the possibility of admitting errors and lead to additional denial, which itself must be dispelled.

THE NEED TO LOVE AND BE LOVED

John went through a real metamorphosis when he broke his ties of corporate dependency with General Electric. When he chaired the annual division planning session, instead of insisting that everything be done his way, he listened to every recommendation from peers and subordinates. He seemed to radiate a new warmth when he discussed proposed personnel changes and department forecast goals. The participants actually enjoyed the session without having to fear the outbreaks of irrational tirades John normally issued.

At dinner that evening with several other vice presidents, one of his staunchest adversaries asked, "What the hell has happened to you, John? You're acting like someone we've never seen before. I've always disagreed with the way you badger people into doing what you want. But now you seem to be kind and considerate. You're actually listening to people. I hate to admit it, but I think we could end up being good friends."

John's reply shocked everyone. "Three months ago I suffered an emotional breakdown. I didn't like or trust anyone and I felt that nobody cared whether I lived or died. Damn near committed suicide. Then I met a lady—I won't go into the details right now—who convinced me to read a book by Charles Colson, Nixon's old crony. That book changed my life. I started looking at people differently—actually began caring for them—and I found out that love is reciprocal. I'm still working at it, but I'm sure now I can make a new life for myself. I now know that caring for others is more important than satisfying my own ego. And I feel terrific."

The final behavior deficiency to deal with is the intense self-centeredness common to most corporate codependents. The need to have everything go their way, the requirement for others to cater to their desires, utilitarian individualism demanding self-gratification, and the "me-ism" influencing all decisions must be changed to a caring, compassionate attitude toward others. The shift from caring for your own welfare to caring for others will result in a whole new set of feelings eventually turning to love.

Most adult males have difficulty speaking of love without wincing and feeling uncomfortable. It's easy for us to express hard feelings such as anger, sadness, fear, ambition, drive, desire. It's not so easy to talk about the soft feelings—kindness, serenity, mercy, and love. Fortunately, most women don't seem to have this problem.

We are all influenced by the connotations of love as romance and sex, but there is another type of love that everyone needs—

especially the recovering codependent. A nonromantic, caring love for your fellow man. During the first phase we gave names to a lot of bad feelings: anger, depression, fear, and self-doubt. During recovery these need to be replaced with good feelings such as love, joy, happiness, contentment, serenity, and peace of mind—feelings we haven't experienced for a long time. In fact, most of us have to learn them all over again, especially love. After working for years in a corporate environment that frowns on such a human feeling, most of us forget what love feels like and how to give and receive it. Yet we all experience the universal need to love and be loved.

M. Scott Peck best expresses what is meant by the need to love in his best-seller, *The Road Less Traveled*.[1] Love is "the will to extend one's self for the purpose of nurturing one's own or another's spiritual growth." Peck further explains, "The act of love—extending oneself—... requires a moving out of the inertia of laziness (work) or the resistance engendered by fear (courage)." He goes on, "When we extend ourselves, our self enters new and unfamiliar territory, so to speak. Our self becomes a new and different self. We do things we are not accustomed to do. We change."[2]

To reach out to another person, extending compassion and assistance beyond the boundaries of self-interest, is a basic need of mankind. We want others to experience the good feelings we have experienced. By reaching out to help others grow, by making an extension of ourselves, we are in effect causing ourselves to grow.

We also want this wonderful experience of love to happen to us. We want to be loved by others. We want our family, friends, business associates, and society in general to accept us; to approve of our appearance, actions, and thoughts; to actually love us for who we are, not for what we have done, how much wealth we have accumulated, or how smart we are. Fortunately, love is a two-way street: If we extend ourselves in the act of loving others, we will find that love comes back in the form of acceptance, friendship, and caring. But love takes courage. It's not easy. It doesn't just happen. The act of loving requires a conscious effort on our part to cast aside prejudices and to accept others for what they are—not for what we want them to be.

Within the corporate life-style, the disenchanted executive experienced debilitating fear. The act of giving oneself to others is also a fearsome task with a high potential for rejection, and this risk stimulates the fear of failure. What if I open myself to love another and that person doesn't want my love? How can I stand rejection when I have laid myself bare? How will I handle the ridicule when my friends and family think I am nothing but a foolish romantic or a religious fanatic? This is what courage is all about. To have the courage to love you must control this fear. As M. Scott Peck relates: "Courage is not the absence of fear; it is the making of action in spite of fear. . . ."[3]

To break the bonds of codependency, a person must believe that love is not only possible, but also probable. You must acknowledge to yourself and to others that love is a prerequisite to a happy and satisfying life. Love can not be attained without moral growth. A basic commitment to moral values not only makes love possible, but mandatory. Once moral growth begins, the act of giving and receiving love becomes a natural phenomenon, and to deny this need would be tantamount to denying the desire for recovery.

All the other good feelings you need and want emanate from love. Once the barriers to loving yourself and other fellow human beings are broken, all kinds of good feelings occur: joy, happiness, contentment, self-confidence, and hope. Love is the foundation without which these good feelings cannot be achieved. Therefore, to become serious about traversing the road back we must first learn to love ourselves and then to reach out and love other people. With a genuine love for others, self-centeredness disappears as if by magic.

A REORDERING OF PRIORITIES

Personal values are not easy to change, but change they must on the road back to sanity. The essence of recovery from disenchantment with corporate values is change. Values taught by the corporate world are what caused your psychological problems to begin with. Now it's time to realize that they don't work. A reordered system of personal values consistent with moral growth and psychological health must replace utilitarian corporate dogma. And this set of values must include love and compassion. Priorities must change. You no longer owe your time, effort, and very existence to the corporation. You now owe your life to yourself and to others.

The following priorities are at the heart of a new system. A person's beliefs and standards must be founded on this order of personal responsibilities, or roadblocks will appear:

1. Your first responsibility is to yourself.
2. Your second responsibility is to your wife or husband.
3. Your third responsibility is to your children.
4. Your fourth responsibility is to your parents and other relatives.
5. Your fifth responsibility is to your friends.
6. Your sixth responsibility is to your employer.

Compare this with your current paradigm. If an employer or former employer rates higher than sixth, or if parents, spouse, children, or friends are more important than yourself, it's time to realign your thinking.

Some people will respond that putting oneself first is selfish, contrary to moral teachings, and can only lead to more of the "me-ism" philosophy we're trying to get away from. Without engaging in theological or sociological dialogue, the answer to these critics seems self-evident. If we are not mentally, morally and emotionally strong, we are no good to others. If our own feelings and thoughts are mixed up and we are disappointed with our own lives, how can we ever give love to others? Moral conscience is the essence of a person's very existence. Putting oneself first is putting moral consciousness first. This is not selfish—it is selfness. The addicted codependent who lacks self-esteem, harbors guilt and fear, and regards himself as inferior, is selfish. The healthy, morally strong, and emotionally secure individual recognizes the need to master himself before he can help others.

This does not mean that you should look out for yourself and your own welfare to the detriment of others. On the contrary, selfness provides the foundation and the moral strength to be a giving, loving person with genuine care for others rather than self-centered and always looking out for your own best interests. Responsibility to yourself first is mandatory to recovery. Without such self-love, you cannot follow the Nine-Step Program. While assisting other codependents in changing personal attitudes, I developed the following Guidelines to a Better Life as a daily

---

Guidelines to a Better Life

I promise myself that starting today:
1. I will live each day as if it were the last.
2. I will listen to my conscience for guidance.
3. I will not worry about other people's problems I am unable to help with.
4. I will let events occur in their normal fashion without trying to change things to my way.
5. I will not be afraid to admit I am wrong.
6. I will be honest and open with my family, friends, employer, and subordinates.
7. I will not berate another person whom I think is wrong.
8. If angry or fearful or depressed I will talk to another human being about it and express how I feel.
9. I will not blame others for my mistakes and errors.
10. I will accept whatever tomorrow brings tomorrow, without fear or prejudice.

---

reminder of what we are trying to do in a recovery program. I keep this list posted in my office and refer to it whenever I feel myself wavering. You might try the same tactic.

As mentioned earlier, there are several outside sources of support available to the recovering codependent. Once new behavior patterns have been identified and a person becomes willing to give and receive love, the implementation of these changes will be enhanced by the active solicitation of support from: (1) the real family unit, (2) a cadre of friends, and (3) a true community of peers.

FAMILY SUPPORT

The road back to sanity is full of potholes. A person needs all the help he can get. Ideally, that help should begin with his real family. A good listener is essential to recovery and an understanding spouse who takes the time to become a good listener can be invaluable. So is encouragement and compassion from other members of the family unit—children, parents, brothers and sisters, or other relatives. But to get their support, you'll probably have to make some changes in relationships.

Until now, working 10-hour days and six- or seven-day weeks at the office, in the shop, or on the road has left you little time and energy for family activities. This must change. You must make the time to be with your family, to listen to their problems, care for their needs, and reenergize a feeling of togetherness before you can expect them to reciprocate. To reenter the family unit you must take the time to get to know family members all over again. Learn their interests, likes, and dislikes. Learn their values—they may have changed since you last looked! Then make the effort to include them as participants in new interests and adventures. Do new things together as a family. Go fishing, play golf, or remodel a bathroom. Work toward common interests to be shared with all family members.

Don't forget to be honest about the horrors of corporate addiction. Relate the anger, fear, depression, and self-doubt you've been through. Let them share the grief (they will want to), but share the good feelings too. Let them know you love them. Practice caring and kindness. Show them with concrete examples that you have changed and are willing to change even more to remake the family unit. It may take time to develop a warm, supportive relationship, but don't be discouraged. It's a vital part of the recovery process. Don't worry if it takes weeks, months, or even a year to rebuild the family unit with you as an integral part of it. It's all part of the process. And be patient. Remember, your family has been forsaken for many years while you preached the corporate gospel at every turn. It's natural for them to be cautious in accepting changing attitudes and values.

Changes in relationships are difficult. Family members may have become disillusioned themselves. Waiting all these years for the executive to participate in a home life may have soured his spouse. To survive in his absence, a spouse, children, or parents may have changed their own attitudes and values. When you finally do return, it's to find a household of strangers. They are not the same people you forsook for the corporation years ago. They now have their own lives, and you are the intruder. They have learned to survive without you and may reject your efforts to reenter the family unit. This is a major stumbling block to recovery and, unfortunately, one which psychologists, psychiatrists, and other behavior scientists often have difficulty coping with in prescribing healing processes. The family that turns its back on the recovering codependent can easily delay or prevent recovery.

A long-term friend of mine and practicing psychologist has dealt with repeated cases of executive disenchantment and subsequent recovery programs. He relates the following case history of a middle-aged aerospace engineer recovering from corporate codependency.

"Michael was well on his way down the road to recovery from the psychological trauma of being fired. He was undergoing continual therapy with a psychiatrist who felt that he had reached a dead end. The psychiatrist asked me to perform a series of tests with Michael to try to understand the root cause of his blockage. A battery of tests and several sessions later the following story came out. As Michael related, 'I know I need to have the support of my family. Dr. Miller was very clear on that. The problem is that my wife is unwilling to give me that support. I finally got her to talk to me two weeks ago and she refused to answer when I asked her if she still loved me. She did say she didn't like me anymore. Didn't like what I had become. And I can see that she has changed, too. I hardly know her now. She has a new job with a good income. She has a whole new set of friends, many of whom I don't like and most of whom I don't even know. Her interests have changed, and she isn't the person I married 25 years ago. I don't know when it happened, but she changed—radically. And now she won't give an inch to support what I need to do to make my own changes. She says whatever I want to do is OK with her. Just leave her out of it.' Clearly, Michael could not move forward with his recovery without coming to grips with this serious deterioration in his family relationship. I understand from Dr. Miller that Michael was unable to break the family barrier and has now relapsed into a serious schizophrenic breakdown."

Unhappily, there is no easy way out of this dilemma. Family relationships disintegrated beyond repair are of no use as a support mechanism, and other groups must be substituted. You must have someone; you cannot go it alone. As we shall see a little later, such support does exist from friends, or even complete strangers who have formed a true community.

If your spouse has given up, one answer is a temporary separation – at least until you have regained enough emotional strength to cope with a rocky marriage. Not that I favor divorce. On the contrary, I strongly believe in the marriage commitment – for better or worse. A recovering codependent, however, doesn't yet have his emotions under enough control to cope with both his own changes and a rocky marriage. It's far better to traverse the road to recovery alone for a while than to be constantly on the defensive against your spouse and kids. I know it's a hard step to take – especially if you love your family – and I do not recommend a separation lightly. During the recovery period a codependent needs family support more than ever before.

Another condition is even more dangerous: having a spouse who is also an addicted codependent. Two emotionally weak people depending on each other for support need to have an exceptionally close marriage to make the recovery together. As with an alcoholic or a drug addict: one slip and either one or both are back to square one. It makes no sense to live in an environment fraught with the same emotional dangers you experience at the corporation. And your spouse will also need help to recover. Separation, at least for the short run, is often the kindest solution for both parties. Occasionally, recovery can be a shared experience. During the morning break at a seminar on personal relationships and profitability, a young couple approached me with their story of recovery from emotional turmoil.

Mary Beth and Jeff were a career couple. Both were 36 years old. She had worked her way up to assistant administrator in a local hospital; he had progressed to manager of a 55-man engineering department at an electronics company. They both were earning good salaries and showed promise for advancement. However, they had also become completely disillusioned with the lack of interest either employer showed in the government's insane policies on the wars being waged in Central America. This realization of corporate indifference translated into a disenchantment with many, if not all, of their respective organization's goals and policies. And both realized how dependent they had become on the continued goodwill of their companies to support their emotional, social, and financial needs.

Mary Beth sought psychiatric assistance from a highly recommended therapist. The psychiatrist invited Jeff to participate in the therapy sessions. He suggested they work the recovery program together, since they both were suffering the same disorders from apparently the same causes. Regular attendance at these sessions, active efforts at self-analysis, and a moral awakening by Mary Beth in four months and Jeff in six enabled them to leave therapy within the year and begin the recovery process on their own.

That happened three years before I met them, and both Jeff and Mary Beth confirmed that if they had to go through the recovery process alone rather than together, either one or both would have had a relapse by now. As it was, both were well along the road to recovery. Their faces sparkled when they confirmed that the success of the program was due to their joint effort, working together toward a new life-style. And both young people confirmed, lovingly, that their marriage was now spiritually stronger and emotionally more secure than ever before. Incidentally, Jeff left his job with the electronics company and began an engineering design business of his own. Mary Beth still works for the hospital, but no longer depends on her work environment to provide emotional and psychological support.

Although requiring a very strong, loving relationship, a joint recovery effort can work wonders, as Mary Beth and Jeff proved. If your spouse wants to participate in the program, by all means agree. Your marriage will probably end up stronger than ever before.

In addition to offering psychological support, the family unit can be of immense help in another area. If an executive is out of work and searching for a new beginning, financial support must come from somewhere and the best source could be his spouse. If he or she will take at least a part-time job to provide some income during this period, progress will be faster. Even if he remains with the corporation, a second source of income can provide the reassurance of financial security necessary to reduce the fear of losing his job. Tight budgeting can actually forge a tighter bond between family members. Pitching in to work out a bare-bones budget can bring family members—children as well as spouses— together in a common goal of survival and can provide mutual support for financial, as well as emotional, difficulties.

SUPPORT FROM FRIENDS

Friends can also be enormously supportive. Some people are hesitant to admit they were fired from their job, or worse, that they have experienced emotional dysfunction. Even though the psychology of failure is tough to deal with socially, to follow the Nine-Step Program seriously, you must be honest with friends. Tell them exactly what happened. If you were caught in a retrenching, admit it. If you were fired because of a disagreement with the boss, talk about it. If you quit because you couldn't stand the corporate environment any more, freely discuss the situation. Be honest with everyone. *No more lies!* That's part of the therapy.

Also, don't be ashamed to talk about changed moral values, especially if the change has evoked a real awakening. The feedback will be surprising. After my own experience, I hesitated mentioning to anyone how radically my moral outlook had changed for fear of ridicule. As courage mounted, I began talking about it in open conversation. Much to my surprise I found that many, many other people have experienced the same miracle. Most people are hesitant to open the conversation but once you begin to speak freely, they also open up. Speaking freely and openly about your new ethics is part of the Nine-Step Program. If you are fortunate enough to have experienced a rejuvenation of moral criteria, don't be afraid to broadcast. It will only help your cause.

The resiliency of friendships always amazes me. Friends you abandoned during brainwashed days in the business world will welcome you back to the land of the living with open arms. Trying to follow the Nine-Step Program, I wanted to renew old friendships wherever possible. Without exception, everyone I had cast aside during the days of my corporate addiction took the time to listen. As I admitted my defects and related my recovery experiences, each one welcomed me back as if nothing had ever happened. In fact, several friendships are stronger now than ever before.

Just as with the family unit, friends form a much needed support group to reinforce the implementation of new behavior patterns. The recovering codependent has convinced himself that he is OK, not a bad person: emotionally weak, yes, but also morally strong with new appreciation for the need to engender soft feelings. Now he needs to test these convictions on other people. He needs to have others agree that he really is OK and that his new behavior meets with their approval. He needs to be sure that he isn't just talking himself into believing something that can't be true. He needs to rebuild his damaged ego. And friends can do that.

The best, and probably only, way to rekindle old friendships is to be forthright in admitting your personal defects. Acknowledge past actions that have hurt people. Admit continuing emotional weakness. Remember, it's all right to be you. It's acceptable to be weak. It's normal to express feelings. Such openness will almost always be reciprocated. After all, as the saying goes, "A friend in need is a friend indeed."

One night about midnight, on the way home from the airport with my wife, daughter, and a trunk full of luggage, my car stopped running 20 miles from home. I could not get a cab or a ride from anyone. There were no motels nearby, and I couldn't think of anyone who could help us. I reluctantly called Bob Eke, an old friend whom I had treated badly for several years but who lived only half a mile from my house. "Of course I'll help, Larry. I'll slip some clothes on and be there in half an hour." When he dropped us off at our home at 1:30 I thanked him profusely, feeling sheepish. His only comment was, "What are friends for, if they can't help each other?"

A True Community of Peers

Strangers can also be a source of support and become friends of a different sort. Outsiders who share the common belief in an open expression of feelings, strangers who are willing to accept each other for who they are—these are the new friends developed in community.

Rugged individualism has been used to describe the current American culture. Constant competition, more and better material possessions, an obsession to succeed, and belief that the end always justifies the means all make it difficult, if not impossible, to be honest with and about ourselves. To survive in this environment we must continually fool ourselves into believing that, regardless of obstacles, with individual initiative we can succeed on our own. Weakness must not be tolerated, for with weakness comes failure. Nor must we allow anyone to know our inner thoughts, for with this knowledge we can be controlled.

Yet, as seen earlier, the opening of a person's heart to another human being is an essential step in the recovery process. Even though revealing inner weaknesses can backfire, the risk must be taken. The intense desire for the quick fix attainable through utilitarian individualism must give way to a renewed dependence on community. As Willard Gaylin so aptly phrases it:

> We have seen, particularly in America, an extraordinary overemphasis on the individual. The question of collective good versus individual gratification is only recently beginning to reemerge in moral argument. I am confident we will rediscover the biological meaning of community if we have the time, and if the damage of an overextended individualism allows for the privilege of return. We are just beginning to see some cautionary anxiety about whether we have taken our individualism too far.[4]

To journey the road back to sanity requires continued admission of vulnerability. It is mandatory in steps five, seven, and eight of the Nine-Step Program. But how does one keep admitting weakness without undue risk of retaliation or rejection? Where is this safe person who will not use our admissions against us later on? One such safe house outside the family is the group of people who form a true community. The word community has many meanings. Webster's *New World Dictionary*, Second Edition, has no less than 10 different definitions of the word, although the closest fit in the context of this book is, "friendly association; fellowship."

In *"The Different Drum,"* M. Scott Peck discusses community as "a group of individuals who have learned how to communicate honestly with each other, whose relationships go deeper than their mask of composure, and who have developed some significant commitment to 'rejoice together, mourn together,' and to 'delight in each other, make others' conditions our own.'"[5] Some community groups are large and impersonal, such as Alcoholics Anonymous and other anonymous support groups. Some are very small and meet in the basements of homes or churches, or in offices. One of the purposes of such groups is to give members a safe place to lay open their hearts, concerns, fears and angers; to become vulnerable to others; to share joys and miseries openly and without fear of prejudice or repercussions; and to cleanse their souls.

Communities often form in times of crisis. Sharing emotions following the death of a loved one, during and immediately after a natural disaster such as a tornado or fire, or in the event of a national crisis such as the declaration of war (although a community the size of a nation is too broad for purposes of this book) often results in the formation of groups of people who can be free and open with each other. Community can also be experienced without a crisis, and sometimes without planning for it at all. As Peck explains: "Because our need—our subliminal yearning—for it [community] is so compelling, we sometimes fall into community by accident, even when there is no apparent crisis."[6]

Where do you find such a community group? You might check around your immediate neighborhood to see if one is meeting nearby. If it is, you may certainly join in, because a true community is inclusive of everyone and its members know this. If you can't find a suitable community nearby, contact *The Foundation for Community Encouragement, Inc.*—a public foundation "to encourage the development of community wherever it does not exist,..."—either to learn of existing community groups in your area or to get information to begin such a group yourself. The address and phone number are: P.O. Box 50518; Knoxville, TN 37950-0518; (615)690-4334.

A true community group is more than a safe house to display emotions, however. In its purest form, it creates a unique opportunity to experience pure love between human beings: honest sharing of feelings and genuine caring for others. As one woman remarked on her way home from a community meeting, "I feel cleansed all over, like I have taken a shower, both inside and out."

In some quarters, rugged individualism as an ideal is gradually giving ground to belief in the need and benefits of community. We are rapidly learning there are some things an individual just can't do alone. Nuclear power, the potential of space warfare, and the destruction of the ozone layer dictate a sharing of technology and concern in worldwide community. Restoration of our waters, forests, and land pummeled by industrial greed mandates a sharing concern at the national community level. And the staggering increase of mental and emotional disorders, suicides, and the deterioration of marriages provokes the need for caring for each other in community at the individual level. As Willard Gaylin states, "I am convinced that we have reached the limits of individualism and our survival depends on rediscovering our need for community. In that process we have the opportunity to rediscover love."[7]

Participation in a community group is a helpful step in solving the emotional dysfunction caused by corporate disenchantment. You will be surprised at how many other people have gone through the same turmoil you have and at how they have managed, and still continue, to lift themselves out of the morass.

BROADENED HORIZONS

In addition to building ties with family, friends, and community, developing a range of new interests can offer you important assistance in gaining control of your emotions and straightening out your personal values. Doing new things with new people, experiencing new challenges and new ideas hastens the change process. For an employee, new interests are easiest to structure as leisure-time activities. In many cases, however, they can lead to new perspectives on human relationships both on the job and off, or can even lead to a new life-style.

Why new interests? Because the road back to sanity requires change in perspectives and changes in working, and perhaps living, environments. And new interests force a new outlook—they force change.

Several years ago, my son Charles decided to make a change in his life-style. He had a successful contracting business in New

York but decided that there must be more to life than 10-hour days, more and more money, and deteriorating mental, spiritual, and physical health. Both he and his wife Maggie (who worked as a nurse and experienced the same psychological disillusionment) consciously developed a new interest in sailing. They read about boats, visited boat shows, and spoke with a number of boat owners. One day, they disposed of their living quarters, packed their belongings, invested their life savings in a sailboat, and began a new life-style cruising the world. They have never looked back and have never been happier. Although dependent upon pick-up jobs for financial survival and living on sparse income they have found peace of mind and new moral growth through their broadening of interests.

There are any number of ways to develop new interests. Try projects around the house: electrical or plumbing repairs, building an addition, or landscape gardening. Explore new hobbies: model trains, boat building, golf, or tennis. Perhaps broaden your world perspective by taking an overseas vacation, or cruise a freighter to Antarctica. Develop those latent design skills with a new invention. Become an active participant in clubs, associations, or other social groups. Run for political office. Take a college or trade school course. There are an unlimited number of options. Just do something to expand your horizons, meet new people and gain new perspectives on life.

Change is frightening, but it also stimulates the mind. Right now, you need to do something to take your mind off the ever present psychological trauma of corporate disenchantment. New horizons, new interests, and new people supplement and reinforce changes in behavior and beliefs and provide the opportunity to develop and practice your new morality. A new beginning mandates new interests.

NEW GOALS

The culmination of the process of change is establishing a new set of personal goals. Goals you were coerced into accepting as a corporate codependent are now archaic and must be thrown out. Promotions, higher salaries, more perks, and a larger office are no longer relevant. Rediscovered moral criteria and a redefined set of personal values form the foundation to develop new goals. These goals will reflect not only how you want to lead your own life, but how you can mesh your desires and talents with those of family and friends. The need to fulfill responsibilities to yourself is paramount, but you also need to structure goals to enhance the lives of your loved ones and other fellow human beings. You must strive for selfness—not selfishness.

Twelve Rules to Live By

The Nine-Step Program is the foundation upon which to build a future life. Following the program provides increasingly more distinct insights into your own abilities and desires. The further along the road back to sanity we travel, the clearer new goals will become.

Obviously, each person must set his or her own goals. Although the list I developed for myself has proven workable for many people, other goals may better meet your needs. Just be sure they conform to the new set of values established earlier. Following these new goals should put you back on track whenever the temptation arises to vary direction. Goals are a personal set of rules to live by. Nobody else needs to see them, so be as personal as you wish. The main idea is to give careful thought to what you really want to be, what is really important to you, and how you really want to live the rest of your life. The answers to these questions will be your goals. Put them down on paper. Hang them on the wall. Keep referring to them daily. They will eventually become second nature.

OPTIONS FOR A NEW LIFE

Well along the road back to sanity, you should be feeling better by now: the battle is being won. You should also have a pretty good idea what went wrong at the corporation and what to look out for to avoid a repetition.

Armed with new goals, you can expect a new life-style right around the corner. An endless array of possibilities present them-

---

Twelve Rules to Live By

1. I will try to be objective in dealing with my fellow employees without prejudice toward what might be best for me.
2. I accept myself the way I am, recognizing I am not perfect.
3. I accept other people for what they are, recognizing that their opinions are just as valid as mine.
4. I will give credit where credit is due without usurping other people's ideas and actions as my own.
5. I will try to treat everyone with respect and human dignity without trying to force my beliefs and values on them.
6. I will support my employer with as much loyalty as possible without sacrificing my personal integrity and moral values.
7. I will be patient with my peers and subordinates at work.
8. I will try to dispel anger as soon as I recognize it but will not consciously hurt anyone else.
9. I will deal with fears as they arise, knowing I have the strength to survive anything the corporation can throw at me.
10. I will try at all times to maintain a caring and compassionate attitude toward all others and try to promote love and community between all people.
11. I recognize my priorities and will always place the needs of myself, family, relatives, and friends before my employer.
12. I will actively strive to build and maintain a warm and sharing family unit.

---

selves. The only limitations will be self-imposed. A new start in life, although a bit frightening, will also be a great adventure. Look forward to it with anticipation. Although having suffered batterings from the corporation, you have not succumbed. You have succeeded in pulling yourself up by your own bootstraps. You have a new family relationship, better than ever before. You know friends will stand by you no matter what you do. And best of all, you know yourself and have confidence in your ability to cope with anything. By this time you probably also love yourself—at least a little bit. But if not, that will come in time. Don't worry about it. The following chapters explore how to achieve eight different and new life-styles, some within the corporation or your own business, some without. Each has advantages, and each has risks.

Nothing is of value unless we risk something to obtain it. But avoiding risks is as much a failure as taking a chance but not achieving our goals. We must take risks every day—in our cars, in planes, on the ski slopes, and with our associates and friends. There are also risks in venturing out into the unknown of a new career or a new job. Will you succeed or will you fail? Will you be happy once a new life-style has been achieved or will it merely be a repeat of your experiences with the corporation— or worse? Those are the risks, and no one can be sure at this point what the outcome will be. Not even you. If you don't try, however, you'll never know, so you might as well go ahead. What is there to lose? If you don't go after a new life-style the only choices are going back to addictive behavior or finding some desert island to hide out.

Just keep in mind that nothing is certain. There are risks in everything, so don't hide your head. You're a stronger person now. You've got everyone on your side. Lead with your best punch and get going.

Changing life-styles—the third stage in the recovery process —is absolutely mandatory. Everything accomplished to date will be wasted unless you take the final step. Even if you stay with the corporation, or with your own company, there are a myriad of changes to make in your living pattern. There are no guarantees, but the probabilities of success are high if you're serious. Changing can be a lot of fun if you approach it with the right frame of mind. It's an event. It's a challenge. It's invigorating. No telling where the changes will take you, but the odds are high that a new approach to life will breathe fresh air into your tired, confused frame. As your new goals begin to be realized, don't be surprised if your appearance changes so radically that acquaintances you haven't seen for some time fail to recognize you.

Each alternative in the succeeding chapters will be highlighted by true stories of others who have risked the change. Some have won, some have lost, but all have tried and are better for it. Good luck.

ENDNOTES

1. M. Scott Peck, *The Road Less Traveled* (New York: Simon & Schuster, Inc., 1978), p. 81.
2. *Ibid.*, p. 131.
3. *Ibid.*, p. 131.
4. Willard Gaylin, *Rediscovering Love* (New York: Viking Penguin, Inc., 1987), p. 232.
5. M. Scott Peck, *The Different Drum: Community Making and Peace* (New York: Simon & Schuster, Inc., 1987), p. 59.
6. *Ibid.*, p. 81.
7. Gaylin, *Op. Cit.*, p. 243.

CHAPTER 4

I'LL STAY WHERE I AM:
ADAPTING TO CORPORATE LIFE

"Damn SQR all you want. The fact is, my girl, you're stuck with it!" As she put the finishing touches to her face that Monday morning, Mary Alice knew she couldn't quit. Chief designer at SQR, a major New York fashion house, she was sick of the corporate rat race. For seven years she had been riding the commuter trains to New York from her home in suburban Philadelphia—nearly five hours each day. Leaving at 5:45 A.M. and returning at 7:30 each night left her exhausted. Frustrated with the perfectionism and obsessions of her new boss at SQR, she began suffering all the anger, fear, and self-doubt of corporate disenchantment—yet she knew in her heart she was trapped.

Two years earlier, Mary Alice had given her husband most of her savings to invest in his new restaurant. This most recent entrepreneurial scheme would probably be another loser, just like all the others he had tried. Even with a salary of over $60,000, supporting three kids in college and a husband with little income, left Mary Alice virtually nothing for a rainy day. Plus, she loved fashion designing and couldn't think of anything she would rather be doing. If only SQR weren't such a horrible place to work!

Even though Mary Alice felt emotionally drained, suffered daily headaches and frequent depression, drank too many manhattans for lunch, and had put on an extra 10 pounds last year, she didn't dare leave the corporation. She was stuck and she knew it. But still, she had to make some changes or she would explode.

Sound familiar? It should. Many executives facing corporate disenchantment are stuck with their companies and jobs whether they like it or not. They cannot quit the corporate life-style or even seek out a new company. Unwilling to risk entrepreneurship and not ready to retire, they are frozen in their tracks. Most executives between the ages of 35 and 60 choose to remain with their present company for a variety of reasons, even at the expense of being dissatisfied and unhappy. They cope with emotional turmoil by withdrawing from company activities, isolating themselves from friends at work, starting destructive rumors, chastising corporate policies and employing a variety of other defense mechanisms. They repress anger and, fearing loss of income, hang onto their jobs in spite of personal hurt and emotional illness.

The corporate web has tightened and they cannot break away. Changing to a life-style outside the corporation sounds wonderful, but without financial independence and strong family support it's impossible to do. How many executives, managers, professionals and employees of any rank dream of finding a job in another company closer to home, with better benefits and higher pay, with a more considerate boss, or with more chances for advancement? How many fantasize that given a different work environment they could certainly be happier than they are now? Given the opportunity, how many wouldn't willingly trade the frustrating, grueling, unfulfilling job they now have for something new—either on their own or with another company? But they can't bring themselves to cut the umbilical cord. The corporate web remains securely fastened around their necks. Corporate dependency has become a way of life they cannot exchange. They must hang on and make do the best they can, even if it means ruining their emotional and mental health.

This is the toughest road to travel. A person fired from his job, although distraught and discouraged, at least has change forced upon him. He must do something new whether he wants to or not. He can find a job with another company, become an entrepreneur, change careers, or even retire. But a disenchanted codependent, stuck with a job in an addictive corporation, has only two choices: muster the courage to quit and voluntarily risk a new venture, or remain in place and try to cope with disenchantment. The latter choice is certainly the more common.

Financial security isn't the only consideration preventing the disenchanted executive from fleeing the corporate coop. Age, family responsibilities, and level of earnings also have a major interactive influence. A manager in the 25-to-35 age bracket, single, with no family responsibility and a base salary of $35,000 to $40,000 a year generally has no difficulty quickly finding another job—usually better than the one he has and with a higher salary. If he becomes disgruntled with corporate dependency, the choice to leave is his and his alone. There are virtually no ties to bind him to the company. If he recognizes the symptoms of addictive codependency, the options of staying, looking for another job, or becoming an entrepreneur are his alone. Risking termination by changing behavior patterns to cope with emotional dysfunction is much easier for young executives than for those on the other end of the spectrum.

An executive past 50, with kids in college and a salary of $75,000 or more can have a very difficult time duplicating job responsibilities and salary. He has two strikes against his making a career or job change before he even gets started. If he is fortunate enough to find a job with another company it will most likely be with a small to mid-sized organization. The owner or president is willing to pay a high salary for experience because the company is in trouble and he hopes new blood will bail them out. Addictive behavior is often the reason for the trouble in the first place, however, so changing from what he has to such a new position won't help the recovering executive solve his problem. His risk in taking the recovery road is far greater than that of his young counterpart.

Most managers fall between these two extremes with varying degrees of restrictions or difficulties in relocating, but the closer one gets to the second example, the higher the risk in changing and the easier it is to stay stuck. Of the three restrictive categories, age is by far the most difficult to overcome.

Despite federal age discrimination laws and despite the excruciating need in the business community for heavily experienced managers, the willingness of companies to hire or promote a person decreases with the person's age. American veneration of youth and the corollary disregard for the elderly punish executives more severely for every year added to their personal calendar. In most other industrialized nations—and even more in developing countries—the elderly are revered and honored. Young people look up to their seniors for guidance, learning, and stability. But not in America. Here, the eternal search for the fountain of youth desecrates the aged. Without a beautiful body and several decades of work ahead, an executive finds it difficult to interest any employer in hiring him.

The greatest responsibility for this cultural aberration rests with the corporate world. Enormous salaries to beginning employees bearing no relationship to contributed value; mockery of the moral virtues of honor, loyalty, respect, and community responsibility; glorification of the "something for nothing" attitude; and ad campaigns promoting sexual freedom, the body beautiful, and a pleasure-seeking society all emphasize the "live today because tomorrow may never come" approach to life, and all work toward the casting off of older executives. In corporate America, 50, the prime of life, is defined as "old."

Although coping with an addictive organization or boss is significantly more difficult for older employees, with added willpower and perseverance it can be done. A person caught in this trap can successfully recover from corporate codependency if he really wants to do it. There are definable, workable ways to achieve emotional stability and personal independence while living a happy, satisfying life *within* the addictive corporation. It takes a little longer and some extra effort, but it can be done. To begin with, it involves changes in relationships with and attitudes toward (1) the boss, (2) the peer group, and (3) subordinates. It is necessary to change how a person appears to these people, how he addresses his needs from them, and how he reacts to their attitudes and demeanor. But change means risk—and risk means the possibility of failure.

THE RISK OF CHANGE

In Chapter 3, we saw the necessity of taking risks to achieve any of the steps along the road to recovery. The risks of discovering one's true self and the possibility of rejection from others had to be taken to begin the journey. Structuring a life-style for psychological survival within an existing addictive corporation means assuming additional risks of rejection by incurring disfavor or even malice from a boss, peers, and subordinates. A corporate codependent, indoctrinated with the fear of failure, finds these risks awesome. It takes a major effort and courage to risk behavior changes in the face of this feeling. However, risk you must. There is no other way.

On the other hand, just starting down the recovery trail has been an enormous risk in itself. You've admitted addiction, risked an intense self-evaluation, and accepted the Nine-Step Program. You've risked rejection or retribution by becoming vulnerable to another human being. You've risked ridicule from your friends and family by acknowledging your need for moral growth. By taking these risks and relying on rediscovered moral principles for survival, you have developed strength of character and convictions. The risk of disfavor from the boss is nothing compared to what you have already gambled.

There are two aspects to changing behavior. The first is to acknowledge how you want your behavior to change, which we've already examined in Chapter 3. The second is to implement these changes in everyday living conditions. Wanting to do something and knowing how to do it are a far cry from actual implementation. Putting any change in behavior patterns into practice can be a lot more difficult than merely defining and acknowledging the need.

We all tend to get stuck in how we interpret and react to circumstances in our jobs, marriages, and our interactions with other people. The older one gets, the more stuck one becomes. Even knowing that what we do or say is wrong or harmful to others, we still do and say the same things over and over again. Why? Because we're stuck. We can't seem to unglue ourselves from past habits. As Dr. Sidney B. Simon explains:

> When you are stuck your ability to do anything about your situation seems to disappear. Nothing seems able to get you moving, not your desire to be better, not your treasured goals and aspirations, not even the pain you feel. Threats, bribes, and impassioned pleas are not enough to move you.[1]

Even when a corporate codependent recognizes the changes he should make, it's too easy to procrastinate and hope the bad feelings will go away on their own.

For the disenchanted executive there are three primary reasons for being stuck: (1) fear of reactions from others, (2) lack of personal initiative, and (3) lack of self-confidence. All three are interactive, but it's clearer to deal with each separately. You must find a way to unglue yourself from the panorama of sticky excuses for not changing. The beginning should come from knowing that your moral principles and conduct are right regardless of criticisms from others. Knowing you're right generates courage to risk the ridicule of bosses and others.

Fear of Reactions from Others

But it's not easy. As we saw in Chapter 2, fear of rejection can be a dominant force in stalling a recovery program. No one likes to be held up to ridicule in front of friends or business associates. We all want to be accepted for who we are and what we are. As a recovering codependent with a new set of values and redefined behavior standards, you must translate these changes into everyday living in the work environment as well as at home and with friends. The sooner the boss realizes you are a new person and will not put up with addictive corporate dependency any longer, the sooner you can get on with normal work activities and be productive for the company.

But a boss can be intimidating. The art of intimidation characterizes nearly all power-addicted bosses. To protect their position in the corporation they have honed this skill to a very fine edge. They know that by creating an air of intimidation, they can coerce subordinates into doing almost anything. They can control their employees' actions and thought processes to further their own gains. Their most effective tool in practicing this skill is their subordinates' fear of rejection.

Whenever a subordinate recommends a solution to a problem, or a new procedure or approach, or a different way to handle something, the addicted boss quickly puts him down with, "Oh, that will never work," "I've thought of that but rejected it as impractical," or most likely "I don't like that idea." After having his creative ideas rejected a few times, the subordinate becomes intimidated from suggesting further changes.

Vicious intimidation occurs at group meetings conducted by the boss when he redresses and admonishes the subordinate publicly: "What a dumb idea. Anyone with an ounce of sense would know that won't work," or, "Why can't you solve the problem and meet the sales forecast? A good salesperson would have no trouble doing it."

A more insidious form of intimidation flowers when the boss lets it be known indirectly, through the grapevine, that he is dissatisfied with your performance—but never addresses you directly. One morning a subordinate or someone from your peer group approaches you with, "I understand the boss is really on your back about meeting the increased production quota this week. Too bad." But you haven't heard anything about an increased production quota.

After one or two of these put downs—it doesn't take very many—a person comes effectively under the control of the boss and, fearing further rejection, ceases to recommend changes, take initiative, or express his opinion. Withdrawing into his shell, he becomes an obedient servant of the boss and sinks deeper into addictive codependency.

One effective trick in dealing with an intimidating boss is to play the game for a while. Agree that his way is always best. Make him feel important and the best judge of any and all decisions affecting the company. Intimidating power bosses nearly always lack self-confidence. They are unsure of themselves and their abilities, and by intimidating others they allow a false sense of security to pervade their intellect. By playing up to this addictive weakness, you can often get the boss to stop intimidating you. When that happens, the likelihood of rejection of your new behavior patterns diminishes.

If that approach doesn't work you might have to ask for reassignment to a new job or a new work location, perhaps assignment to a different division or department within the company, or maybe a different job working for the same boss, but with less responsibility. Such a request might solve the problem—or it might be met with resistance. If the latter occurs, you should begin looking for work with a different company. As a recovering executive, you must change your behavior, and if the boss won't accept your new outlook, there really is no alternative but to face the consequences.

Rejection by a peer group might not have such far-reaching ramifications as rejection by the boss, but it can be even more damaging to the individual psyche. Over the years, one learns to look for endorsement and reassurance from the peer group to support one's actions in the work place. Being social animals, most people require daily interaction with business friends and associates. In many cases it's even harder to practice a new morality with peers than it is with the boss. When you sit at the lunch table and for the first time interject your new moral beliefs and soft feelings into the conversation, you can be certain there will be shock and disbelief from peers. After the initial shock wears off, small group discussions and debate about your new morality can easily undercut your resolve to continue. In the case of Jack Rose it was almost the undoing of his recovery program.

Before tackling his boss, the manager of contract administration, Jack decided to try out his new philosophies on business friends. They were a close-knit group of five, sharing fishing vacations, winning last year's bowling league championship, and attending dinners and cocktail parties at each other's homes. The group had noticed Jack change from a bitter, critical opponent of the company to a warm, caring person who seemed to radiate serenity and peace of mind. When Jack told the group of his inner changes, the universal comment was, "You've got to be kidding. The only way to survive in this company is to be as ruthless and conniving as everyone else. You start sounding like a religious fanatic preaching goodness and light and you'll be out on the street in a day. And don't look to us for help. We've got our own jobs to protect." Jack was decimated and bewildered. Had he really taken the wrong path?

Unfortunately, risking ridicule from a peer group is just as necessary to recovery as risking the wrath of the boss. Rejection is a very real possibility. Nevertheless, at least try to include work associates in the recovery program. It will help. One way that works for some people is not to say anything about addiction or codependency, recovery programs or morality, ethical standards or behavior patterns. Just go ahead and begin practicing them. Pretty soon, your behavior will begin having a positive effect on the behavior of others, and they won't even realize it. During my initial recovery program I decided to stop swearing—a small change, but one I felt was important. Within a week there was a noticeable change in the language used by my associates at work, and within a month no one was swearing, at least not in my presence. I also stopped telling little white lies, and again, in very short order, others responded with cleaner slates as well.

Rejection from your subordinates takes on a slightly different tone. When they see you actually listening to their suggestions, soliciting help with problems, asking about their family's well-being, and generally exhibiting a caring attitude in place of dictatorial behavior, their initial reaction is fear. What does the boss have planned for us now? When will the ax fall? Who's on the way out? What are the boss's motives? And defenses will be raised. Upward communications become stilted and incomplete. Some subordinates begin to bypass you and go to the next step up the hierarchal ladder. Political intrigue fosters rumors, and nonproductive time is wasted as small groups debate your demeanor. Unless you can get your message across quickly, rejection by subordinates can do more long-term harm than anything else. You depend on their support to get the job done; if they reject your new ethical behavior, you're done for in the company.

Jack Rose had more problems with his subordinates than with his boss or peers. No one believed the new Jack was for real. Lines of communication were severed. False information and data began filtering in to him. The rumor mill abounded and productive effort in his department came to a standstill. Soon, employees began looking to Jack's peers for advice and even started going directly to his boss for instructions. This rejection, together with rejection from peers, almost ruined Jack's chances for remaining with the company. He was firmly stuck in the quagmire. His worst fears were realized. Change looked impossible.

Lack of Initiative

Lack of initiative can also become an unyielding adhesive cementing the executive to inaction. Although he recognizes that dishonesty, denial, obsessive perfectionism, and self-centered behavior must be abolished on the job as well as in his personal life, he can't seem to muster the drive to get going. Inertia acts like a stone wall he can't seem to push over or get around. Instead of talking to the boss, peers, and subordinates about his new beliefs, or even beginning to practice them without saying anything about changes, he withdraws into his protective armor and continues to act in the same addictive manner.

It's easier to go back to the same old ways of behavior because the pattern is firmly established and everybody knows what to expect from you. Success in the political arena confirms that your survival techniques have been perfected. You know what to expect from the boss by practicing the old habits. It's just more comfortable not to change, and it doesn't take long to convince yourself that changes in moral values and ethical behavior are fine outside the work place, but on the job it's much easier to go along with the old ways.

This is a sure road to failure. A recovering codependent cannot have two sets of values—one for his personal life and one for the work place. What is right at home is right on the job. Dishonesty at the office falls into the same category as lying to a spouse. Caring and consideration toward fellow employees matches the same ethical standards as kindness and sharing with friends. Two codes of ethics are impossible. Either you want to change or you don't. If you do, then take the initiative and start dealing with that brick wall.

A brick wall can't be pushed over all at once, but it can be dismantled one brick at a time. To break the inertia try changing one behavior at a time, perhaps a small one to begin with—as I did with swearing. Maybe you can't stop lying, denying, and controlling all at once. If the wall looks too high, take one step at a time and, as on the roller coaster ride in Chapter 2, momentum will quickly build.

Many times, the initiative or willpower to change becomes stymied by fear. A person just doesn't have the courage to make the changes he knows are necessary. He's afraid of what might happen in the future, and this robs him of the willpower to proceed. Fear is still very real, even with reassurance and support from family and friends. For years, he was immobilized by fear of potential reprisals, failure or even termination. It's no wonder that when it comes time to change work habits, the willpower to do so seems lacking. But somehow fear must be overcome. Changes must be made.

One way to think about change is to recognize that it happens to everyone, every day. The only constant in this life is change. The age of computers has made information instantaneous and the future has become a calculable quantity. There's no need to fear change. Change will always be with us. It is good, it is healthy, and it is stimulating. As Leo Buscaglia states in his book, *Bus 9 to Paradise*:

> This ability to see, experience and accept the new is one of our sav-
> ing characteristics. To be fearful of tomorrow, to close ourselves to
> possibilities, to resist the inevitable, to advocate standing still
> when all else is moving forward, is to lose touch. If we accept the
> new with joy and wonder, we can move gracefully into each tomor-
> row.[2]

Of course, if a person lacks the self-confidence to change and doesn't even have the initiative to try, then all will be lost.

Lack of Self-Confidence

One of these bad feelings caused by corporate dependency that we saw in Chapter 2 was self-doubt. When a person doubts his ability to handle a situation, or when he has strong concerns about his ability to survive the adversity caused by taking a specific action, he will avoid the situation and never try the action.

In dealing with an addictive corporation or boss, one way to build self-confidence is to create a safety net. An acrobat failing to negotiate the tight rope will fall into a net, unharmed. A diver whose equipment fails can rely on his diving buddy to pull him to safety. A recovering executive also needs a safety net if his attempted changes are rebuffed. There's always the possibility that honesty, openness, and kindness will not be tolerated by a boss, peers or subordinates. Before even trying such changes he needs a safety net to assure that he can survive financially, regardless of the reactions of others. You must believe that you can pay the rent and buy the groceries even if the corporation and its leaders do not accept your new code of conduct.

You must also have the psychological confidence to weather the storm—even if you must eventually quit your job and seek a livelihood elsewhere.

The starting point in building this safety net is to restructure your life outside the corporation. To build the confidence to cope with change two programs should be implemented:

1. Establish a second source of income, independent of the corporation.
2. Develop new talents, skills, and interests other than your current occupational skills.

Not only will these conditions provide a safety net, but the mere initiative they require also gives a person a new sense of worth. With this net, he can go on to make the requisite changes in on-the-job behavior patterns, secure in the knowledge that even if they are not acceptable to the corporation, he can survive.

FINANCIAL INDEPENDENCE

For most employees, the greatest fear in risking change is loss of income. How can a person—dependent on the good graces of the corporation to provide income for rent, college bills, or retirement—be expected to take a stand against this same employer? Fixed mortgage payments, astronomical costs of health care, usurpation of Social Security reserves by the federal government, and visions of unemployment compensation lines and decrepit nursing homes for the elderly make it impossible to risk losing his job.

Dependence on the corporation for a sole source of income precludes the possibility of taking control of your own life. Bills must be paid, groceries must be purchased, debts must be settled, and your family must be provided for in the event of your death. Financial dependence is like a hangman's noose—the more you pull on it the tighter it gets. As long as you count on that monthly paycheck to meet all financial obligations, the corporate web cannot be broken. There must be a way to generate a second income outside the corporation. It doesn't have to match your existing salary. In most cases that would be difficult, if not impossible. But you can generate at least some income to tide you over in any emergency. Roy and Sharon Frederick found the solution in flowers.

Roy and Sharon, both 33, lived in a typical upwardly mobile suburb of Cincinnati. Sharon's days were filled with raising two children and maintaining their four-bedroom colonial. Roy was vice president with a mid-sized conglomerate. Although still satisfied with his job and without malice toward the company, Roy listened to my advice as I counseled a mutual business associate. After the session, Roy mentioned he was thinking of starting a small business on the side, to be run by Sharon, and asked for suggestions. A new shopping mall was currently under construction near his home and I suggested that perhaps a florist shop in the mall might be the answer. Roy picked up on the idea, and he and Sharon were off and running.

The couple researched the florist industry and, after considering a franchise, decided to go it alone. They negotiated a lease for space in the mall, located appropriate sources of store equipment and floral supplies, and successfully negotiated a Small Business Administration guaranteed loan for $50,000. Sharon was delighted and proceeded to build a thriving plant and flower store.

In the beginning there wasn't much income; in fact, for the first three years Sharon barely broke even. But during this period, tax breaks from the business enabled Roy to save nearly a quarter of his personal taxes, and by the fourth year the shop was turning a profit. By the following year, Roy and Sharon netted over $25,000 from the plant and flower business.

During this period, Roy became dissatisfied with the progression in his job. Political infighting increased. Stress mounted, travel became a burden, and restrictive corporate policies drained his enthusiasm. With the flower business in the background, Roy's confidence remained high. Even though disillusioned with the corporation, he stuck it out for another year, secure in the knowledge that in a worse-case scenario he and Sharon could survive with the income from their flower shop. Eventually, Roy did leave the corporation and decided to move to Philadelphia. Selling the flower business, the couple realized sufficient gain to tide them over until Roy could either find a new job or buy a business.

The psychological security from his second source of income allowed Roy to weather the storm of disenchantment until he succeeded in shedding the corporate yoke.

Not everyone can find a second business netting $25,000, and not every disenchanted executive has a spouse ready, willing, and able to assume management of a business, but everyone *does* have the ability to locate or create some type of second income. The following are some of the possibilities I have recommended to clients:

1. Part-time bookkeeping or tax service.
2. Interior design.
3. Computer instruction school.
4. Rental real estate management.
5. Stock investment portfolio.
6. Part-time house painting.
7. Part-time tree service.
8. Furniture refinishing.
9. Antique furniture store.
10. Pet training and grooming.
11. Office services: telephone answering, copying, fax.
12. Typing services: resumes, reports, contracts, books.
13. Ghost writing.
14. Part-time teaching of evening adult education classes.

All of these income-producing activities can be accomplished on a part-time basis either by yourself or your spouse. There is no need to give up your primary job, nor to invest large sums of money. All it takes is a little initiative and ambition.

Mohammed Shamir, a securities analyst with Morgan Stanley & Co., approached the problem of financial independence somewhat differently. He found financial security outside the corporation by using the knowledge gained from his employment to build a private investment portfolio. Years passed without any substantial gains in managing his investments. The combination of dividend income and capital gains on his tax returns averaged only $5,000 a year. But Mohammed was patient. Progressing up the corporate ladder, he gained confidence in his ability to select and manage more winners than losers.

As the bull market of the 80s continued its rapid ascent, Mohammed's boss was promoted and a new vice president took over the department. Mohammed felt he should have been given the job, and an intense rivalry developed. Beginning to show the symptoms of corporate codependency, Mohammed learned quickly that cutthroat tactics were the new rules to follow. But the more he tried, the worse he felt. Anger, remorse, disappointment, and feelings of inadequacy eventually led to an emotional breakdown, forcing him to take a three-month leave of absence. Rediscovering a new morality and redefining personal goals led Mohammed down the road to recovery. But he still feared reentering the world of high finance with an antagonistic boss.

After replacing his old codependent behavior of dishonesty, obsessive control, denial, and self-centeredness with a softer, more moral pattern of compassion for his coworkers and even his boss, Mohammed went back to Morgan Stanley. Though he was somewhat fearful of expressing his newfound attitudes toward others, the financial security from his personal investment program gave Mohammed the courage to try. Two years later we met for lunch and Mohammed related his story of success. But he was quick to point out that without the knowledge that he could survive financially without the corporation—at least for a time—he would not have had the courage to practice the Nine-Step Program.

Whatever path you choose, the mere fact that you have income-producing interests outside a regular job can ease the fear of practicing the recovering program. It gives a person confidence to know he is not tied to the corporation forever, not dependent on success in the corporate political arena for the preservation of his livelihood, and not restricted from making the other changes necessary for personal survival. Even though an executive stays with the corporation and will probably never need to depend on a second source of income, the psychological comfort he derives from knowing it is there removes much of his fear of the future. It also enables a person to take those actions for controlling his life that he knows are right. A second source of income is a prerequisite to recovery if he stays with the corporation.

A FALL-BACK POSITION

Concurrent with establishing financial independence–even if it is only for psychological reasons–it's a good idea to start a personal development program to discover new talents, skills, and interests outside the corporation. On the surface, this sounds unimportant. One may say, "Of course it would be nice to have the talent and ability to do something in addition to my current job but it can't be crucial to the recovery program. Besides, I don't have the time. My job takes everything I've got." That's a very normal response to such a suggestion. But don't be fooled. This is an important step if you are really stuck with a company.

Corporate dependency is voluntary. Only if he wants to be dependent on the corporation must a person continue addictive behavior patterns. We get stuck in a job because we do not have the confidence to risk a change. The main reasons we don't have confidence are financial insecurity and a narrow vision of our talents and skills. A corporate lawyer will always be a lawyer if he doesn't exercise his innate talents in the theater or as a teacher. A sales manager will always be in sales if he won't explore hidden skills in public speaking or conducting leadership courses. A financial manager will continue to be a bean counter if he believes manipulating numbers is his only talent. And a corporate president or vice president will manage corporations forever if he doesn't realize he can do just as well organizing social programs or managing political campaigns.

Developing hidden talents and skills is just as important to recovery from codependency as an independent source of income. The mere fact that you know you can succeed in a line of work different from your current job adds a strong sense of survival. It gives you confidence. Just like a second source of income, it allows you freedom to exercise the Nine-Step Program without fear of ending up in an unemployment line. An alternate vocation frees the psyche from corporate dominance.

Almost everybody has a talent or a skill with which to earn income from other than his chosen profession. I call this a "fall-back position." Many of us began our careers doing something specific but different from the job we have at the corporation. Perhaps it was as a bookkeeper, a shoe salesperson, a brick layer, or an auto mechanic. Maybe an undergraduate degree in sociology or chemistry led to an MBA, which launched your business career. Work as a hotel employee while earning an engineering degree may have provided a limited background in the hospitality industry. Most of us have something we can do as a fall-back position in the event of an emergency. At the time, we never thought we would have any use for such skills, so we buried them in our memories. Now is the time to resurrect long-lost talents and keep them visible in your mind. Once recognizing such a talent it's possible to begin exploring a part-time vocation in that field while still working full-time for the corporation—as Mary Coogan did.

Mary worked as a nurse's aid in a hospital while earning her bachelor's degree in business. Upon graduation, she accepted employment with a local bank. Twenty years and three banks later, Mary had managed to become senior vice president of a mid-sized New Jersey bank. She had put her hospital experience out of her mind long ago and concentrated on making it in the banking industry. But now a proposed merger with a large Philadelphia bank seemed imminent. Although assurances were given that none of the senior officers would lose their jobs, Mary felt threatened and stress began to build. While negotiations proceeded over the ensuing six months, Mary's headaches and backaches increased in severity and frequency. Denying anything was wrong, she increased her work pace and quickly became a workaholic, obsessed with driving herself and her subordinates mercilessly.

The merger finally occurred and Mary kept her position as senior vice president of the merged conglomerate, but her physical ailments continued. Through professional help, Mary recognized her addictive codependent behavior. Advised by her analyst to resign her position, Mary could not bring herself to take the step. She did, however, remember the good times and satisfaction she felt many years ago working in the hospital. Over the next nine months, while continuing her job at the bank, Mary organized a neighborhood trauma support group of volunteers to assist medical teams with newly arrived patients at the hospital. The hospital administrator was so impressed with Mary's efforts that he offered to put her on the payroll as a part-time assistant in the trauma ward. Mary gracefully refused the offer—for now. But the fact that she now knew she could earn income in a field other than banking furthered her recovery and allowed her to begin practicing her new behavior pattern at the bank—much to the surprise, and delight, of her new boss.

If for some reason you don't already have a fall-back position, it's never too late to learn another trade or vocation. Graduate degree programs in many professions are available in most cities. Adult education classes teaching specific skills proliferate in nearly every region of the country. Correspondence courses are available to everyone. Perhaps you can expand a hobby or a volunteer activity into a second vocation in an emergency. It's never too late to broaden your horizons and either brush up on long-forgotten old skills or develop new talents. Either way, as a recovering codependent, a fall-back position is crucial to your recovery program.

With a second source of income and a fall-back position firmly in tow, a person's confidence to implement changes in behavior patterns at work will expand. The ability to survive financially eases the fear of rejection from bosses, peers, or subordinates. It also tends to provide the initiative to make changes.

Changing work habits is risky. No question about that. Rejection, ridicule, and even the possibility of being fired can make implementing new, nonaddictive behavior patterns perilous. But once again, there are support mechanisms available. You need not go it alone. There are ways to get bosses, peers, and subordinates to provide you with support in the recovery process. And with others involved in what you are trying to do, the risk of making changes diminishes. The secret lies in subtle changes in your attitudes toward others. In Chapter 5, we'll see how these subtle changes can affect relationships and provide yet another safety net for the recovering executive.

ENDNOTES

1. Sidney B. Simon, *Getting Unstuck* (New York: Warner Books, Inc., 1988), p. 5.
2. Leo Buscaglia, *Bus 9 To Paradise* (New York: Random House, Inc., 1986), p. 96.

CHAPTER 5

A NEW EXECUTIVE: CHANGING
BEHAVIOR PATTERNS IN THE
CORPORATION

Having put a safety net firmly in place, a recovering executive should be ready to face the difficult but necessary next step: making appropriate changes in his personal behavior and approach to dealing with others in the corporation. With your new code of ethics as support, you should be ready to substitute new behavior standards for your old codependent traits. Honesty should replace lies, recognition of the human dignity of individuals should overshadow the obsessive need to control, and an altruistic concern for others should supplant egotism. Your new ethical behavior standards must be implemented in the work environment, not for any economic gain, but because you cannot recover from codependency if you practice two sets of values—one at home and one at work. Such dualism will inevitably impede all attempts at recovery. To regain your sanity, you must learn to practice traditional moral principles in everything you do—including your actions and decisions in the work place.

This doesn't mean a person should show up for work one day with bugle blowing and an unfurled flag proclaiming his new found morality and renouncing addictive corporate policies. On the contrary, implementation of behavior changes mandated by the Nine-Step Program is subtle, quiet, and nondisruptive for others. If you maintain a nonjudgmental attitude and go about your business as normal, you will almost always enlist others' unannounced help in making your changes. It can be done quietly, almost imperceptibly. Unconsciously, bosses, peers, and subordinates will act as support mechanisms to your recovery.

The key to this vault of support lies in your recognition of what relationships and behavior are really important and what can be discarded as useless or harmful. These changes take place in four arenas of the work place: (1) personal behavior, (2) behavior toward others, (3) the imitation family, and (4) moral values.

PERSONAL BEHAVIOR

Before a person can change relationships with others, he must begin practicing new work habits consistent with the Nine-Step Program. The following are the most important habits to develop as soon as possible:

1. Honesty; no more lies of any kind.
2. Open acknowledgment of mistakes.
3. Constructive dealing with anger and fear.
4. Coping with problems as they occur.
5. A new set of responsibility priorities.

To break the addictive power circle a person must be honest with himself and others: no more shaded opinions. Take credit when credit is due, but give it to someone else if it's his or her idea. "It's our opinion that . . . , should be replaced with "It's my opinion that . . . , and Mike agrees with me," or "It's Mike's opinion that . . . , and I agree with him."

Stop fabricating rumors or exaggerations. This is easy. Don't state anything as a fact without the evidence to back it up. Don't guess that something may or may not be the case. If it's an opinion, express it as such. And don't express any opinion about someone else's behavior—unless you can say something good. "I think John is wasting a lot of time"; "It seems to me Patty could be working harder"; or "I understand Eileen and Rick are having an affair" may be juicy items for gossip, but they are judgmental and can only hurt people. This is the type of poor communication typical of addictive codependents. Also if you have something to say to another person, tell him or her directly. Don't delegate your dirty work to someone else. Keep direct lines of communication open with everyone. It's the only honest way to interact. If another person makes a mistake that affects you or your performance in the company, tell him you know about it and that it's OK this time. If the boss calls you on the carpet because of it, don't share the blame or make excuses. Acknowledge openly that it was Bob's mistake, not yours, but that you'll try to help him correct the problem so it won't happen again. You can't afford any more lies or cover-ups. To survive you must accept the responsibility for your own actions, but not for those of someone else.

This doesn't mean you must be perfect. Of course not. We all make mistakes. But when you make a mistake, a bad judgment, or a miscalculation, admit it to the boss. If you fear recriminations for the error, it's better to get it out and air the problem than to be dishonest and try to bury it. Most bosses, even those severely addicted to power, have a hard time punishing someone because of honesty. If the boss's instructions were not clear, be honest enough to admit the misunderstanding. Next time try to clarify his directions before proceeding.

The same principle holds true when dealing with subordinates. If you've made a mistake, or a bad decision, admit it to them openly. A good starting point is an explanation such as, "It was my fault you need to work this weekend. I made a bad judgment about the amount of work the project would take. I'm sorry if it inconveniences you. What can I do to help?" By the way, when was the last time you heard your boss make a similar statement? Probably never.

An executive must learn to deal with his anger and fear in constructive ways within the framework of the corporation. This sounds more difficult than it really is. One trick I developed while still working for a corporation was that whenever I attended a confrontal meeting or when I encountered a particularly tense or difficult situation, I tried to smile. Almost invariably what was slated as a confrontation ended as a peaceful discussion and what could have been an angry face-off turned into an intelligent conference. It's amazing how disarming a smile can be. That may sound trite, but it really works.

When something happens to make you angry and you can't muster a smile, try telling the person who was responsible for the event how you feel. Not with shouting and foot stomping, but quietly and rationally. I once said the following to my tyrannical addictive boss and it worked wonders: "I really wish you wouldn't chew me out in front of my peers. You're angry and that makes me angry. But more than that, it makes me feel bad that I have hurt you. I apologize and will try not to do it again." He was so shocked that he never gave me a hard time in public again.

Fear can be lessened by getting all the facts. Once the facts are on the table they can be accurately assimilated. There is no need to fear something known—it can be dealt with. The unknown must become known as soon as possible.

Lenny, an accountant, had always been timid. One day, directed by his boss to represent the company at a gathering of chemical engineers, he was to report back any developments affecting the outcome of his boss's pet project—the importation of a chemical disinfectant from Brazil. Lenny knew nothing about disinfectants other than what he had picked up reading labels as a consumer. Mixing with all those expert chemical engineers frightened him, but he was even more petrified at the possibility of reporting back the wrong information. So frightened he could scarcely move, he couldn't keep any food down. To assuage his fear he obtained a copy of the printed agenda in advance of the conference and spent three days in the public library trying to learn about disinfectants. On returning from the conference he wrote a three-page memo to the best of his ability—although still not having thoroughly understood what went on at the meetings. His boss was shocked. Lenny had produced an intelligent, well thought-out appraisal of the subject matter together with four recommendations for dealing with disinfectant import restrictions proposed at the conference. He ended up with a small bonus and the gratitude of his boss.

Solving problems as they come up can be a tough assignment for a person with little authority to act on his own. Many times problems might arise through actions of someone outside your circle of authority or from the actions of superiors. There's not much you can do about these problems and they are not the ones to concentrate on. But problems within your control should be dealt with as soon as possible. Don't let a problem fester. If it's something that needs doing, do it. If it's a meeting, hold it or attend it. If it's a personnel problem, talk to the person involved (who can probably solve it a lot faster than you can). If it's a dispute, try to resolve the issue. If it's a tough project, get to work on it. Whatever the problem might be, it's important to deal with it and get it out of the way before its festering becomes malignant. Problems have a way of not going away unless someone does something about them. Unsolved problems lead to fear—usually repressed. They can also cause obsessive behavior trying to invoke cover-ups.

The last of the primary habits to change isn't really a habit at all—it's where a person places the corporation and his job in his personal list of priorities. Chapter 3 listed responsibility to oneself as first, to family and relatives next, followed by responsibility to friends and, finally, responsibility to the corporation. There is a 100 percent certainty that if you mix up these priorities, you cannot recover from corporate dependency. Every time an executive puts his job at the top, the recovery program fails.

The entire rationale for developing a safety net to guard against dismissal resulting from changed behavior patterns is predicated on the recovery priority list. The corporation and your job can't be higher than sixth on the list. If they are, you sacrifice yourself, family, and friends for the corporation—which is what contributed to the psychological mess in the first place.

Although most corporate bosses will disavow any attempt to have you put the company before family and friends, in fact, an addicted power boss expects you to do just that. Overtime, late meetings, weekend projects, and delayed vacation plans all aim toward having you put the company first. However, it won't work to march in and announce, "From here on I won't work any overtime or weekends, or attend late meetings. My family comes first and they need my time more than the company." That's a sure recipe for getting fired. But subtle changes in your work habits can get the message across just as clearly, and if you do it right, no one can blame you for shortchanging the company.

Ginger Blackman was a manager with a mid-sized publisher in Florida. Recognizing the need to straighten out her emotional dysfunction, she decided on the following strategy for keeping her job and the company in the proper priority perspective:

1. She began by instructing the 15 people working in her department that overtime and weekend work would no longer be an acceptable way to get any job done. She expected everyone to be at work by 8:30 and to leave at 5:00, but to put in a full day's work. Those were her hours and she expected everyone to follow her lead. Any overtime had to be approved by her in writing.

2. She told her boss about the new schedule and guaranteed the same or better performance from her department as before. If he wasn't entirely satisfied, she would make up the work herself.

3. She also told him that she could no longer work weekends because she had enrolled in a college course that took all day Saturday, and she needed Sunday to study.

4. Finally, every morning she let her boss know of any plans she had for that evening or any evening for the next four days and asked him to tell her then whether she would be expected to attend any meetings on those nights.

Ginger's boss accepted the first three points without much comment, realizing his escape was to have Ginger pick up the extra workload her people couldn't get done. But evening meetings? He explained to her that all types of emergencies could arise requiring evening meetings—and usually did, at least three times a week. He couldn't possibly let her know in advance, not even a day.

Knowing her boss was a dysfunctional workaholic, Ginger knew she must do something drastic to break this logjam. The next day she handed her boss a letter of resignation outlining his refusal to comply with her request for advance notice of evening meetings as the reason. On the bottom, in small print, she included a "cc:" to the company president. Her boss was shocked and angry but agreed to give her the advance notice she required. Ginger's stand resulted in the abandonment of evening meetings. In addition, all of her subordinates finished their daily work loads in the time specified, weekend work for everyone in the company diminished to a trickle, and Ginger is still employed and doing well as a successful recovering codependent.

BEHAVIOR TOWARD OTHERS

Along with changes in behavior patterns affecting his own welfare, the recovering executive must make adjustments in his relationships with others, both within the company and without. Built on the foundation established by new personal behavior traits, these changes in relationships will inevitably bring others in the company to his assistance and support him in his recovery—even though they might not realize what a supporting role they play. It's convenient to group these relationship changes into four categories: (1) management techniques, (2) relationships with superiors, (3) relationships with peers and subordinates, and (4) family welfare.

Everyone has his or her own management style, whether running a company, managing a department, or heading up a project. We've already seen how power addiction causes managers to obsessively control subordinates and demand perfection. This type of domination is dictatorial management. Power addicted managers won't admit this, but that's what it is. In the recovery process, such behavior is intolerable. A change in management style must be implemented. And the change must be to what I call "merciful management." Others might prefer "benevolent management" but merciful management seems appropriate to recovering codependents. With merciful management you treat subordinates the same way you would like to be treated by your boss: with high values placed on human dignity, compassion for others' problems and misgivings, concern about the welfare of employees both on the job and off, and a generally kind approach that recognizes the very human need of everyone to be appreciated and supported, even loved—although this is a difficult concept for most managers to grasp in the environment of an addicted organization.

In Chapter 3 we saw how love and other soft feelings can open marvelous doors. But loving of your fellow man can be a formidable task. There probably are a number of people in the organization you don't care for at all. Now you're expected to practice merciful management, an altruistic approach that calls for extending a loving hand to them? Yes! Remember, we're talking about people who have the same feelings, fears, and desires you have. Everyone has a different personality and set of opinions. It is a recovering codependent's responsibility to accept these different traits and reach out to help people wherever and whenever possible. When the opportunity arises—and it certainly will—where there is a choice between being kind toward someone or being ruthless, take the former approach. You are learning to accept people for what they are, not for what you want them to be, and this is love.

Changes must also occur in a recovering executive's relations with the boss and other leaders of the corporation. When something doesn't go the way he wants, a codependent usually reacts in one of two ways: by becoming critical of those in authority or withdrawn and secretive. Both reactions lead to a breakdown in communications and allow the disappointment, hurt, or disagreement to fester. Such an open sore further alienates him from the boss and increases the breakdown in communications. Criticizing the leadership either openly or subtly increases the executive's feelings of anger and betrayal—although his boss may be unaware that anything is wrong and therefore cannot take action to correct the problem.

Part of the recovery program is to be honest and open in communications. To practice this habit, the executive must address his wrongs directly with the boss when they occur, not days or weeks later when the boss has probably forgotten what happened. The best way to handle this is to force direct and continuing communication. This becomes quite difficult with a power-addicted boss because one of his control mechanisms is to avoid any direct communication with subordinates that might lessen confusion and thus endanger his position of authority. Many times it is difficult to get to see him. He's in a meeting, out of town, on the telephone, or behind a closed door. If you make an appointment to see him, he will forget it or say something has come up that's more important. Instead of telling you directly that he can't meet, he will dictate a memo inferring that such a meeting is unnecessary. An addicted boss can find any number of ways to avoid direct communications with his subordinates.

Yet, part of the recovery program demands open communications. Somehow, you must find a way to break this communications barrier. Waiting outside the boss's door for a meeting or phone call to finish, having his secretary alert you the moment he is free, and calling him on the phone are some of the ways you can get through. Phoning him at home in the evening or on weekends might break the logjam, even though telephoning is only a shade better than written communication. When a misunderstanding or disagreement arises, the only way to resolve the issue—and resolve it you must—is to have a direct, face to face discussion. Open and clear communication are so crucial to the recovery process that if the boss flatly rejects your overtures, your only choice might be to resign.

A second change in relations with the boss is to practice the same compassionate attitude toward him that you do toward subordinates. Get close to him. Try to get him to talk about his problems and concerns. Find out what's bothering him and why he is insecure. Let him know you really do care about helping him solve whatever problems he may have with *his* boss or with a difficult project. What can you do to help him further his career? This can be a very disarming attitude for a boss to handle. Most will not expect it and be somewhat reticent to open up to a subordinate. But with persistence it usually works.

After Ginger Blackman's boss, Roger, overcame his shock and anger at Ginger's stand against his workaholic addiction, he became more accessible to her. Ginger used the opportunity to follow up with her second punch. About a month after their confrontation, she asked for a private meeting to discuss a reorganization of her department. During the meeting, Ginger turned the conversation to Roger's apparent dedication to the company and how he spent every waking hour on company business. With a little probing, she learned that his wife was suing for divorce and their eldest daughter had taken his wife's side against Roger. These twin catastrophes drove him to seek refuge in his work. Ginger had no solution to his problem, but listened carefully and sympathetically while Roger unburdened his heart. After that meeting, their relationship changed. Roger was no longer demanding, unreasonable, and uncommunicative; Ginger was no longer rebellious. By exercising a little compassion, Ginger not only furthered her own recovery program but also, by helping him recognize he wasn't alone in his agony, actually helped Roger to begin his own journey out of the morass of emotional dysfunction.

This same caring attitude can be utilized to improve relationships with peers and subordinates. Both power addicts and codependents of power addicts expect their behavior to be mirrored in those around them. A demanding, dishonest, workaholic boss expects his subordinates and peers to behave the same way. Since he can't recognize the harm in his own actions, he expects everyone else to act the same way. Before beginning the recovery program, you probably acted similarly.

With such a history, a caring attitude is the last thing anyone expects of you now. The case of Jack Rose in Chapter 4 is a perfect example. When he began listening attentively to his subordinates and peers at the planning meeting and actually accepted suggestions from others, everyone was shocked. Even his staunchest antagonist was won over. It's very difficult for anyone, peer or subordinate, to resist reciprocating kindness. Merciful management of subordinates demands a compassionate attitude. As you practice this approach it won't be long before your peer group learns of the change. At first, suspicion runs rampant. What is he after? What does he know that I don't? Has the boss promised a promotion? Has he taken the credit for one of my projects? Will he beat me out of the next raise? These questions and more are bound to be raised by the peer group. Changed behavior, even for the better, is disarming and raises red flags. The reason is competition. In the corporate arena, internal competition for the boss's favors is a way of life.

How then can you cope with potential disbelief from your coworkers? And how can you reach out to help others who are competing against you, trying to beat you out of the next promotion, conniving to put you down in front of the boss, and otherwise practicing corporate political gamesmanship? It's not easy, but it can be done.

As the saying goes, "It takes two to tango." It also takes two to compete. If you refuse to continue playing the competitive game and let adversaries have their way without a struggle, the challenge of winning will soon vanish. When two boxers enter the ring both must box or there isn't any fight. If one refuses to raise his gloves, the other boxer will return to his corner after a few light punches. He will win the fight but will never challenge again. In the corporate arena it's a little different, but not much. Practicing compassion toward your enemies will quickly take the competitive edge out of relationships. Without the threat to their security or advancement, adversaries can no longer be antagonists and can't hurt or embarrass you or beat you out of anything.

Judy and four other nurses were competing for the recently vacated head nurse's position in a hospital in upstate New York. The subtle, and sometimes not so subtle, competition had been going on for over two months. The date for naming a successor was rapidly approaching when Judy had her emotional break-down. In her first two therapy sessions, her competitive nature was uncovered and her therapist recommended she withdraw from competition for the head nurse's job. On returning to the hospital the next day, Judy wrote a letter of commendation to the nursing board suggesting that either of the other three women were more qualified than she and pointing out virtues and abilities of each. One of the three did get the job and Judy was relegated to her normal nursing duties. However, relationships changed. Knowing Judy's actions, the other losers became her friends instead of enemies. Her new boss regarded her in a new, favorable light. A year later, when a teaching assistantship opened up, Judy was highly recommended to fill the job—without competition from anyone else.

Practicing merciful management techniques can work wonders with both peers and subordinates, but not everyone reciprocates with warmth and consideration. Some of them will try to take advantage of your apparent acquiescence. Some will see kindness as weakness and become even more disparaging. They will kick and shove and push, and they will win some battles—be ready for it. But few can hold out against compassion very long. As soon as the glory in winning has run its course, they usually accede. In the long run you will be the winner, but even if you aren't, you have no choice. The road to recovery demands concern for other people and you must follow your new goals.

Judy won her war because she refused to compete with her associates on the level they demanded. This doesn't mean Judy stopped competing. It means she stopped destructively compet-ing. As long as a person works for the corporation there will be competitive pressures—it's the nature of the corporate game, and an executive can't run away from it. But he can compete on his own terms. Instead of worrying about false accusations, inferred incompetence and exaggerated rumors, concentrate on your job performance. When others realize you are no longer in the political game, they'll leave you alone. And to ignore an outstanding job performance would put the boss in a bad light. Compete the right way and you're bound to win—if for no other reason than nobody else is in the running. It's just one more fine line to walk between patterns of addictive corporate behavior and your new personal goals for survival. It takes some high stepping and finesse, but it is achievable. Not all competition is fair, however. As we saw in Chapter 1, the boss has his own agenda for survival that everyone is expected to support. A subordinate's recovery program has little meaning to the boss if it conflicts with his personal goals. The assistant, vice president, or staff person who flagrantly furthers the boss's goals will inevitably gain favor. Competition for such favor is keen because by speaking up for a subordinate the boss can make the difference between that subordinate's keeping a job and losing one. So everyone ends up catering to the boss's whims. Backing out of this competition may leave you wide open to criticism and even termination.

But you don't have to drop out of the race. Compete for the boss's favor, but do it honorably. As long as your actions don't hurt yourself or anyone else, what harm can come from supporting the game plan? If playing up his management abilities is honest, can further his career, and harmless, then why not compete for a ranking in the boss's camp? On the other hand, if such action would be harmful either to yourself or to others, then you owe it to the boss to explain your position and let the chips fall where they may. If such a stand means termination, then other recovery efforts will probably not be tolerated either and you're better off leaving.

By keeping new ethical goals in the forefront of all business decisions and interpersonal relations, the recovering executive will probably not only be successful in mastering the competitive environment, but also cause others to change to his way of thinking. Caring for others is contagious. It has a way of spreading even in an adversary organization. You must follow this path anyway, and you might be surprised at what happens to those old antagonists.

Changed behavior patterns outside the company environment will inevitably affect a person's demeanor at work. It's difficult, if not impossible, to practice ethical standards of behavior at
home without doing the same at the workplace. Reprioritized
responsibilities that put family welfare above the corporation
demand compliance with family needs first. If a family member
is ill and requires care, then take time off from work. If your
spouse, child, or other family member has a problem and needs
help, it's more important to handle that matter first rather than
rushing off to the office at 8:00. Even if it means sacrificing an
important business meeting, not completing a project on time, or
incurring the boss's wrath, family welfare comes first. This is just
one more risk a recovering executive must take. If the company
can't or won't allow him this necessity, quitting is probably the
only solution, as David learned the hard way.

David has been an obedient corporate employee at a New York
investment banking firm for six years. An effective wheeler and
dealer, David rose through the ranks quickly and at 33 earned a
tidy six-figure salary plus a bonus and other fringes. But the
price he paid was high. Distraught, nervous, and disenchanted
with the morality required in deal making, he had severe
headaches that finally caused him to recognize his emotional dysfunction, reassess his personal values, and enter a recovery program. Shortly thereafter, David's wife entered the hospital for
emergency surgery. David notified his boss that he needed to be
with his wife in the hospital and wouldn't be in for a few days.
When he returned to work, he found an angry boss and one of his
major deals taken over by another project manager. Confused and
afraid of losing his job, David promised his boss that such an
absence wouldn't happen again. That was the end of his recovery
program and David sank back into the quagmire of corporate
dependency. Six months later, David had succumbed to three-
martini lunches and three packs of cigarettes a day to ease the
psychological burden of his emotional dysfunction. He knew he
was losing the battle.

About that time, David's teenage son suffered a nervous
breakdown and his wife desperately needed David's help to cope
with this catastrophe. That was the final straw. David finally rec-

ognized his family came first. He told his boss that he would
return as soon as he could, but not until his son's condition was
stabilized, and went home. A week later his son was recuperating
in the hospital and David went back to work—only to find that his
desk was occupied by a new body. His boss called him in and
informed David he no longer had a job. If he wasn't responsible
enough to take care of business matters first, he could look elsewhere for employment.

The risk is great in slighting the corporation—but then the entire
recovery process is an enormous risk. All the steps in the process
must be followed religiously—including reprioritizing
responsibilities—or recovery will never occur and all those bad
feelings will only get worse. If you are unwilling to make the commitment and then live with it, you might as well give up now.

HANDLING THE IMITATION FAMILY

As seen in Chapter 1, corporate leaders often insist on membership in the corporate family. Attendance at company picnics,
dinner parties, and other social events; active participation
at meetings and seminars; strict adherence to company policies;
and encouraging subordinates to become involved in corporate activities and accept corporate philosophies all prove a person's willingness to be a part of the family. The reputation of
IBM as the epitome of corporate togetherness is well known.
The familiar "Big Blue" nomenclature is designed to encourage
esprit de corps among employees. "Family" obedience requires
compliance with a variety of written and unwritten dress and
behavior codes. The idea is that people who look the same and act
the same will think the same. The imitation family unit thus
remains a strongly knit group.

General Electric, Arthur Andersen, many of the national
banks and investment banking houses, Merrill Lynch, and other
large conglomerates have this same public image. Togetherness
and employee esprit de corps imply competence and a competitive
edge in the market place. Many lesser known mid-sized corporations are even more dogmatic in their requirements for family

membership. If your company is one of these addictive organizations insisting on active participation in imitation family activities, be very careful. This is just another way for the corporation to exercise control over your thoughts and actions, and that is something you, as a recovering codependent, cannot afford to let happen.

On the other hand, in continuing to work for the corporation a person must find a way to follow his new personal goals and still not conflict with corporate policy. This can be accomplished by separating the "look right" from the "be right." The corporate family cannot be ignored. Nor can a person go against its policies and still keep his job. He must continue to abide by the rules and participate actively in company functions. This is the "look right" and should be sufficient recognition of the imitation family to please the boss and other corporate leaders.

But you do not have to rely on the imitation family for psychological, social, and moral growth and well-being. Nobody can force you how to think. No corporate leaders or set of rules can dictate what you believe in or what your values are. There isn't any requirement that a person must forsake his own family for the corporate unit. On the contrary, successful recovering codependents usually develop a much stronger real family bond than they had before. They follow corporate policies and regulations on the job but rely on their real families and friends for emotional and moral support. This is the "be right" and is the direction you must take on the road to recovery. There is no alternative.

Lawrence was a dictator. He ruled a mid-sized food processing company from his presidential suite with an iron hand. Elected five years earlier by the board of directors for his reputation as a "get-it-done," two-fisted throwback to the turn of the century industrial barons, Lawrence proceeded to clean house of deadwood management, to implement tight controls, to force wage and benefit reductions, and to trim the workforce by 25 percent. He insisted that management, as well as all other employees, participate in planned corporate activities. Workdays became 10 hours instead of 8, and nearly every weekend included a company meeting or function that demanded attendance by one or more groups of employees. Loyalty to the corporate family became the rule of thumb for anyone who wanted to remain on the payroll.

The effect was remarkable; for the first time in a decade the company experienced three successive years of increasing sales and earnings. Shareholders were delighted and stock prices quadrupled. Lawrence had led the company from the brink of disaster to a major force in its industry segment.

But then a national recession hit and the company suffered declines along with many other companies in the industry—all except the industry leader, which seemed to thrive on adversity and registered an increasing market share and improved profitability in the face of the recession. Board and shareholder pressure mounted against Lawrence. "If they can do it why can't we?" was asked at every monthly board meeting. The policies that had worked to buoy the company profits were now failing. Key executives resigned, the union threatened a strike, sales were plummeting, and auditors questioned the veracity of the current inventory valuation practices.

The world was turning against Lawrence—or so it seemed. Stress increased, and along with the added tension and pressure, his annual physical exam revealed skyrocketed blood pressure and a small ulcer. His drinking had increased along with his food consumption and the doctor warned him to slow down and change his approach to life or he would soon be dead.

Lawrence asked for a 30-day vacation and retreated to a small mountain resort in Colorado—by himself. There, in the quiet and solitude of natural surroundings a strange thing happened. Lawrence the hard-boiled, intransigent, ruthless corporate leader experienced a rejuvenation of his spirit. It was as if he suddenly realized the difference between right and wrong, an awakening of long dormant moral values. Not that he tried; it just happened. He changed, and changed radically.

Returning to his presidential post, Lawrence began changing the very policies he had sanctioned several years earlier. He consulted executives before making key decisions. He implemented improved benefit programs and an employee stock option plan. Caring for other's problems became a byword in the management circles. Overtime was forbidden and employees were encouraged to spend free time with their families. The company even closed for Good Friday, which hadn't occurred since Lawrence's predecessor held the reins. Employee productivity began showing marked improvements. The board couldn't believe what they were seeing. A man hired because he was tough now turned out to be benevolent—and it was working. The employees, customers, the community, and even competitors were responding with overwhelming enthusiasm. Even better, the company once again showed earning improvements and the stock price rose.

When asked by a major shareholder at the annual meeting what had happened, Lawrence answered: "Nothing very complicated. Before I left for the mountains, my 20-year-old daughter told me to seek refuge in my conscience. Whatever I decided to do, she said, I could count on her. Her support gave me strength. Then, while in the mountains, I came to understand that as president I have a responsibility for the well-being of my employees and customers and the best way I can exercise this responsibility is to encourage people to be themselves, like themselves, and act for their own well-being. That means caring and kindness from their superiors and support from their families. Like I said, nothing very complicated."

MORAL GROWTH

Chapter 4 examined how inertia and lack of initiative can easily hamper the implementation of changes in behavior patterns. This initiative, or willpower, is tough to maintain, yet somehow you must find the strength and determination to begin the implementation process and then keep going. By this time you should already have begun the recovery process and therefore must have a genuine desire to succeed; otherwise, why bother? But when the going gets tough, when the boss appears completely unreasonable, when peers begin the customary political infighting, when the company issues new policies that you know are wrong, when your spouse or children treat your recovery program with skepticism or even disdain, when you've had enough and are ready to call it quits—that's when your need for willpower to keep going is greatest. And that's when you must rely on your new code of moral values: your regenerated moral convictions of right and wrong, of what is worth doing and what is not. So when the road get too bumpy and you feel yourself slipping back, call up that moral conscience you've rediscovered. Take time to listen to that still, small voice within. Rely on instincts and intuition. Then go ahead and do what you know is right.

How will you know the right thing to do, the right decision to make, or the right way to handle a situation? You'll know. We all know. We always have known. Moral growth is the same for all of us and it always guides us in the right direction, if we will only listen. Remember steps two and three of the Nine-Step Program:

2. I have the inner strength to make whatever changes are necessary to regain my sanity.
3. I will follow my conscience to temper intellectual decisions with moral determination.

The Nine-Step Program is not just a rhetorical exercise. It is a way of life—the rules by which you agree to live when entering the emotional recovery process. The whole purpose in rediscovering moral values is to provide direction and inner strength for recovery. Moral growth serves as the bastion of resolve in coping with disenchantment, frustration, and confusion. You can deal with rejection, ridicule, disappointment, failure, and even getting fired by believing in and adhering to your inner conscience, that still, small voice controlling your deepest feelings and convictions. It's the only real strength any of us have.

Even more exciting, implementing moral conduct in place of addictive behavior can influence an entire organization: Your caring in dealing with people and your honesty in handling problems will be visible at work. There is no way to cover up these changes and still function productively. This doesn't mean making soapbox speeches proclaiming your rediscovered moral virtues—although the desire to do so may be strong. Nor does it mean attempting to convert others to your way of thinking. All it really means is that you have come to grips with yourself. You have confidence in your ability to do what is right, and you can act with the best interests of other people in mind without advertising your moral convictions: Be a loving, giving person while still commanding the respect of others. Joy, happiness and personal satisfaction will show through, and when others receive compassion they will reciprocate. It is even possible that eventually your ethical standards may permeate the organization and reach the corporate leaders.

CAN YOU MAKE IT?

So that's how to cope with corporate disenchantment and still keep your job with an addictive corporation. To make it easier to follow, let's summarize the tactics:

1. Continue to follow the Nine-Step Program.
2. Make appropriate changes in relationships with the boss, peer groups, and subordinates.
3. Get unstuck by overcoming the fear of reactions from others, initiative inertia, and lack of self-confidence.
4. Develop a safety net with a second source of income and a fall-back position.
5. Implement personal behavior changes.
6. Implement behavior changes toward others and deal honorably with internal competition.
7. Learn to live with the imitation family without succumbing to its dominance.
8. Rely on your moral conscience when things go wrong.

Following this path probably won't make the company any more palatable, but at least it should make life bearable—and it will certainly break the corporate web. Can you make it? Yes. Many other people have and are continuing to enjoy prosperous and satisfying lives while working for addictive organizations. Will you make it? That's up to you.

But don't be too upset if, after you implement all these suggestions, it's still impossible to combine the recovery program with your present work environment. It is not at all unusual to strike out in at least one or two of the eight steps. Sometimes it's not feasible to implement all of the steps simultaneously. A recalcitrant boss, uncooperative subordinates, or a company hopelessly enmeshed in addictive policies can nullify even your most ardent efforts at making a recovery program work. If this sounds like your company, then trying to adjust personal behavior patterns while continuing to mollify an addictive boss becomes a fruitless task. You're far better off looking for work elsewhere. Ideas in Chapter 6 for finding another job should ease the pain and provide you with the wherewithal to break the corporate web.

CHAPTER 6

ANOTHER CHANCE:
MATCHING A NEW COMPANY
WITH A NEW PERSON

"I don't want to set the world on fire. I just want to do my job the best I can and be left alone," replied Frank McGinty, a recovering executive, when I asked him how he liked his new job.

I met Frank when we worked for a subsidiary of IU International. Both of us were fired on the same day, along with seven other middle managers, during one of the IU house-cleaning moves. In those days the Walworth Corp., a large manufacturer of industrial valves, was losing money faster than could be accounted for. Cash was nonexistent. Bills went unpaid for months. Management turnover measured close to 75 percent. The industry was changing, and Walworth was dying. Top management of the parent company determined that the solution was to hire new operating management continually, so every year or two there was an almost total house cleaning. Frank and I avoided the first three, but in the fourth, we were caught in the vise.

While I went to another corporate conglomerate, Frank opted for a production job with a privately owned mid-sized company. When we next met several years later, I was becoming increasingly disillusioned with corporate life whereas Frank seemed happy with his new company and his life-style and enthusiastic about working as production superintendent. He held no delusions of grandeur and didn't want to take a bigger job. He told the owner and president that he would continue to do his best for the company, but because of his inability to cope emotionally with corporate politics he requested that he not be considered for any advancement in position. The owner understood Frank's position and honored his agreement.

At the time, I thought Frank was crazy and chastised him for giving up the corporate battleground. Several years later, when suffering from the psychological trauma of losing my biggest, and last, corporate political battle, I began to understand the wisdom of Frank's philosophy.

For the disenchanted executive finding another job can be a nightmare—particularly if he is past 50. Federal age discrimination laws have done little to help the older executive. In spite of their excruciating need for solid experience, many companies find a variety of excuses for not hiring an executive over 50—and in some cases the cutoff age is 45.

As Hilda Scott and Juliet F. Brudney point out in their book *Forced Out*:

> To the public in general, and even to older people who aren't job hunting, the unemployed older worker evokes stereotyped reactions: If they had been any good they wouldn't be out of a job. They must be slowing down, out of date. Or, if it has been established that the older worker is a victim of a mass layoff or merger, they aren't looking hard enough; don't know how to present themselves . . . ; or are too fussy. They want too much money, or they won't consider changing fields. They won't or can't develop new skills. Maybe they're unwilling to relocate.[1]

A recovering codependent has another strike against him: he must find a company where he can continue to practice his recovery program.

Of course there are many choices other than taking another job. You could retire, become an entrepreneur, or even change careers outside the business world. However, most middle-aged executives do not have the financial resources—not to mention the mental discipline—necessary to retire. An even higher percentage do not have the inclination nor the financial wherewithal to become entrepreneurs. Nor do most of them have the financial security, personal characteristics, or desire to make a complete change in careers.

The only choices remaining, then, are either to stay with the same corporation and try to change behavior patterns to cope with the addictive work environment, or to find another job in a different company. Obviously, if you have already been terminated, the first choice becomes moot and you're left with finding another company.

What special problems does the recovering codependent encounter in finding a new job? Plenty. But there are also some unique ways of finding employment in an environment where his recovery program can continue unabated.

Changing companies is at best traumatic; at worst, it can be a nightmare. Just finding the right company to consider can be difficult and may take a long time. Perhaps it will require relocating or retraining. Thankfully, there are some proven methods that have been used successfully by other recovering codependents for finding the right job in the right company. While using the normal job search resources such as recruiting agencies, want ads, and personal contacts, keep in mind the following tested guidelines and special techniques specifically applicable to a recovering codependent. They will help you select the right company to fit your moral criteria.

THE START-OVER ATTITUDE

One of the best ways to avoid another psychological disaster is to approach a job search with a "start-over" attitude. The very first step in the Nine-Step Program is to acknowledge that you have no control over the corporation or events emanating from corporate policies. The start-over approach acknowledges this and goes one step further. It means that a person will not even try to exert such control. It means he will accept the policies and directions of company officials as their prerogative—not his. As a recovering codependent, he wouldn't accept an addictive management position even if it were offered.

The start-over approach means the executive is willing and ready to begin a new page in his corporate career. It means he is amenable to performing his job without trying to win another person's position. He is willing to support the corporation but will not become married to it. And he flatly refuses to accept membership into an imitation family again.

The start-over approach means a new set of goals: a new code of ethics and new moral values defining what is important. These moral values should be compatible with the company's goals, but if they are not, the recovering codependent promises himself that he will not change his values to fit the corporate mold. Neither will he try to get the company to change to fit his standards and beliefs.

The start-over approach means that a person likes himself just the way he is. He'll perform the job to the best of his abilities but will not, under any circumstances, change his convictions to comply with company philosophies. He will continue to follow the personal goals outlined for himself. They are important to his sanity. He steadfastly insists that that's how he will live his life, both on the job and off. He'll be honest with himself and with his employer in all things—regardless of the consequences.

The start-over approach means that your responsibility priorities are to yourself, your family, and your friends in that order, and that they take precedence over your responsibilities to the corporation. The start-over approach literally means a person is willing to start over in a new job as a new person, not necessarily at the bottom of the ladder—his talents and skills will probably overshadow those of many of his coworkers—but in a noncompetitive position. He must take steps to ensure that superiors, peers and subordinates realize he is no threat to their jobs or security. He is, in fact, a new person. Previous corporate achievements are of no significance anymore. Holding the position of company president or department manager in the old company is immaterial now. When you start over in a new company with a whole new set of values, your new employer must understand that you are willing to start over with a clean slate. If he can accept you as you are, chances of your success are high.

SIGNPOSTS AND DANGER SIGNALS

When you begin to look at new job opportunities, it's important to be constantly aware of both visible and hidden characteristics of the company. Always guard against the possibility of ending up with another addictive corporation or working for another addictive boss. But how does a person identify whether either a boss or an organization has addictive characteristics? Some signs are obvious to an outsider and some are hidden except to existing employees.

Addictive organizations are basically dysfunctional—that is, abnormal, impaired, or incomplete. They seem to be on the brink of disaster. They use slogans, posters, banners, and clever phrases to pep up the morale of employees. Public relations efforts keep the company name in the media limelight as a great place to work, as selling terrific products, or as supporting worthwhile causes, but when you meet someone who has worked or is working for the company, he or she admits that, inside, the company is in turmoil. Annual reports to shareholders are thick, pretty, and full of glowing remarks about how great the employees are—but the numbers show a dismal record of performance and you wonder how the company can afford the fancy report. Announcements to analysts and the financial community always stop short of describing what is really going on behind the company's doors. No officer ever announces that the company made a mistake or a bad judgment. Problems are always explained as caused by external events.

An addictive corporation is always led by addictive management—it can be no other way. There are usually four sure signs that the management of a company is power addicted: (1) confusion, (2) denial and dishonesty, (3) competition, and (4) obsession with control.

Confusion reigns supreme. Today's problems are always put off until tomorrow. No reasonable explanation is ever given about how problems arose. Saying "That's just the way it is in this industry" is a favorite method of escaping responsibility for anything bad. Employees never seem to know who their real boss is. Organization charts are nonexistent, out of date, or so poorly composed nobody can read them. Lines of authority continually cross so no one manager or executive is responsible for anything specific. Crisis management is practiced with great proficiency. No one has time to make long-term decisions because they are always putting out yesterday's fires. There's always a current crisis to be handled now, right now, today.

Personnel practices extend the level of confusion. Management avoids true measurements of individual performance. People are judged in magical ways using mysterious weighting charts, questionnaires, and evaluation forms. The end result is that people are told what they are "worth" rather than made to feel like human beings. Arbitrary behavior standards are established to protect the top management of the company. People are judged by who they know rather than how well they perform.

Denial is another favorite trick used by addictive managements to obscure the truth. For example, a company may deny the harmful environmental effects of products it produces: "Nothing wrong with insecticide sprays—they make the fruit look good." Dishonesty is not only tolerated, but it is also expected. People are not allowed to say what they think or feel, only what their boss wants to hear. Addictive corporations practice dishonest, manipulative advertising. Some products don't work as advertised; other products damaging to one's health and well-being are glorified as making their users sexier. A new sports car is shown as attracting flocks of young starlets or musclemen.

Internal competition is not only tolerated, but also expected and emphasized: to win at any cost; to smash the opposition; to get the promotion, a raise, the new project, or more customers regardless of who gets hurt. Finally, addictive corporate leaders are obsessed with control. As we've seen, power addiction can only be fed by control of events and people. Addictive management employs this control to mete out punishment if unrealistic goals are not achieved, or if rebellious executives disagree with the boss or refuse to play by the Rules of the Game.

Communication in addictive corporations is also mixed-up. Nobody says what they mean or means what they say. Written memos are everywhere. Seldom are one-on-one meetings held to resolve issues or confront problems. Third parties are used to carry messages in order to avoid face-to-face meetings. If someone has a complaint, instead of taking it to the source, he or she discusses the problem with others who have no authority to resolve it. Gossip and rumors proliferate. Secrets are a way of life. Bosses believe they know what is best for employees to hear or know about. Enormous amounts of time are wasted passing rumors in small groups.

An addictive corporation is grossly inefficient. Corporate leaders tend to overlook the important issues and concentrate on small, easily solved problems. Schedules are missed, reports are late, and meetings begin late. Forgetfulness by employees is a recurring condition.

The primary mission of the corporation is usually totally ignored. Corporate leaders go off on tangents; they make acquisitions that have no relationship to the company's mission, try to influence government legislation, become involved in international politics—everything except what they have told stockholders they are in business to do.

Addictive leaders blame others for their own shortcomings. They blame foreign competition and government trade policy for the company's profit decreases. They blame unions for low productivity of workers. They blame the IRS for lack of capital investment. The cause of poor performance or even failure is always portrayed as external to the corporation, its leaders never at fault.

Such tactics are fundamentally unsound and, for the recovering codependent, deadly. Such nonproductive policies encourage the employee to concentrate his time and energy on activities that cannot produce, sell, or distribute goods or services to consumers. The corporation gains nothing toward its avowed mission of increasing earnings. An addictive corporation is not only harmful to the individual employee but also to its customers and to society. Inefficiency and wasted resources contribute nothing toward the betterment of mankind.

Clearly, the recovering executive searching for a new job must, above all other considerations, avoid the addictive corporation. Many are easy to learn about simply by reading the newspapers and newsmagazines or watching TV. Others, particularly smaller companies, can be identified as addictive during the interviewing process.

Now that you know what to guard against, there is no excuse for falling back into the addictive trap. But what about the positive elements? What characteristics should a company possess to aid in the recovery process? Any executive is fully aware of the need for an adequate compensation package and good personal chemistry between the employee and his boss. There are two other positive criteria to look for in a job search, however, which are even more crucial:

1. The company must be "people-oriented."
2. The company must place a premium on individuality and creativity.

A PEOPLE-ORIENTED PHILOSOPHY

How do you identify a company that considers people its primary asset? Certainly not from its advertising campaign. "We care!", a popular slogan to attract public goodwill, tries to convince the public that a certain company is people-oriented. However, in practice, the company is obviously addicted to material goals.

You probably cannot identify such a company from its annual report or sales literature either. These documents are also constructed to create favorable public opinion. You certainly cannot tell from its top executives, who broadcast the virtues of the company at seminars and on TV commercials. Once again, these addresses are aimed at establishing a good image of the corporation.

The best results usually come from talking to as many employees of the company as possible. At times, the closest you can get is during the interviewing process—and that's OK. With eyes and ears open, you can tell pretty quickly how the structure and policies of the company influence actions of its employees. Some personnel representatives can be very polished and can put on a beautiful show of company loyalty, but once you get past them, the rest of the people you interview should be more forthright about the company. The following are some of the key questions to get answered:

1. When was the last cost-cutting reduction in the workforce? If the answer is "never" or "too long ago to remember" you are probably safe. At least the belief that poor profitability can be solved by firing people isn't prevalent.
2. What is the turnover rate in management ranks? If more than 5 percent of the supervisors and managers have left

within the past three years, this probably reflects a problem with people relations.

3. What happened to the person who had this job before? If he was fired, why? If he quit, why? If he was assigned to a different job, why? Is it OK to talk to him about the company? If it's a new position, then what has changed in the business to require this new position?

4. Why not promote someone from within the company? If no one can do the job, what makes it so unique? Or doesn't anybody want the job? If not, why?

While interviewing for a Division Controller's position with a multinational conglomerate I asked why the company didn't promote from within to fill the job. "We've looked for six months but there just isn't anyone on board who meets the qualifications of the position," was the answer from the Personnel Manager. It seemed strange that a corporation known for its financial acumen and heavy staffing of field controllers couldn't locate one person capable of filling this position. However, I was so thrilled with the opportunity to join this company I closed my eyes to the potential problem.

Six months on the job revealed the real answer. Not only was my boss a confirmed power addict, but he was also firmly addicted to alcohol – to the extent of keeping a fifth of Johnny Walker in his desk drawer. Known for his tyrannical management methods, no viable candidate within the company would even remotely consider taking the job and become subjected to the constant barrage of insults, tantrums, and irrational behavior of this Division General Manager. In fact, they all breathed a sigh of relief when I accepted the position. Excuses for not wanting the job were no longer necessary.

If you get a chance to walk through the company's offices or plant, observe the demeanor of the employees. Is there laughter? Is the tour guide greeted warmly? Do people take the time to say hello to you? Or is everyone concentrating on work? The latter probably indicates an undercurrent of dissatisfaction. People are afraid to stop working, even to observe common courtesy. This is obviously not a people-oriented company.

INDIVIDUALITY AND CREATIVITY

It's a little tougher to ferret out a company's attitude toward individuality and creativity. Because many corporations make either a conscious or an unconscious effort to squelch individual thinking and personal growth, the assumption should be made that, until proven otherwise, such attributes are not tolerated. No specific questions asked at the interview will yield a straight answer on this matter. Seldom, if ever, will a company representative deny that individuality and creativity are desirable traits. It's good image building to promote the individual's importance to the company—whether it is true or not.

Probably the best way to determine the level of tolerance for individual thinking and action is to listen and observe. No matter how much a corporation wants to hide its personnel sins from the outside world, listening to how questions are answered and observing the demeanor of people working at the company can provide clues about the type of management behavior. Private meetings with employees can also indicate whether individual initiative is valued or thwarted. Trust your intuition; it will always be more accurate than what you are told.

Several years ago, while interviewing for a financial executive position at a major tire and rubber company in Akron, Ohio, I was enthusiastic about everything I saw and heard. A week later I was offered the position at a salary 35 percent higher than that I earned at my previous company (from which I had been terminated in a cost-cutting move). However, something didn't ring true. Intuitively, I knew something was wrong even though the company appeared to be people-oriented and proclaimed the value of individual initiative and creativity. So I asked the Executive Vice President (who was to be my boss) if I could visit the facilities one more time before giving my answer. He agreed.

This time, I knew what I was looking for. During a luncheon inveigled with one of the department managers who would be reporting to me, I popped the $64,000 question: "Jim , if you had your 'druthers,' all things being equal—compensation, benefits, and so on—and assuming you felt qualified technically, would you rather have the job I am offered or run your own small company?"

"That's easy," he replied. "I'd much rather run my own company. Then I could be as creative as I wanted. No one could tell me my ideas weren't any good. I could be myself and have the freedom to succeed or fail on my own."

That was all it took. My intuition was correct. Creativity was not valued in this company and individual initiative was probably not tolerated. I rejected the offer, and a year later I heard that four top executives had been terminated—including the new financial vice president who had accepted the position that had been offered to me.

It is sometimes easier to find appropriate people-oriented policies in a smaller company than in a large corporation. Although many executives from large conglomerates find opportunities for advancement, high salaries, and attractive benefit packages less prevalent in smaller companies, the underlying management philosophy may very well be more adaptable to the recovering codependent.

SMALL OR LARGE

The choice between a large company and small one seems to create an eternal struggle for executives trying to change jobs, particularly if they have been weaned in a multinational environment. The obvious pros and cons are just that—obvious—and we won't bother with them here. But distinct differences in company size relate to the needs of the recovering codependent. Is he any safer in one size or the other? Can his goals be realized more easily and more completely in a small or a large company? Are his financial criteria more apt to be met by a smaller or larger company? These critical questions must be addressed from the outset. Obviously, a clear advantage of one size over the other precludes wasting time on the loser.

Generally, the smaller the company, the closer relationships are between employees and company leaders. There are fewer corporate structures to deal with, less pressure from other executives, and certainly cleaner lines of communication to the top management level—whether it be the owner–president or the board of directors. Especially with a small, privately held company, an executive should be able to exercise a greater degree of initiative and creativity. Policies, job definitions, and responsibilities must be broader because there are fewer specialists. Usually, an executive in a small company must wear many hats and be proficient in a variety of functions requiring individual initiative to solve problems. A small company also tends to be more people-oriented than a large conglomerate. Almost by definition, to obtain maximum creativity in the decision-making process, the boss must be cognizant of the needs and desires of his subordinates. Motivation techniques directed toward cooperation are often predominant in this type of organization.

But there are also risks. Many small companies are run by dictators—some malevolent, some benevolent. Either way, the boss's opinions are going to rule. His desires and needs must be met. His rules will be played and his conscience kept clean. Is there room for the newly hired executive to be himself? Is there an open morality permeating the company? Or is the owner or president so dictatorial that he uses his personal agenda to manage? Not infrequently, an owner–manager is so addicted to power that conditions are worse than in a large company. At least in a large public corporation, the president is answerable to the board of directors. In a privately owned company, the owner answers to no one.

Are the financial rewards of working for a small company sufficient? Small companies offer a greater chance for individuality, but many are unable to match the compensation package offered by a larger corporation.

Most codependent executives leaving a large corporation find it difficult to go back to another of the same size because finding out the true character of a large corporation or of its top executives is very arduous unless there are public events which reveal their true nature. It's much safer to choose a smaller company as your first venture back into the corporate world. Smaller companies are not necessarily any freer of addictive behavior than large corporations, but generally the smaller the organization, the easier and faster one can determine the true nature of the boss.

A NEW INDUSTRY

Another avenue often helpful in the recovery program is to find a job in a completely different industry. If you've been in banking, try manufacturing, or move from retail to financial services, or from manufacturing to computer services. Many times, such a break from the past can be beneficial in providing the impetus to change. With no frame of reference to earlier addictive situations one should find it easier to implement new behavior patterns.

Larry tried unsuccessfully twice before to shed the bonds of corporate codependency. His first shot, with another large corporation, ended in dismal failure. His second attempt was with a mid-sized company manufacturing products for the same markets as his earlier employer. Once again, he became caught in the corporate web. Distraught and confused, Larry couldn't bring himself to go after another job as an employee, so he began a small consulting practice. On the way to recovery, he found he needed an extra push to break the inertia of inaction and made a conscious effort to locate an engagement in an industry different from those in his background—preferably in financial services. Being with another manufacturing company, even as a client, would bring back too many memories dangerous to his recovery process, whereas a financial services company would hold no past associations. Eventually, Larry negotiated a consulting assignment with a small investment banking firm in New York. It was to be for an indefinite period of time and a full-time engagement. It was almost like being an employee again. And it was a complete break with the past. It was part of the recovery program.

There was nothing mystical about investment banking—no business or organization problems Larry hadn't encountered many times before. But the problems were packaged differently. Solutions required slight variations from prescriptions in a manufacturing environment. In the end, these small differences forced a reorientation of his thinking and allowed Larry the final dissolution of 20 years of corporate brainwashing.

It's interesting to note, as Larry related after the engagement ended, that this small firm of fewer than 12 employees was proba-

bly as addictive an organization as any he had seen before–
including such giants as General Electric, Chase Manhattan,
Boeing, and ITT. Paranoia and neurotic behavior ran rampant
throughout the organization, for employees as well as the owners.
All the characteristics of addiction were present. It was impossible to distinguish between addicts and codependents, but everyone was one or the other. As Larry remarked, "Just goes to show
that addiction and codependency don't discriminate by size of
company or type of industry."

The change in industry, however, did serve its purpose in his
recovery process. To this day, he firmly believes that without such
a break, he would not have been able to finally cast off the old psychological nightmares. So don't brush off the possibility of a new
industry as part of your therapy. A change in scenery can help.
Just be careful of the traits of the company. Small companies as
well as large ones can be infected.

FINDING THE RIGHT JOB

How do you actually go about getting a new job? Particularly
when merged out, fired, let go, or otherwise released by your old
employer? As shown earlier, the business world holds a widespread philosophy that losing a job means failure. The higher one
climbs the corporate ladder, the more difficult to overcome the
stigma of failure attached to being laid off.

It's not necessary to explore here all the banalities of how to
find a job. You know most of them by now anyway, and if you don't
there are plenty of books available with explicit instructions.
However, the following examples illustrate how two recovering
codependent executives used their ingenuity to find good jobs
against the odds. The first case was related to me by a client who
ran his own executive recruiting agency. One of his candidates,
Judy Wy, a recovering codependent, used this approach in a successful bid to locate a new job during her recovery period.

Judy Wy worked her way up the corporate ladder to the position
of Vice President for a mid-sized advertising agency in New York.
At the age of 47 she realized the fallacies of corporate programs

she had blindly accepted and even advocated to customers for over 23 years. She became totally disenchanted with her company and recognized her own symptoms as codependency. She left the agency and began her recovery program.

Within a year she felt strong enough to begin a job search but couldn't face up to the normal harangue of personnel managers or to playing the recruiting game—which she knew only too well, having changed companies six times in her career. There must be a better way to find a job, she reasoned. Armed with a lot of heart, courage, and moral strength, she risked her entire meager savings on three full-page ads: one in an advertising trade journal, one in the *New York Times*, and one in *Iron Age*. (Several of her former-ad agency accounts were in the steel distribution and metal fabrication businesses.) She structured it to be a situation wanted ad, complete with her personal vita, her picture, and in broad, bold letters, "I AM A RECOVERING CODEPENDENT FROM THE CORPORATE RAT RACE" and beneath that line in small type, "I Am Weak, But I Am Willing, And I Need A Job."

Within two weeks Judy received 48 replies; 15 looked like positive job opportunities, 3 were offers to co-write a book of her experiences, 20 were offers of marriage and/or dates, and 10 were from "kooks." She accepted a job offer three weeks later and has been happily employed at that company ever since. Interestingly, of the 15 answers representing job opportunities, all but one extolled Judy's honesty in admitting codependency, acknowledged that their companies recognized the disorders of addiction, and commended her for the gutsy job solicitation technique.

Another interesting approach was used by Ed Coglio. An engineering manager with Grumman for 24 years, Ed was approaching his 58th birthday when he was informed that the recent cost-cutting program eliminated his job. On the street, angry, disenchanted with corporate platitudes, and frightened that at his age other jobs were few and far between, Ed gave up. He withdrew $10,000 from his savings account, told his wife he'd return in six months, and left for an island in the Caribbean to sort out his emotions.

Ed took a job as bartender in a small resort, but he didn't last long. His anger showed through and in six weeks he was fired.

Decimated, he retreated into his shell. He let his hair grow, dressed in beachcomber togs and spent his days walking the beaches and forest trails, sleeping under the stars wherever he could find secluded surroundings.

One morning, Ed awoke with a start. A little ragtag Cruzan boy was skipping stones in the water. He came over to Ed and asked for a quarter—said he wanted to buy a cup of coffee for breakfast. Ed accompanied the child, met his mother and 11 sisters and brothers living in a one room shack, and for the first time in his life realized how lucky he really was. Without going into all the details, it can be said that this encounter caused Ed to experience a moral awakening. He suddenly realized that self-pity was a cop-out. Others were far worse off than he was, and never complained. The kindness and faith extended by this wretched family shook him loose. Three days later he was on a plane home.

Armed with moral courage, Ed tackled the job hunt in a very simple way. He sent reśumeś to the three largest engineering consulting firms in Philadelphia, offering to go to work doing whatever had to be done for a salary of $5,000. Two out of the three responded with an offer. One of these was clearly an addictive organization, and Ed realized it was only interested in taking advantage of his plight. The other one appeared to be genuinely interested in his background and Ed accepted a position as a designer. Within a year, Ed was promoted to department manager—at a $65,000 salary. A short time later, Ed related that his boss had mentioned over dinner one night that Ed got the interview because of his unique offer to work for $5,000, but that he was hired because his boss believed he had met the first genuinely good person in his career and hoped Ed could influence others in the organization.

These unique approaches may not work for you; on the other hand, they might. They do illustrate, however, that there is more than one way to get a new job. A recovering executive has a great deal to offer a company. The trick is to let your new ethical approach to life shine through. Don't let rejection through the normal channels get you down. If answering ads, using recruiters, or writing blind letters doesn't work, why not try something creative, as Judy and Ed both did? What can it hurt?

Creative Interviewing

You probably know more about professional interviewing techniques that I can ever assimilate. But there are some considerations in presenting oneself during the interviewing process that are unique to recovering codependents. Honesty is one of the changes in personal behavior the executive must make early in the recovery process: being honest with himself as well as others. This sounds like a platitude, yet many people tell themselves they will be honest, but fail. Lying about personal values, capabilities, and achievements to obtain a new or better job has become accepted practice in the interviewing process.

The interviewer himself makes lying easy because he always wants to know what you have accomplished in your career. He wants to know your past performance that demonstrates that you can do this job. As an interviewee, you respond, "In my last job I was responsible for a 10 percent profit improvement," "I developed a new marketing technique which produced a 25 percent increase on sales over a two-year period," "I recruited a new staff of managers for the division home office," or "I improved productivity by 15 percent." You really mean that you participated, along with several other people, in a series of decisions and actions that resulted in these improvements or changes. It boosts your ego to claim the achievements for yourself, but this is lying.

The recovering codependent cannot afford to lie anymore. He must continually be on guard against the temptation to glorify his past actions. He does not dare fool himself or others into believing he was, or is, something other than himself. One of the steps he has agreed to follow in changing his personal values is to be honest with himself and other people. Elaborating upon past achievements will only lead to failure in the recovery effort.

Some interviewers expect the candidate to amplify his past work history. They want to believe that he is someone who can bring a new approach, a better talent, or a different outlook to the company. This becomes an "easy" sell and typifies the kind of overachiever so sought after by the addictive corporation. But this is not what the recovering executive wants. He should not be interested in a company that advocates dishonesty, and if he finds himself in such a circumstance, he should walk away from the interview.

On the other hand, there are interviewers and companies who value honesty, and they are easy to spot in the interviewing process. If you maintain a posture of honesty and integrity about your past performance, acknowledge that you were only one part of the decision-making process, and openly confess codependent weaknesses and vulnerability and you still get an offer, then chances are high it will turn out to be the right job. If you do not get an offer, then you shouldn't be interested anyway. To admit personal fallibility and to discuss concerns about addiction and codependency in a new company may cost you the job offer, but at least it will keep you on the road to recovery. On the other hand, a positive response by the interviewer is assurance that here is a company you can effectively work for.

Interviewing Gamesmanship

Avoid interviewing gamesmanship! We have all been on both sides of the interviewing table fully aware that the question and answer process is nothing more than a game of wits. Each party tries to read between the lines and seek out hidden agendas in the other party's questions and responses. Some professionals in personnel management intentionally create tension to determine the other party's mental toughness. Key questions are phrased not to get accurate information but merely to establish control of the meeting. Physical surroundings, body language, attire, and personal demeanor are all used to establish control over the other person. The interviewer is not trying to understand the capabilities of the candidate, but to show him or her who's in control. The candidate doesn't try to learn about the company and the job, but only tries to boost his own ego by dominating the agenda. This gamesmanship is one of the traits you are trying to obliterate. Obsessive control got you into trouble in the old company. To continue to try to control other people's lives and actions will only drive you further into the hole.

Joan was interviewing for the position of sales manager of a small computer services firm. My client asked me to handle the recruiting for this position as well as two others. I knew of Joan's codependency disorder from checking personal references. She came across as aggressive, intelligent, and performance-oriented—an ideal candidate—until we took a coffee break. She then began interviewing me! How did I feel about the feminist movement? What experience did I have in sales management? Did my wife have a job, and where? How did my kids view all my travel away from home? Try as I might, I could not swing the interview back to learning about her qualifications. She had granted me the first hour, but after that the agenda was hers. Her need to control was so intense that when I refused to play her game she began to perspire, twitch nervously, pace the floor, and in fact lose control of herself. She had not yet taken control of her own life and had not even honestly begun the recovery process. Obviously, she didn't get the job.

Control is one form of interviewing gamesmanship. There are many others, as most executives are well aware. To play the game is not to be honest. And honesty is a prerequisite for a recovering codependent. If the interviewer insists on playing games, stop the session and walk away.

SYNERGISTIC VALUES

Personal values and work standards of a potential new boss and peers should be similar to yours. The interview is the place to make the judgment. Now that you have made the effort to reconstruct your own life based on new standards of morality and work ethics, to take a job with a corporation whose leaders advocate diametrically opposed viewpoints would be disastrous. Remember, new goals emphasize personal and moral growth, honesty, open relationships, and a caring and compassionate attitude.

There are several questions to pose at the interview to clarify the position of the corporation's leaders:

1. How do the top executives communicate downward? Memos, media news releases, face-to-face meetings?
2. How will your new boss communicate? Memos, formal group meetings, informal one-on-one meetings?
3. What is the primary mission of the corporation?

4. What were the principal causes of poor financial performance, union strikes, or other adversity?
5. Are people's performances measured against a formal plan
or forecast? How and by whom are merit salary increases
and promotions determined?
6. What role does internal competition play? What happens
to the losers?

The company is a safe work place if the answers are:

1. Face-to-face meetings.
2. Informal one-on-one meetings.
3. A clear and concise statement of its mission.
4. Internal reasons, not external.
5. Measured against plan. Judged by immediate supervisor,
against plan.
6. Minimal competition. Losers are not losers.

Any other combination of answers to these questions spells trouble; the risk of an addictive corporation and leaders is too great.

Creativity

The encouragement of creativity on the job is probably the best
insurance the recovering executive can find to manage his own
actions and life-style. One way to assess the importance the corporation's leaders place on creative thinking is to examine the process of annual budget preparation. If financial standards are
dictated from the top—either from corporate leaders or department managers—then little emphasis is placed on the
individual's creative performance. On the other hand, creation of
goal-oriented performance criteria by the executive responsible
for performing against these measurements requires a high level
of creativity. The importance of creativity to the corporation can
be easily determined by probing the procedures for the preparation of these annual performance yardsticks.

Another measure of the value corporate leaders place on creative thinking is the importance they place on new ideas and suggestions for operating improvements. How are suggestions for
improvements communicated to the boss? How many employee

suggestions were received last year and how many were accepted? Were employees rewarded for making suggestions? How? These questions can all be asked legitimately during the interviewing process. A corporation that values creativity will be anxious to brag about the results. A company that prohibits employee creativity will be hesitant to acknowledge a working employee suggestion system. The interviewer from such a company will invariably answer with, "Yes, we have such a system in place, but it doesn't work very well. People seem hesitant to make suggestions." This is a clear signal that creativity enhancement is missing.

THE EIGHT-STEP SEARCH

As seen in Chapter 4, one of the most difficult barriers to break is one's lack of self-confidence resulting from emotional upheaval. The fear of slipping back tends to make one overly cautious in searching for a job. It's natural to feel insecure at this point in the recovery program. Lacking confidence to handle threatening situations, you don't dare make another mistake, so you continue to search for just the right job in just the right company. This leads to failure; you can never find the perfect solution to your problems. You must take a risk.

Everyone who has traversed this road has recognized the need to try to make a new start. Some have failed. Those who have made it realize that no new job is perfect, and that every company and every boss has some traits that are uncomfortable or disagreeable—but they also recognize the need to compromise. By following the Eight-Step Search, you can improve your chances of success. If you ignore this program, your risk of failing escalates significantly. To summarize the Eight-Step Search:

1. Utilize the start-over approach.
2. As much as possible, avoid addictive organizations and addictive bosses.
3. Look for a people-oriented company with a noncompetitive environment.

4. Promote yourself and establish expert credentials before you start the search.
5. Be honest with a potential employer about your codependency background.
6. Avoid interviewing gamesmanship.
7. Insist on maintaining your individuality.
8. Look for common values.

While it won't guarantee success in finding the right situation, following this program does improve the chances. The Eight-Steps Search really works. Give it a chance.

On the other hand, if you just can't bring yourself to go to work once again as an employee in the business community, a career change may be in order. There are a number of opportunities in the nonbusiness world for executives with sound business backgrounds; the next chapter explores some of these possibilities.

ENDNOTES

1. Hilda Scott and Juliet F. Brudney, *Forced Out* (New York: Simon & Schuster, Inc., 1987), p. 54.
2. Anne Wilson Schaef and Diane Fassel, *The Addictive Organization* (San Francisco: Harper & Row, 1988), pp. 137–176.

CHAPTER 7

A FORK IN THE ROAD:
A MID-LIFE CAREER CHANGE

The Director of Planning for a multinational NYSE conglomerate, Frank had been with the corporation for 12 years, and even though he no longer believed in the corporate propaganda, he didn't have the nerve to call it quits. Also, he really enjoyed the planning activities of his job, although he knew most of it was just window dressing for the security analysts. Still, he began to have doubts about the whole spectrum of business philosophy. The need to bring in greater earnings per share every year escaped him. Personnel policies that clearly discriminated against older executives made his hair stand on end. House-cleaning layoffs every three years, labeled cost-cutting by the CEO, began to look suspiciously like an acceleration of the youth movement. Anger and self-doubt hammered at his psyche, and the thin veneer of the company's employee welfare programs began to melt away. The corporate family just wasn't standing up to the test of time.

Frank strongly believed that young people held the key to the future and became increasingly agitated at what the business schools of the country were teaching these leaders of tomorrow about the morality of business ethics. At age 52, he finally recognized that if he really wanted to help these youngsters he must take action to change his own life-style. Practicing the hypocrisy of business ethics was inconsistent with his personal beliefs. A mid-life career change seemed imminent.

Having always been intrigued by the social opportunities in college teaching, Frank decided one day to throw in the towel, leave the corporate world, and become a college professor. Until his death two years ago, Frank was one of the foremost proponents of benevolent management practices and a loud critic of the harsh corporate treatment of long-term employees.

IS A CAREER CHANGE FOR YOU?

There are thousands of executives in large and small corporations who, if given a choice, would opt to leave the business world. But the corporate web is strong. Financial rewards, status, hope for a better tomorrow, and fear all work against any thought of leaving the corporate family. Yet these same executives broadcast their displeasure with business morality at cocktail parties, social events, and the dinner table—anywhere someone will lend a sympathetic ear. They complain, but they don't act.

Sooner or later, however, an event occurs that pushes them to a decision: a new company president, an argument with the boss, a lost promotion. The event causes a real hurt to the executives' psyche but also provides the impetus to change. When this happens, a vacuum occurs. They don't want to remain in business but don't know what else to do to earn a living.

A good friend of mine, frustrated, disillusioned, and in his third job in three years, approached me for advice about what to do with his career. Recognizing the nature of his codependency, we worked through a self-evaluation, new goals, and the necessity of following the Nine-Step Program. But he still didn't know how to go about selecting a new life-style: he was stuck. I advised the following procedure, which I have used myself to sort out the vast possibilities for a new life.

1. On a large piece of paper, make a list of all the things you would like to do if you had the opportunity. It makes no difference how absurd or far-fetched the list is, but it should include everything you can think of that you would like to do: perhaps take a cruise around the world, buy a Cadillac, go skiing, date a movie star, learn to program a computer, be president of a company, teach in a college, move to a desert island.

2. Put priority numbers after each wish—1, 2, 3, 4, etc. Count halfway down the prioritized list and tear off the second half of the sheet; you'll never get to those items.

3. For the remaining wishes, write down opposite each one the results of achieving it. Do a "what if" exercise: "If I did this, what would happen?"

4. Ask yourself how you like the results of each wish. Those you would be unhappy with, throw out. Keep evaluating until you are down to five or six wishes that have results you could live with.

5. Take another piece of paper and list all the things that are important to you. This must include everything. Your wife, kids, level of income, a big house or a condo, annual vacations, playing poker on Saturday night, helping other people, going to church, and so on.

6. Put priority numbers after each one and tear off the sheet halfway down.

7. Match up the remaining important items with the remaining wish list, correlate the two, and reduce your options to the top three wishes. These are the options to explore. One of them will probably be the right one.

This exercise resulted in two viable options for my friend; however, both were related to doing something different within the business world: buying a business or starting one from scratch. Though he is still employed, the time is drawing near when he will feel that he has enough financial security to take the gamble and kiss the corporation goodbye.

This simplistic method usually produces enough choices to provide a hope that there may really be a life after the corporation—though such a life might involve a fairly drastic mid-life career change. Give it a try. You might be surprised what you come up with. I certainly was. But a mid-life career change is a frightening thought. Regardless of how one defines the term *mid-life*, whether it be 35 or 65, to throw over a lifetime of business-oriented philosophies terrifies most people, and the stumbling block is usually financial.

Fortunately, there are a number of ways to generate income outside the business community that, though they require radical changes, are doable in a reasonably short period of time. This chapter will explore five areas: (1) government agencies, (2) the professions, (3) college teaching, (4) social services organizations, and (5) political office.

Each of these alternatives has both advantages and risks, so before choosing one you should weigh the likely result against criteria for each risk as it relates to the recovery program: (1) psychological compatibility, (2) philosophical symmetry, (3) social acceptability, and (4) financial considerations.

PSYCHOLOGICAL COMPATIBILITY

As a recovering codependent, you have acknowledged that your life has become unmanageable and you have already made some radical changes in your system of values. Conditions acceptable in the past must now be avoided. Other environs must be sought after.

As in changing companies, the two situations to be avoided in any career choice are addictive organizations and requirements to control others. Addictive organizations exist outside the business world as well as within. The recovering executive must try to avoid any organization or relationship that exhibits such behavior attributes. How do you know if addictive behavior patterns exist? Observe the functioning of a given organization in reference to definitions of addictive behavior given in previous chapters. The following are some of the questions you should ask:

1. Does the performance of the organization reflect ignorance of its stated mission for existence?
2. Are communications within the organization predominantly in written form?
3. If an organization has financial, credibility, or personnel problems are the reasons for these problems blamed on external situations?
4. Is there strife within the organization that promotes competition between its members?
5. Does secrecy play a major role in the internal operations of the organization—secrecy between the organization and the outside world, and secrecy among its own members?
6. Does the organization have a reputation for dishonesty?

An affirmative answer to any of these questions offers proof of addictive organization behavior. Many governmental agencies exhibit these characteristics, as do some churches, religious groups, and educational and social organizations. In making a career change, try to do sufficient research to avoid inadvertently walking into another addictive organization. The second time around can be a lot more devastating.

A second feature to avoid in a career change is an organization that fosters control of the individual either by its policies or by its practices. Several religious groups inflict heavy penalties on church leaders who disobey dogma. The American Medical Association, another organization that tries to control the actions of its members, tolerates only those medical practices and procedures sanctioned by it.

Controlling practices are easy to spot in well-known organizations. They are not so easily recognized in an organization out of the public limelight, such as a large law practice or accounting fir. However, the same control techniques used in the business world apply to these organizations:

1. Membership in an imitation family.
2. Dedication to the organization's goals.
3. Commitment to the boss's objectives.
4. Internal competition.
5. Use of greed, fear, and promises as control tools.

The recovering codependent must also recognize that control is a two-way street. Clearly, he must not put himself in a position where others exert an unmanageable degree of control over his actions. Neither can he afford to choose a career that demands that he control others. Both are equally harmful. Control of his own life is paramount; control of or by others is addictive behavior.

Stress is another one of those two-way feelings. In the business world, severe cases of executive stress create mental and physical disorder. Stress in this form should obviously be avoided in a new career. On the other hand, one of the conditions you will probably search for in a new career is intellectual stimulation. Practicing the Nine-Step Program demands the stretching of your mental capabilities. You have probably already found mental skills you didn't know you possessed. In a new career, continuing intellectual stimulation can be extremely rewarding and, surprisingly, controlled stress can provide inspiration.

Jerry Smyth retired from a corporate staff position with a major conglomerate after recognizing he could no longer put up with corporate betrayal. In his search for a new life-style, he succumbed to pressure from his neighborhood supporters to run for office on the local township board of supervisors. Having won the seat after a fiercely competitive race, Jerry found the problems facing the new board extremely stressful. Concerned about his ability to handle this stress, he quickly considered resigning; fortunately, he was dissuaded.

One night over cocktails, he seemed particularly cheerful and self-satisfied. I asked him if this was due to winning some political battle at the supervisor's meeting. No, Jerry replied, but the stress of dealing with township problems forced him to begin using his creative instincts for the first time in years, and these intellectual exercises provided him great joy. His mind was no longer dormant. Stress had cleaned out his mental chute and opened his thinking process to a whole new adventure in learning. That's why he was so happy.

There are also positive psychological factors to look for in a new career, one of which is instant or long-term recognition of your talents. Public recognition builds the ego, and the recovering executive desperately needs to be regularly reassured that his demeanor is acceptable to others. When deserved, ego building can be a marvelous way to achieve this reassurance. Public acceptance as a compassionate person gives the recovering codependent the confidence to continue in his chosen new career and invariably nurtures further improvement in his emotional health.

Be careful of pride, however. Unfettered pride can be deadly and leads right back to addictive behavior. Pride fosters power, and we've seen how addictive power can be. Pride also gets in the way of moral growth. Reassurance brings good feelings and emotions, but unleashed pride caused by praise and fawning only brings harm.

PHILOSOPHICAL SYMMETRY

Presumably one of the reasons for seeking a new career is that you question the immorality and unethical practices in the business world. Philosophically, it isn't right to place the profit motive above the needs of the individual. It seems inappropriate to produce products that are intentionally harmful to mankind (weapons, environmentally hazardous substances, unhealthy consumer products). The absence of compassionate management appears consistent throughout the corporate empire. Moral growth, stagnated by material gains, has become practically nonexistent.

However, nonbusiness careers also pose ethical questions. Is a social service organization or university any less materialistic than the corporation? Can government bureaucracies offer a work environment any more moral than that of a business enterprise? Do standards of performance in the professions promote higher ethical behavior than those in a profit-oriented business?

Look before you leap! The philosophical standards of a new field of endeavor must meet your new objectives of promoting moral conduct and ethical behavior. Some executives feel particularly strong that their mission is to help others. In that case, choosing a career whose underpinnings support compassion for others (such as nursing or psychology) synchronizes philosophically, whereas one advocating dictatorial powers (such as work in several government regulatory agencies, some political offices, or parts of the criminal justice system) does not. The importance of finding a career in a field with philosophical symmetry is crucial. Without such mutual human goals moral growth will be impossible, and without constant attention to the development of moral consciousness you won't make it through the recovery process.

SOCIAL ACCEPTABILITY

In the corporation, the executive had the imitation family for support. Now, recovering from psychological disenchantment, he must have the support of his real family and other community groups. It's difficult for the recovering codependent to handle personal rejection, and the main purpose of support groups is to continually reassure the acceptability of self. This reassurance tends to smooth the waters whenever rejection appears. Rejected recommendations or opinions in the daily activities of the executive's new vocation result in an increased need for support from family and friends.

Therefore, the choice of a new career depends to some extent on the acceptability of such a choice to others. Obviously, if your spouse is an atheist, your new career in the ministry won't solicit much support. Or if most of your friends are predominantly law-abiding citizens, a career as defense attorney for hardened criminals won't garner much reassurance either.

However, you need not have the blessing of all your friends to make a certain career choice, nor does complete concurrence from a spouse insure success. But these matters should be considered, and if you feel a strong need for continual reassurance, it doesn't make sense to choose something alien to either family or friends.

FINANCIAL CONSIDERATIONS

Marcia was terminated from a large Midwest printing company after the owners sold out to a German conglomerate. The new owners deemed Marcia's job as Vice President–Employee Relations redundant, and turned her out, with a month's salary as severance pay. The devastation to her psyche was mild compared to what the firing did to her pocket book. Earning only $41,000 and supporting three kids–one in college and one in prep school–had left Marcia little to invest or save. The day she hit the streets she had a total of $11,825 in CDs, 50 shares of GE stock, a house with a $30,000 mortgage, and $500 per month in alimony payments.

Marcia knew she was sick. The merger, which took three years to culminate, left her emotions in disarray. She drank too much, ate too much, couldn't sleep, and was always angry with her daughter who was still at home. She knew she had to make a change, and the layoff forced her into action. Since childhood, Marcia had wanted to teach, so on the advice of her friends she contacted the local university about part-time teaching while earning her PhD. She was accepted into the PhD program that fall and began her new career path.

One year later, while making good progress toward emotional recovery, she ran out of cash. Medical emergencies ate up all but $3,000 of her savings, the stock was sold, her daughter was ready for college, and Marcia was still two years away from finishing the PhD program. She had no choice but to drop out of school, take another job on the west coast, relocate her family, and go back to the corporate rat race. Today she is a bitter woman, still working at her corporate job, but without enthusiasm and feeling more trapped than ever.

Before making the decision to change careers, take a hard look at your financial resources and requirements. The following eight steps provide an outline to follow:

1. Prepare a written budget of your living expenses, eliminating all superfluous expenses.
2. Convert all possible assets to liquid investments.
3. Estimate the minimum income you need by month for the next three years to cover living expenses.
4. Determine what contingency funds could be raised through borrowings in the event of an emergency.
5. Calculate as closely as possible how much cash you will require to get established in your new career.
6. Estimate as closely as possible how much time you will require to make the career change.
7. Decide if you need to relocate and determine what it will cost.
8. Finally, combine all of the above elements into a monthly financial plan and make a judgment of the feasibility of a career change at this time.

SOME NEW CAREER POSSIBILITIES

These then are the criteria—psychological, philosophical, social, and financial—to examine before you begin down a new career path. Each career choice has a different mix of these elements, some good, some bad. Only you can weigh the significance of the risks against the benefits. The combination is different for each person, and the value placed on each set of conditions varies. But there are some general characteristics of each career choice which can be examined before the election is made and do not require a lot of time on research.

Government Agencies

There are many government agencies—federal, state and municipal—that desperately need the talents of an ex-corporate executive. From the Environmental Protection Agency and the National Forest Service to the Social Security Administration, the Federal Bureau of Investigation, the Foreign Service and the U.S. Military, there are literally thousands of federal agencies needing talented help. If you are interested, the quickest way to learn what openings are available in which agencies is to contact the parent department directly. If you are interested in the Internal Revenue Service, contact the Department of the Treasury; Forest Service, the Department of Interior, and so on. State and municipal agencies and departments also have openings; talented executives should contact the governor's office or the mayor's office directly for information. Sometimes a federal or state senator or member of congress can be of assistance.

There are some distinct advantage to choosing government service as a career:

- Age is generally not a barrier.
- Salaries are fairly competitive with the business world in executive-type positions.
- Pension and retirement programs are highly competitive.
- Health insurance is included.
- Executive stress is usually not a factor.
- The mission of some agencies is to help people.
- There is little pressure from an imitation family.

However, on the downside, there are also a number of risks to government service:

- There is little need for creativity.
- Many top positions are political appointments, and when the boss goes there is often a house-cleaning of his subordinates.
- There is strong control of an individual's actions.
- Internal political maneuvering is as bad, or worse, than in business.

A government agency may also be an addictive organization. Addictive behavior such as deviations from stated mission, secrecy, poor internal communications, and claiming external reasons for failure are common in security or law enforcement agencies. It appears that the more power granted to the agency by law, the more addictive the agency's behavior. The Central Intelligence Agency (CIA) bears closer resemblance to an addictive organization than does the National Park Service. The U.S. Military exhibits more addictive behavior than the Fish and Wildlife Service or the Weather Service.

The Professions

John Q. Wesley, 43 years old, was a vice president at an electronics products division of Westinghouse Corporation. By all outward standards, John was a successful corporate manager following his chosen career path to top management. Earning over $80,000 a year, John began to feel the pressures of corporate life. Maybe the climb to the top was not all it was cracked up to be. Increasingly unhappy with his daily routine and directives from his boss, be began to recognize that a change was probably in order. However, the idea of going through the job search process again was disheartening. That would only mean more of the same, and John didn't think he could stomach another go-around of corporate political battles. He was not particularly aggressive nor interested in having his own business. In fact, the thought of being on his own in the business world frightened him.

John had long dreamed of becoming a respected estate lawyer in a small midwestern town where he could make a significant contribution to the well-being of the people in the community. Until now it was only a dream. The cost of three years of law school looked prohibitive. However, disenchanted with the corporate life-style, he revived his dream once again. His only hesitancy in proceeding concerned the financial commitment.

John had saved nearly $75,000 during his tenure with Westinghouse, and it gave him a feeling of security to know that even if he was ever out of work completely, his family could survive for quite a while. However, when calculating that a law degree would cost over $40,000, leaving the balance of his savings to live on for three years, it didn't seem to be enough.

When approached with the dilemma, his wife responded, "As far as the money is concerned, I'll get a job—which will help— and I can't see any reason why you can't apply for a part-time teaching position at one of the local business colleges while attending law school. Between the two, we can make it. And the kids already have enough money in their college fund to survive. Just do it, and the sooner the better. I'm tired of having you mope around the house every weekend like a sick dog."

With that kind of support, John decided to go for it. That fall, he enrolled in the University of Illinois Law School and accepted a part-time position to teach two courses in production control and inventory scheduling at a local community college.

John graduated from law school with honors and today is practicing estate law in a small community 70 miles from Chicago. Although still struggling financially, he is a happy man and has never regretted the decision to change careers. The new life-style allows him more time with his family and friends, his practice seems to be growing a little more each year, and at last he is doing something for other people. Still teaching one business course at the local college, John is also a Boy Scout leader and active in community welfare programs. His daily headaches vanished, his blood pressure subsided, and he is altogether a new man.

John's advice to other corporate managers who feel boxed in or frustrated by the corporate treadmill is to understand themselves first, develop a strong ethical value system, and then have the courage to find a new life-style. As John stated in his Kiwanis speech, "Man is never too old to change, and with faith in God and your fellow man, anything can be accomplished."

As a recovering executive, you must realize that large professional organizations can be just as addicted to power and control as a business corporation. In fact, large law firms, accounting firms, hospitals, and clinics are businesses. No longer pursuing a narrow mission of professional proficiency, these large organizations have a life and goals of their own that decry the use of the word "profession." They are, in fact, large corporations with a variety of objectives only remotely associated with professional practice. The recovering executive who chooses a professional career change should bear in mind that joining one of these professional businesses is no different than going back to an addictive corporation. Fortunately, many small professional firms, hospitals, and clinics do continue to practice professional standards and are relatively safe for the recovering codependent.

And, you always have the option of starting your own practice. A profession remains one of the last bastions of income-producing activities founded on helping other people. The desire to help others might well direct the recovering executive to such a career path.

Another frustrated executive, Alice had rediscovered her moral consciousness and strongly felt that dedicating her life to helping other people was her true mission. As an officer in a major financial institution, her training and experience had been focused on business subjects. Now at age 43, she left the corporation and entered a three-year nursing program to develop new skills for helping others. It was expensive and time-consuming, but after 20 years of having fought business battles, Alice at last found peace of mind in a new career that meant something positive to her.

John Wesley chose law; Alice chose nursing. You may consider another profession as a new career: medicine, dentistry, the ministry, psychology, architecture, public health, or any number of other possibilities. A career in the professions can satisfy the need to give of yourself to others. It can also enable you to exploit your creative urges and can provide the vocational foundation to a more peaceful, fulfilling life-style.

On the negative side, however, a professional career will probably involve extensive schooling or training. This can be very expensive and time-consuming, and there is no guarantee that once you begin to practice you will be able to make a living at it. Stress can mount as cash vanishes and income remains meager. The biggest risk of all to the recovering executive is to become involved in trying to solve other people's problems—the principal activity of most professions. As we'll see in Chapter 8, it's especially dangerous in the management consulting profession. Others can always solve their own problems better and faster than you can. Listen, advise, comfort, and support but don't try to make decisions affecting someone else's life. This always leads to heartache and frustration and can only drive you deeper into the hole of codependency. Be constantly aware of the dangers of becoming too involved.

College Teaching as a Career

Corporate executives tend to overlook the possibility of college teaching as a viable alternative. Although many colleges and universities require a person to have a PhD to be considered as full-time faculty, several of the smaller private or state colleges are eager to reap the benefits of having an experienced business executive in their classrooms. More and more colleges are recognizing that the best way for students to learn business techniques is from an experienced practitioner, not an academician. For years, doctors have taught in medical schools and lawyers have taught in law schools, but only recently have business schools begun to draw on the wealth of knowledge in the business community.

Current salaries for first-time business school teachers are a far cry from corporate structures. I doubt if colleges will ever pay as much as the business world does, so if high income is a major criterion, look elsewhere. Nevertheless, in many schools, particularly in the East, faculty salary levels are increasing, and $30,000 to $40,000 for a beginning assignment is not bad, particularly when the workload consists of two or three classes.

Learn about college teaching opportunities by going directly to the college or university of your choice. Put together a professional resume that accents your achievements and reflects your abilities in managing people and teaching skills to subordinates. Highlight those skills definable in terms of a college curriculum, such as elementary statistics, basic cost accounting, computer programming, human relations theory, production management, and so on. Company presidents may be offered honorary degrees or part-time assignments to teach seminars, but if you can't bring your experience down to the detailed level of a college curriculum, it will be tough to get a full-time faculty position.

Armed with a professional resume, contact local schools to find out which ones offer full-fledged business degrees. These schools have the broadest business curriculums and hence the greatest need for instructors. Be sure to get the name of the dean or other person in charge of selecting faculty. Sometimes you can get this information from the library, but using the telephone is quicker. Write a literate cover letter to accompany your resume. If you have difficulty with such a cover letter, perhaps your local high school English department will help. (I tried this once and it was the best letter "I" ever wrote.)

Be persistent. Most colleges fill their faculty positions in the early spring for the fall semester. Your timing might be bad the first time around, but try a follow-up in a few months. College administrations are notoriously inefficient, and your letter may very well get lost before it ever reaches the right hands, so keep trying. Chances are high that at least a part-time position will be forthcoming in a few months. Perhaps working part-time while you are still with the corporation and then branching out into a full-time position as an opening occurs will work best. Either way, if you have any inclination at all for the teaching profession as an alternate vocation, it is not only possible but also highly probable that a complete change can be accomplished within a year.

Like the professions, college teaching offers the executive an opportunity to devote his energies to helping others. It also provides ample opportunity for creativity. Stress is normally quite low, and choosing the right college or university can insure a symmetry of philosophies. But once again, many institutions of higher learning, particularly large state-endowed universities, encourage addictive behavior. The effect can be mitigated somewhat if you choose an institution organized so that enough space exists between yourself and the administration. However, one must still be cautious.

Social Services Organizations

The Philadelphia telephone directory lists over 500 social services organizations ranging from the Children's Aid Society and the Hearts & Hands Foundation for the Handicapped to the YMCA, Action Alliance Of Senior Citizens, and the Traveler's

Aid Society. If you have an interest in a new career in social services, the best source of information on what might be available in your area is the local chamber of commerce. Most chambers of commerce will gladly provide listings of organizations, addresses, and telephone numbers. The whole idea of social services is to provide help to needy people or for socially worthwhile causes, and most organizations readily accept people committed to these beliefs.

Perhaps the work will be voluntary for a while, but with a little ingenuity and foresight, most people can get a paying job eventually. Additionally, these organizations provide an ideal outlet to practice your new moral values. Most do not offer high-paying positions—certainly not in the same league as the professions—yet the opportunity to help is ever present and assistance is desperately needed.

Once again, the major risk in such a career, other than low wages, seems to be that the organization may encourage addictive behavior. Even in social services organizations, selfish people have created addictive environments. They are not difficult to spot, however, and as long as a person is consciously aware of the danger, he should be all right.

Private international organizations such as Amnesty International also offer unique opportunities. Amnesty International uses nonviolent methods to try to free people unjustly incarcerated for their religious and political beliefs: "Prisoners of conscience," as Amnesty calls them. Amnesty's techniques include:

> campaigns on particular countries or human rights abuses; mobilizing professional occupational groups on behalf of colleagues; publicizing patterns of human rights abuses; missions to talk with government representatives; or, in cases where torture or death are feared, a network of volunteers to send urgent telegrams signaling international concern.[1]

Talented people are constantly needed to coordinate or manage these activities as well as to perform actual vigils. As Peter Benenson, founder of Amnesty International so aptly put it:

> The candle burns not for us, but for all those whom we failed to rescue from prison, who were shot on the way to prison, who were tor-

tured, who were kidnaped, who "disappeared." That's what the candle is for .... [2]

Surely, few organizations are involved in a more widespread effort to promote the cause of human rights than Amnesty International. You can contact Amnesty at the address and telephone number listed in the Appendix.

Greenpeace is another international social services organization. It is dedicated to preserving the world's natural resources, including all living creatures. Information about Greenpeace can be obtained directly from its Washington office, also listed in the Appendix.

The Peace Corps is an excellent organization promoting assistance to underdeveloped nations. It provides an opportunity to practice caring and compassion, make a concrete contribution to your fellow man, and personally benefit from a wide variety of experiences. Currently, a two-year overseas assignment pays all volunteers' travel and living expenses and, when the assignment is completed, $200 for each month served ($4,800.) The Peace Corps welcomes older executives with almost any productive or human skills. There is no top age limit and about 10 percent of those currently serving are over 50. If you are interested, you can find the address and phone number of the Washington office in the Appendix or you can contact your local Peace Corps recruiting office.

If you are interested in additional information about international opportunities, contact a local public library or write the Institute for International Economics in Washington, DC. Also, the Appendix lists other humanitarian organizations—mostly volunteer—operating both domestically and overseas.

Political Office

You probably never thought about running for an elected office. A busy corporate executive seldom has time to get involved in serious politics. But now, why not consider a career in politics: state, municipal or federal? The pay isn't bad. Some state legislators make over $55,000 plus liberal expense accounts—for a part-time effort. Fringes are good too: health insurance, pension plans, tax breaks. There is ample opportunity to help other people, and nobody can control how you think or what you do. True, constituents may not vote you back into office for a second term if they don't approve of your voting record, but that is hardly what I mean by control. You would be making a very real contribution to society and at the same time practice creativity as much as you wish.

There are a few risks, however. Getting elected to any office is not an inexpensive process. Advertising, campaigning, and office support all must be paid for. Some campaigns take a long time, and during this period a candidate is without income. So before embarking on a political career, determine how much you can invest in a campaign and whether your total financial resources make such a move viable. Obviously, if not elected, your investment of time and money is all wasted and you are still left without an income-producing career. Or, even if you are elected once, perhaps the second time around the voters will turn to the opposition, and once again you'll be out in the cold. As an alternative, you could try to become associated with someone else running for office with the understanding that if elected, he will find a spot for you in the new administration. The risks in this tactic are self-evident.

Nevertheless, in spite of the high risk of failure, many ex-businessmen do end up in politics—and usually make good administrators. It is certainly something to consider as a new career but perhaps, to mitigate the risks, as a second career in addition to teaching or a profession.

HOW TO GET STARTED

Once the decision is made to make a mid-life career change part of the recovery process, the big question becomes: How do you ever get started? The following program proved useful in making my career change and should be of benefit to others.

1. Research the career that interests you the most. Use library sources, government publications, magazines and books, and career counseling. Talk to friends, visit colleges and universities. Interview people already in that career, and do anything else you can think of to provide a thorough understanding of its specific and unusual characteristics.

2. If your career choice requires additional training—such as going to law school or learning a foreign language—take the appropriate steps to qualify for entrance.

3. Become will-known. Establish credibility as an expert and develop a strong public image as a person with unique abilities. Then market this new image in the career of your choice.

The first two steps are self explanatory and not particularly profound. But the third step is the key to a rapid and successful career change. Remember the story of Judy Wy, the advertising agency executive who took out a full-page ad in two magazines and a newspaper proclaiming her abilities and asking for a job? The same approach can be use in changing careers, except in this case advertise your credentials and opinions or offer your support rather than ask for a job.

A similar approach is to put together a seminar to be conducted at a local hotel or conference hall. The content of the seminar should cover the area of expertise you want to establish credibility in. *Then* run the ad; a local business newspaper is an excellent vehicle. Announce who you are, give a brief vita, tell what the seminar is about, and provide the registration details. The subject matter doesn't make any difference as long as it is something you are qualified to present and is related to your new career goals. It's even immaterial how many registrants show up. Of course it would be good to get enough to cover the rental of the hotel room and the cost of the ad, but even that isn't too important. The more people who see the ad and the more people who hear about you, the stronger your public image as an expert will be. Become a celebrity!

Or, if self-imaging isn't appealing, try writing articles on appropriate subjects for a local newspaper, shopper's guide, tourist bulletin, or other local publication. The subject matter should be appropriate to your chosen career goals, but the type of publication is immaterial. Just pick one with as big an audience as possible so that your views on the subject will become widespread. Become an authority!

If neither of these ideas is appealing, a direct mailing to the organization you wish to join, the university where you want to teach, or the local chairman of the political party you wish to support also works. Compose the letter as a concerned bystander, not a job seeker. When the answer comes, keep the dialogue going and, pretty soon, when you approach someone in the organization for a job or an endorsement, he or she will know who you are and what your views and background are. Become a supporter!

Once you are known as a celebrity, authority, or supporter marketing yourself becomes easy. Let the agency, the organization, or the party know that you have now become interested in joining and will bring your favorable public image to the group. It will be hard for anyone to turn down such an offer.

By now you have learned enough about yourself to be confident of your goals. Marketing yourself in a new career should be natural. You should like yourself better than anyone else, and if you genuinely like something and believe it has value, selling it becomes easy. Becoming self-confident in your own abilities and beliefs is one of the advantages of being a recovering codependent. There are many careers outside the business community that can yield a satisfying life-style; only a few have been touched on here.

On the other hand, if the thrill and challenge of business is still in your blood, perhaps you should consider starting a management consulting practice. This also provides a life-style conducive to helping others and encourages the development of unique individuality. The next chapter takes a look at how to get started in this career.

ENDNOTES

1. *Voices For Freedom* (London: Amnesty International, 1986), p. 7.
2. *Ibid.*, p. 4.

CHAPTER 8

THE SOOTHSAYER: STARTING A MANAGEMENT CONSULTING PRACTICE

> Everybody calls himself a consultant these days—and it's giving the rest of us a bad name. The two primary groups I refer to which give themselves the title of "consultant" are: *the unemployed*, who feel that they dare not say they are temporarily between jobs, and *retirees*, who have been regrettably terminated and are not yet ready for pasture.[1]

When thinking about starting his own business, nearly every executive immediately focuses on management consulting. There appears to be a pervasive belief throughout management ranks that because an executive held a high-paying, high-powered job in the corporation, his talents must be in demand in the marketplace. After all, the corporation thought enough of his abilities to hire him in the first place; why shouldn't other people do the same? Except this time he'll do it alone without the interference and pressure of the corporation. Set up an office, get a telephone, hire a secretary, and let it be known that valuable management talents are available for sale to the open market. Success is right around corner, right? Wrong! More management consultant practices fail in the first six months than any other start-up enterprise.

Why does management consulting seem to hold such promise for the ex-executive? For five reasons:

1. It's easy to join the fraternity. There is no certification of expertise: no exam to pass, practically no licensing requirements (except for some engineering, scientific or mathematics disciplines), no specific educational or experience requirements, no state residency requirements, and no government or professional bureaucracy to define the rules of professional conduct.

2. It's inexpensive to get started. You don't need equipment, personnel, a library, or even an office.

3. The product sold is experience. You don't need any special education, and you have no laws or court cases to reference, medical terms and procedures to contend with, or tax codes to learn.

4. It's an opportunity to make big money, fast. If you choose the right specialty, an annual income of $500,000 is not out of the question.

5. There is not much competition. You sell yourself, so more often than not, personality traits win out over technical superiority. Once your credentials are widely known, there are so many specialties that competition in any one is negligible.

Even though the failure rate during the first six months is abominable–more beginning management consultants fail than succeed–consulting remains a favorite recourse for the disenchanted executive. It is a career he can manage by himself without hindrance from the corporate structure. Financial success is limited only by his own actions. And most important of all, a management consultant has the opportunity to help other people–a prerequisite to recovery.

Management consulting is different from any other professional practice. Medicine, law, dentistry, accounting, and architecture are all fields of expertise in which the average buyer of the service admits little or no knowledge. You hire a doctor to diagnose and treat because you don't know how to do it yourself. You hire a lawyer to defend you in court because of your unfamiliarity with the law. You hire a CPA to prepare your tax return because you don't know the intricacies of the tax laws. Practitioners of psychology, psychiatry, the ministry, and social work are trained to listen, observe, and help the buyer of their services solve his own problem within his own means.

But management consultants possess neither unique training for prescribing remedies nor special techniques for listening or observing. Most management consultants are ordinary business people, trained in business subjects, who sell their advice to other business people trained in the same business subjects.

There are variations, of course. The buyer may be a government agency or department; a not-for-profit organization such as a hospital or a fund-raising organization; or an educational, religious, or social services organization rather than a business enterprise. Still, the management consultant is hired to give business or business-related advice regardless of the form or structure of the client—and this business advice is generally available to the public without special education or technical training.

Therefore, before a client willingly pays for management consulting advice he must first recognize that he has a business problem, and second, must want to solve it. Additionally, he (1) either cannot or will not use his own employees to solve the problem, (2) recognizes that the consultant has solved a similar problem before, and (3) is willing and able to pay for such advice, whether or not it is followed and regardless of the results. Management consulting means exactly what it says: a business person selling advice to (consulting with) the management of an operating organization.

WHAT CAN YOU SELL?

A management consultant generally sells his advice in two quite different markets:

1. To a large organization, functionally structured into areas of responsibility, departments or groups.
2. To smaller organizations with authority centered in a single person or a small group of individuals.

A large organization will usually only hire a management consultant if his expertise is so specialized that an insider can't provide the same service or if the organization wants an independent opinion to verify findings or solutions proposed by internal staff. For example, a college may want to reorganize its administrative functions but doesn't employ a full-time organization specialist, or it may want to verify a reorganization plan proposed by its human relations director.

Large organizations may need help in such areas as organization planning, strategic planning, management evaluation, or surveying a new facilities site. An executive possessing extensive experience in one of these specialized areas can usually find another large company—many times a direct competitor—willing to pay to learn how a similar organization has resolved the same issue.

Smaller companies tend to use management consultants more for project management. Personnel recruiting, data processing installations, arranging new financing, and developing an export marketing program require specialized skills not usually available in a small company. Or perhaps a small company may hire a management consultant to supervise a detailed project such as to develop a long-range strategic plan or to manage the design of a new computer system.

However, the biggest demand for consulting services in a small company arises when the company is in financial difficulty. If the management consultant can offer solutions successfully implemented in other companies, his services will be eagerly sought after. A management consultant is not hired to increase the body of knowledge, but merely to give advice about how to solve a problem.

But beware of small clients. A small business owner usually has an enormous ego. He believes he can run his own business better than anyone else and it is only the occasional, unique problem he may have difficulty solving. Generally, he only wants a consultant when the company has serious financing, marketing, production, or personnel problems. Few entrepreneurs ever hire a consultant to tell them how to run their businesses better or how to increase profits. These are management skills they feel they already have.

So when starting out be careful to limit salable advice to specific areas. One of the biggest mistakes a beginning management consultant makes is being too broad, trying to convince the marketplace that he knows how to run a business better than current management. Following this path makes it difficult, if not impossible, to attract any clients. It doesn't make any difference how successful a person has been in the corporation. If he doesn't have some unique talent or skill that others are willing to pay for, he shouldn't cast his lot with management consulting.

Johnny Wong was Vice President of Engineering for a mid-sized electronics manufacturer. A real whiz kid, he progressed rapidly up the corporate ladder and at age 31 was one of the youngest engineers ever elected to the office of vice president in his firm. A skillful manager, five years earlier Johnny had assembled a cadre of highly qualified engineers to develop a new electronic wave emulator. The success of the department was largely attributed to his abilities to motivate and manage. Impressed by these qualities, the President elevated Johnny to vice president. A year later, the company merged with a British conglomerate and Johnny was laid off. Bitter over the firing and disenchanted with the corporate life-style, this "manager's engineer" tried his hand at management consulting.

Johnny invested $5,000 in full-color brochures, mailing lists, letterhead, and postage, and then waited for the phone to ring. Six months went by with no clients. After a year, Johnny had landed only two projects and had total revenues of $4,000 to show for his efforts and investment.

Although making a number of very serious miscalculations during his start-up period. Johnny's most damaging mistake was to assume that he could sell management talent. He made the cardinal mistake so many would-be management consultants make: trying to get clients to pay for telling them how to manage. Don't believe for a minute that you can convince a client you can run the business better than he can. Even though it might be the truth, he will never pay you to tell him that. To be a management consultant, pick a specialty and sell that.

WHERE IS THE MARKET?

As in any business, a management consultant can only be successful when a specific market exists for his skill. Doing the job is 10 percent; marketing is 90 percent. He may be the greatest expert around, but without a market there's no way to sell the expertise. A manufacturer might design and build the best mousetrap in the world, but if everyone uses poison, no one will buy the trap.

Joan learned the mouse trap lesson in a hurry when she designed a new computer program to analyze the amount of excess plaque in the arteries of overweight females. It could perform the analysis faster and more accurately than anything on the market. When she left the corporation to form her own consulting practice and tried to market her computer program, Joan found that a simple chemical process was available to cleanse the arteries, and no one needed nor wanted her sophisticated software.

A truism in the consulting profession states that if you aren't one of the best in your field, don't try to sell advice. As Hubert Bermont put it in his book *The Complete Consultant*:

> I find that most people who aspire to consultancy are totally unaware that they have to be *tops* in their field to qualify. *Mere competence is not enough*. They do not understand that clients will not pay for mediocrity or for the fact that a self-proclaimed consultant (as we all are) must have more going for him or her than five or ten years in the field.[2]

In other words, advice is salable only if it is expert advice. In this respect management consulting is no different from any other profession—or most service industries for that matter. Clearly, when you ask a lawyer to interpret the law you expect an expert opinion. When a doctor treats an illness you expect that he will make the right diagnosis. And an auto mechanic is expected to fix an engine properly because he knows how to do it. When a consultant is hired it's because he can do a specific task better or faster than the client hiring him.

One exception to this rule involves selling a service traditionally purchased on the outside by the business community on a more or less regular basis. For example, most small businesses do not employ pension experts on their payroll. When a small business owner wants to change an existing pension plan or to set up a new program, he hires a competent pension consultant. He need not search out the best pension consultant, merely a competent one. Similarly, in the merger and acquisition (M&A) field, when a business owner decides to expand through the acquisition of another company, he will generally engage a qualified M&A consultant to assist him. The consultant need not be the tops in his field—in fact, such a measurement is nonexistent—but he should come well-recommended.

However, an aspiring management consultant must have the credentials to prove he is an expert. Public recognition provides the best evidence but if he is not well-known in the trade, he should at least have either professional certification or letters of commendation from prior employers.

Before starting down the consulting trail one should ask the following questions:

1. What specific talents do I have that are different from and better than those of anyone else?
2. Is there a market for such talents?
3. Do I have the required personal traits?
4. What characteristics of the consulting profession will assist me in my recovery?
5. What characteristics will hinder my recovery?
6. Can I generate enough income to meet my living expenses?
7. How long do I have to build a practice before I run out of money?
8. How do I actually begin a consulting practice?

PERSONAL CHARACTERISTICS

Management consulting is one of the very few occupations left in our society where age is a plus. Because experience is the product being sold and because age connotes experience, the older one becomes, presumably the more expertise one has. Although statistics are skimpy, I suspect the average age of successful practicing management consultants is closer to 55 than to 35. In fact, as Hubert Bermont pointed out, older executives often try management consulting as the last stepping stone before retirement. Older executives also seem to have more patience in dealing with cantankerous clients, and this becomes a prime requisite to success in management consulting.

In addition to having a salable skill or talent, a prospective management consultant must possess specific personal traits in order to deal effectively with other people and to cope with the many false starts and rejections common to the profession. To survive in the consulting world you must possess:

1. A genuine desire to help others.
2. Infinite patience.
3. A likable, outward going personality.
4. Willingness to do the work yourself rather than delegating it.
5. A strong sense of integrity.
6. A negotiating rather than dogmatic attitude.
7. Excellent "people" skills.
8. Ability to give advice without seeing the results of its implementation.
9. Strength to handle rejection.

This seems like an innocuous list, and yet without such strengths and abilities you will probably fail or at least have a difficult time getting going. A genuine desire to help others heads the list because this is the foundation of the profession. A management consultant exists to help a client solve a problem. The key word is help. You can't solve the problem yourself; all you can do is help someone else solve it. Many ex-employees entering the consulting profession do not understand this distinction and believe they must actually implement their own recommendations in order to be effective. This approach can only lead to trouble.

Randy had developed an expertise in designing computer-based manufacturing cost systems. When laid off from his job as Manager of Data Processing, he decided to convert this proficiency into a salable commodity by starting his own management consulting practice. His first client, a small competitor of his ex-employer, engaged Randy to help design and install a similar cost system. Eager to please, he dove right in and within three months completed the system design and basic programs.

The client was very pleased with the system, and Randy should have stopped there, but didn't. Implementing the system over the next twelve months proved far more difficult. Business conditions kept changing, key employees left the company and cash problems prevented the acquisition of appropriate computer hardware as needed. The client became frustrated with the difficulties of implementation and took out his anger on Randy. Eventually, Randy saw that it was a losing battle and negotiated out of the consulting contract. When his next client required a reference letter, the first client told Randy he was dissatisfied with Randy's performance and would never give him a good reference. Randy had forgotten the first rule of consulting: help the client solve a problem, do not solve it yourself. He had let his ego get in his way.

Nearly all successful management consultants agree that without a genuine concern for the welfare of others they would not stay in business long. Parts of the Hippocratic oath from the medical profession apply equally well to management consulting:

> I will prescribe regimen for the good of my patients according to my ability and my judgment and never do harm to anyone. . . . In every house where I come I will enter only for the good of my patients. . . .

For the recovering codependent, practicing a compassionate attitude toward others is paramount, and management consulting offers an excellent chance to do just that. Working closely with employees at a client's office or plant, a consultant can instill a genuine feeling of community in place of individual competitiveness and divisiveness.

The teaching of business practices today—as in the past—tends to ignore the importance of working toward the good of the whole. Whether in the nation's business schools, corporate seminars, or on-the-job training programs, the emphasis rests on achieving personal gains. The assumption seems to be that anyone can make a million dollars if he looks out for himself first. Little or no attempt is made to teach that the development of a caring, sharing group will accentuate the personal growth of the individual. Honesty, integrity, and mercy are considered signs of weakness. The young person just starting out becomes convinced that to succeed in the cold world of business he needs to be conniving and merciless. By practicing a caring attitude at the client's place of business, the recovering codependent, as a respected outsider, can make a major contribution toward reversing this attitude. There are many who would scoff at such a philosophy. Nevertheless, for an individual to be successful as a management consultant, his mental and emotional states must be attuned to the needs of others.

Although this basic premise of management consulting–to help other people–is a real plus for the recovering executive, great danger also exists. A person recovering from corporate dominance cannot afford to become too involved in another person's problems. As the third of the Guidelines to a Better Life (Chapter 3) states: "I will not worry about other people's problems I am unable to help with." The inference, of course, is that they can take better care of their own problems than you can. Although it is a natural reaction resulting from rediscovering moral values, getting deeply involved in trying to solve another's problems can only lead to heartache and confusion. Any professional dedicated to helping others–including psychiatrists, psychologists, some religious leaders, some medical doctors, and management consultants–is advised throughout his professional training to guard against the high risk of becoming personally affected by another's problems. Counsel, advise, listen, and care but don't become personally involved. A client might appear eager to have your personal involvement, but when push comes to shove, he will always blame you for not coming up with a satisfactory solution. As your management consulting practice develops, continually guard against this temptation or there could very likely be a relapse.

An ex-corporate manager of human relations and a recovering codependent, Jean left the corporation to form her own consulting practice specializing in organization planning for nursing homes. Soon after starting her practice she was interviewing aged patients in a client nursing home when she made the near fatal mistake of sympathizing with the woes of two sick ladies in their late 80s. They both complained of inattention from the staff and, being bedridden, could not care for themselves. Jean began a personal vendetta to get the state to provide higher funding for additional staff at the home (which went far beyond the scope of her consulting engagement). She could not forget the plight of her new friends and, when she failed to obtain the funding, relapsed into a deep depression, which forced the discontinuance not only of this engagement but all others as well. Fortunately, she sought professional help and today is back in her consulting practice, but wary of taking on other people's problems as her own.

HELP FOR THE RECOVERING EXECUTIVE

In addition to providing a vehicle for practicing good human relations, a career in management consulting can aid recovery in two other ways: by nurturing personal creativity and by providing a medium conducive to moral growth. Creativity is the backbone of management consulting. Any good consultant must be a problem solver, and solving problems requires creative thinking. Management consulting provides an ideal environment for the recovering executive to practice personal growth through creativity. In fact, few other careers offer such an intellectually stimulating atmosphere. Creativity demands imagination. Years of experience in dealing with the intangible problems of corporate confusion stretches the imagination of even the most staid executive. Forcing his little gray cells to create solutions to unsolvable problems, the executive comes well equipped to deal with the imponderable relationships demanded by the management consulting profession.

Creativity also requires intuitive judgment, not only regarding how to solve a problem, but also which solution of several possible alternatives will be best for the client. These are the marks of a successful management consultant: to be able to guide the client to the right answer to his problem, not just a quick fix; to be able to influence a client toward choosing the road that will yield morally right results both now and in the future; and to be able to counsel a client toward outcomes beneficial to him, his employees, and customers. All these paths require creativity and individual initiative and mark the management consultant as a true professional.

Finally, the recovering executive's need for continual moral growth can also be satisfied by the management consulting profession. Helping others help themselves and coming up with imaginative applications of propitious behavior paradigms provide an environment where virtuous ethics can be practiced.

Bob reported to me one day that he had never felt as alive and well nor experienced such peace of mind as in his consulting practice. Fifteen years as a hardnosed negotiator for a major international union had left him callous, convinced that everyone was out for what he could take away from the other guy. Goodness and kindness had long ago been washed from his heart. He was angry, belligerent, and totally devoid of any good feelings for his fellow man. On the contrary, he felt only disgust. Shamed by these feelings, Bob recognized that if he didn't take some action soon, he would sink deeper into the turmoil of self-loathing and hatred toward others. Along with beginning the Nine-Step Program, he decided a career change was in order and selected labor consulting. In six months Bob had a new lease on life and, according to him, the new vocation brought him closer to his inner consciousness than he had ever thought possible. He actually began to like people again and had an intense desire to be of help in whatever way he could. He learned that helping others help themselves has a circular effect. The more you give of yourself the more you receive in return.

HAZARDS OF CONSULTING

Management consulting is not all a bed of roses, however. Some very real hazards exist in the profession that can have severe negative impacts on the recovering executive. Becoming involved in another person's problems is one. Two other dangers are a high rate of rejection, and a heightened level of emotional and mental stress. A close friend of mine who was a recovering codependent wrote the following in a letter to me while trying to free himself from the grip of a severe emotional breakdown.

"Shortly before my second emotional breakdown I felt rejected by clients, family, friends, and even my conscience. It seemed that everything I tried ended in failure. No amount of effort seemed to make any difference. I felt that if I had to suffer through one more rejection—whether it be a rejection of my consulting advice or rejection of my offer of love to others—I would give up everything. The fear of rejection was leading me rapidly into a dark cavern from which I was certain I could never escape. Rejection was something I could no longer tolerate—and it was this more than anything else, which led me to give up most of my management consulting practice. The level of rejection was just too high. I know now that it was the major contributor to my present demise."

Rejection proliferates in the management consulting profession. Most recommendations to clients will not be followed and most advice will be ignored—even after clients pay for it. Suggestions that the consultant knows are right are cast aside as too costly, too difficult, or too time-consuming to implement. A common retort to recommended solutions is, "That will never work. You just don't understand our business." Sound familiar? It's the same rejection encountered by an employee in an addictive corporation. The most difficult part of management consulting is dealing with the same type of addictive behavior patterns from clients as you experienced as an employee—but with one major difference. This time you can walk away from the engagement without being caught in the corporate web.

Rejection can be difficult to handle when you are emotionally disordered. Recognizing this hazard can keep an otherwise qualified executive out of the consulting ranks. If that's how you feel, by all means choose some other career where the amount of rejection will be less.

Stress is another problem encountered in the management consulting profession. Starting any business creates a high level of stress, particularly when the business doesn't grow as fast as originally planned and seed money begins to run out. Management consulting is no different. In some instances, it can be a lot worse than other businesses. Failure to get new clients, erratic income flow, and constant rejection create stress and can easily lead to despondency, self-doubt, and fear.

Many consultants fail within the first year because they cannot handle the strain of getting new clients. Headaches, back problems, eating disorders, and fatigue are common ailments. Stress is also to blame for many consultants turning to alcohol or drug abuse as an escape. And anxiety over future income has caused more than one marriage to break up during this start-up period.

Subjecting oneself to such pressure may be unreasonable. If one's emotional dysfunction is approaching the stage of an emotional breakdown, management consulting is the wrong choice at that time. It would be much better to seek a quiet recovery period, away from the pressures of the business world, before venturing into management consulting. A return to sanity will never work if additional stress, frustration, and worry are heaped on top of an already fragile psyche.

Some people find relief by calling up their inner strength, as in the Nine-Step Program. Others find this difficult or haven't yet progressed far enough in the recovery program to acknowledge that such strength exists. Such an admission must occur at some point in the process, however, or recovery won't work. But if you're not quite there yet, you can still get some relief from friends and family. Don't be ashamed to lean on them for support. Everyone knows the emotional turmoil you have been through and how you are trying to recover from codependency. Few real friends or family members who have suffered with you this long will turn away if you ask for help.

The following is a summary of the pluses and minuses a career in management consulting offers. On the plus side:

1. An opportunity to help other people.
2. A strong need for creative problem solving.
3. Plenty of room for personal growth.
4. A small amount of getting-started capital.
5. An opportunity for reasonably good income.
6. Easy getting-in requirements.

On the minus side:

1. Danger of taking on other people's problems as your own.
2. High rate of rejection.

3. High levels of stress.
4. Irregular stream of income.

Establishing a successful management consulting practice can be very, very difficult, but if you are still determined to go forward, let's look at what steps you should take to get the practice off the ground.

HOW TO GET STARTING IN CONSULTING

Once you reach the conclusion that you have the requisite traits and skills and that the market for your particular talents actually exists, it's time to begin the grueling task of starting the business—and that means getting clients. There are a number of resources a consultant can use to get clients and those who are successful in the profession use a combination of all of them:

1. Direct advertising.
2. Becoming an authority.
3. Word-of-mouth referrals.
4. Friends and personal contacts.
5. Ex-employers.

Direct advertising encompasses newspaper and magazine ads, direct mail solicitations, TV and radio spot commercials, and billboards. Not too many years ago it was considered poor taste for professionals to advertise their services. In the legal and public accounting professions, advertising violated the professional code of ethics and a practitioner risked disbarment or decertification if he advertised. Now, however, the professions are no different from other businesses trying to get a share of the consumer's dollar and paid advertising has become a way of life. National accounting firms such as Peat Marwick and Price Waterhouse have found that using paid advertising is the only way to remain competitive. Law firms such as Jacoby & Myers, medical clinics such as Rosenthal & Associates, dentists, and architects all budget substantial amounts for paid advertising.

For the management consultant, local trade newspapers together with narrowly targeted direct mail solicitations seem to work best for local coverage, and trade magazines bring results in the national market. Unfortunately, there is no single method for all consultants. Each consulting specialty requires a different approach depending on the market.

Paid advertising can be extremely expensive and, for the consultant just starting out, will be the largest expenditure in his budget. For this reason, if you decide on this approach, engage a qualified advertising agency to handle the work. Let the agency formulate an ad program and arrange for layouts, script, printing, mailing lists, brochure design, and media contacts. It's cheaper and more effective in the long run. *How To Guarantee Professional Success*, by Eugene J. Hameroff and Sandra S. Nichols is an excellent reference work that covers more detailed ideas and suggestions for a consultant's advertising campaign.

Becoming an authority means just what it says: develop a planned approach to gain public recognition as an expert in your field. A combination of some or all of the following will establish such accreditation, and the longer the list of credits, the more clients you'll attract:

1. Write articles for magazines and trade journals.
2. Give speeches to civic, community, and business groups.
3. Take a part-time college teaching assignment.
4. Develop and conduct a seminar.
5. Appear on local TV and radio talk shows.
6. Write a book.

Each time you participate in one of these activities it increases public awareness of your expertise. Before long, clients who have read your writings, heard you speak, or learned about you from someone else will be calling. Once that begins, you become a recognized authority.

Word-of-mouth referrals begin after establishing qualification credentials—either by the above methods or by performing consulting assignments. In my particular consulting specialties —turnaround management and M & A work—word-of-mouth referrals were the best source of clients. However, I could never have made it in the beginning without direct mailings to draw in the first clients. And major clients would never have been attracted without my first establishing credentials as an expert with other smaller clients.

Friends and personal contacts can be another valuable source of referrals. Although I have never received any clients or referrals from friends, other consultants have. Success in getting business through this medium depends on your specialty and how broad your base of friends and personal contacts may be.

Don't overlook your ex-employer as a potential client—at least in the beginning. Many times, an executive terminated in a cost-cutting move possesses special knowledge not found anywhere else in the organization and his leaving creates an enormous vacuum of talent. Not infrequently the very company terminating the executive as an employee will hire him back as a consultant to work on a specific project or problem.

Herb, a technically competent HVAC engineer, was laid off during a cost-cutting effort at a division of ITT. Within a month the company discovered it could not get along without his particular expertise and asked him to come back. "Thanks but no thanks," was Herb's answer. But he did agree to a consulting contract at twice his original salary!

Marty was also brought back by his ex-employer as a consultant to assist with the annual audit. Joan returned to her old company for a six-month consulting contract to teach a replacement how to manage a complicated revenue bond portfolio for a large client. Renee returned for three months to assist in the transition during relocation of the corporate office. All had been terminated during reorganizations, mergers or cost-cutting programs, and all were called back as consultants.

Administrative chores

As in any new business, there are a host of administrative chores to handle. Such matters as (1) setting up a functional office, (2) acquiring necessary office fixtures and equipment, (3) determining a fee schedule and billing procedures, (4) establishing expense budgets, (5) getting liability insurance, (6) keeping records for tax purposes, and a myriad of other nonproductive, administrative activities must be handled.

In the beginning it's foolish to rent office space. There will never be a need to meet a client at your office; his office, a restaurant, or your club will suffice. Use a spare bedroom, a basement, or some other free space in the house. You will, however, need the following to get started:

1. A private telephone line.
2. A desk or table, a chair and a lamp.
3. A small personal computer or word processor.
4. Letterhead and brochures.

That's all! Wait to embellish the office until the clients come.

Setting a fee structure can be tricky. Some consulting specialties, such as M & A work, have widely accepted standards (Lehman Scale formulae). Most management consultants charge by the hour, however, and the hourly rate will vary by type of client, type of engagement, locale, competition, and what the traffic will bear. Hourly rates comparable to the mid-range charged by lawyers and CPAs—currently between $75 and $150 per hour-are generally acceptable. Some consulting engagements are structured at a flat fee for the entire job. Then you must estimate how many hours it will take, add 20 percent for contingencies, and price it at your hourly rate. Some assignments require reduced rates, such as for a start-up client. Some command a higher than normal rate, such as special projects for larger organizations. Flexibility is the key, and in the beginning fees must be structured to what the traffic will bear. Just don't undersell yourself— that's one sure path to failure.

Record keeping for any small business is painful and seemingly nonproductive. For a consultant, however, accurate record keeping—of expenses particularly—can significantly reduce the tax burden. Many expenses considered personal for the wage earner are deductible for the self-employed consultant: allocated house expenses for his office, auto expenses, client relations and entertainment, club dues, and so on. Even though it is painful, record keeping must be done, so ask your accounting friends for help in getting the records set up or pick up one of those small bookkeeping books at the office supply store. Better yet, with a personal computer, there are now bookkeeping software packages available for under $100 that anyone can use, even with no experience keeping a set of books. An example is *One Write Plus*, available from Great American Software, Inc.; P.O. Box 910; Amherst, NH 03031

Eleven Golden Rules

When I decided to take the plunge, it didn't take long to learn that starting and building a management consulting practice was tough. Many things were done backwards, some steps taken too late, and learning by trial and error was extremely costly. Little research material was available to help pave the way and nothing I learned in school or in corporate life prepared me for the agony of getting clients. As a result of trial and error, and subsequent advice from other consultants, the following Eleven Golden Rules for starting a management consulting practice evolved. They have been used by several other executives starting consulting practices and, although perhaps not all-inclusive, can get a person over some nasty hurdles in the beginning:

- Rule 1: Before starting out, do a self evaluation of personal attributes—and be honest. It's better to find out that you don't have the right personality before you leave the corporate nest rather than afterward. If you can't do this evaluation on your own, consult your spouse, friends, business associates, religious leaders, or even a professional counselor (although that's expensive!).
- Rule 2: Define a specialty where you are a recognized expert in the field. Don't try to be too many things to too many people. It is harder to sell generalities than specific techniques.
- Rule 3: While still employed and contemplating venturing out on your own, check the economic timing. Surprisingly, consultants are less in demand during a recession than in good times. If the timing looks wrong, be patient. All business and economic cycles have highs and lows, and it's far better to eliminate at least one variable before beginning.
- Rule 4: Establish credibility in your field of expertise. Write articles for business journals, take a part-time job teaching in a college or night school, work with the SBA as a voluntary counselor for SCORE, give speeches on your specialty before civic and business groups, write a letter to the editor of a local newspaper on an important current topic. An ad in the local paper extolling your reputation is expensive, but can also bring in business.

- Rule 5: Plan, plan, plan. Don't make a move without a well thought-out and documented plan. Try to imagine all the things that can go wrong, and if you think you are unable to cope with any of them, don't begin.
- Rule 6: Before starting out, obtain enough seed money to keep going at least a year without any income, and two to three years with less income than necessary to live on. Pressure to create an income stream is a certain road to failure. Plan on three years for financial viability.
- Rule 7: Keep overhead costs to a minimum. Don't get a big head and think you need to rent an office. A spare bedroom or the basement is sufficient to start. There won't be any clients visiting anyway. Don't hire a secretary or any other personnel. Whatever you can't do yourself just won't get done.
- Rule 8: Budget enough money for advertising and marketing. Clients won't just walk through the door. They need to know that you are there and what you are selling. The only way to get those messages out to the public in the beginning is to advertise: brochures, newspapers, local trade journals, and trade shows. A planned marketing program is well worth the costs.
- Rule 9: Use friends and business associates. Let them know you're in business and need their active help. Sell yourself at cocktail parties, golf games, and civic luncheons. Don't be afraid to tell people you are just starting. Everyone loves an underdog.
- Rule 10: Don't let pride get in the way. It doesn't matter that some people consider you a failure for quitting the corporate game. In the beginning, you'll be swallowing pride over and over again. Always remember that consulting is a personal services business where you may not always be right, but you do have to get along well with people.
- Rule 11. Be sure of total family support and commitment *before* making the decision to venture out. There will be many months of stress and frustration—even despair—and it is very difficult to go it alone. There will be an overwhelming need to hang onto something when the going gets tough.

Although all are important, Rule 4—establishing credibility—is especially crucial. Being an expert is necessary, but if the market isn't aware of your expertise, there won't be any clients. Establish credibility before starting to spend money on brochures, telephone solicitation or mailings. Take the time to cultivate local social, civic, and trade groups. Write some articles for a local newspaper. Volunteer for speaker assignments with the SBA. All these methods work with little or no outlay of money. If you take the time to build credibility in the beginning, your client base will increase much faster later on.

Management consulting can be a rewarding career for the ex-corporate executive. There's plenty of opportunity to help other people. It requires creativity, can be financially rewarding, and doesn't cost much to get started. However, if starting a consulting practice holds no interest for you, perhaps starting a different type of business would be more palatable. That's the subject of the next chapter.

ENDNOTES

1. Hubert Bermont. *The Complete Consultant* (Washington, DC: Bermont Books, Inc., (1982), p. 10.
2. *Ibid.*, p. 19.
3. Eugene J. Hameroff, and Sandra S. Nichols, *How to Guarantee Professional Success* (Washington, DC: Bermont Books, Inc., 1982).

CHAPTER 9

TO CHASE A DREAM: FRANCHISING AND STARTING A BUSINESS

"Failing on your own is 10 times as devastating as failure while an employee. And make no mistake about it, the failure rate of new business start-ups is astronomical. Look before you leap!" I cautioned an audience of graduating seniors. As a guest lecturer, shortly after starting my fifth company from scratch, I was trying to point out the advantages of getting a sound training in business fundamentals and economics as an employee before attacking the world of entrepreneurship. Most new businesses fail for one or more of the following reasons. The would-be entrepreneur:

1. Is psychologically unable to cope with the risks.
2. Lacks family support.
3. Picks the wrong time to start.
4. Chooses the wrong business or the wrong location.
5. Is unwilling to make the required financial and other commitments.
6. Lacks financial resources.
7. Has inadequate training.
8. Does not have a thorough knowledge of the market.
9. Structures the business wrong.
10. Has weak management skills.

PSYCHOLOGICAL CONSIDERATIONS

A recovering executive is especially susceptible to the temptation to venture out on his own. Wanting to rid himself completely of any structured environment smacking of the corporate lifestyle leads to the natural conclusion that being his own boss will solve the problem. In some cases this works; in others it leads to disaster. Some of the major differences lie in the personal characteristics, goals, and emotional and mental strength of the executive. The following questions must be dealt with before going any further toward entrepreneurship:

1. Do you have the right mental attitude and enough emotional stability to cope with the risks and pressures of making all the decisions?
2. Can you manage your personal life to ensure the continued dedication and commitment required to be a business owner?
3. Is your physical stamina sufficient to weather the long hours and hard work?
4. Have you mastered the moral determination to get through all the setbacks, disappointments, and hard decisions of starting a business?
5. How far along the road to emotional recovery have you come?

Most important of all: How many addictive behavior attributes have you changed? Certainly not all. By recognizing which are still at the danger level, you can avoid getting into a situation that will only aggravate the disorder.

In addition, there are 10 personal characteristics required for success as an entrepreneur. You must be:

1. Aggressive, determined, and ambitious.
2. Caring and compassionate toward others.
3. Self-confident but not arrogant.
4. Marketing-oriented—a good salesperson.
5. Optimistic.
6. Honest, with a high level of integrity.
7. Trusting but not gullible.
8. Physically fit.
9. Fearless yet cautious.
10. Morally strong.

During the morning break in a seminar on "How to Get Started in a Business" sponsored by the Philadelphia SBA, a middle-aged engineer challenged the probability of anyone possessing all these traits. He argued that anyone honest with himself would realize there are always degrees of aggressiveness and optimism and that every entrepreneur can't be a super salesperson. The point was well taken and before my next presentation I devised a more flexible way to judge entrepreneurial abilities using the following questionnaire. Of course, some traits are more important than others:

Self-Assessment for Entrepreneurship

How I feel about business

A. Compared to other people I am usually:
____ 1. Much more aggressive
____ 2. Somewhat more aggressive
____ 3. Less aggressive

B. My ambition to gain power and money is:
____ 1. Important but not crucial
____ 2. The main reason for starting my own business
____ 3. Overwhelming

C. If I fail in my own business:
____ 1. I'll try something else
____ 2. It will be devasting
____ 3. Not a major consideration because I won't fail

D. I am confident I will succeed in business because:
____ 1. I will give it my best shot
____ 2. I have never failed
____ 3. I am an expert in my field

E. My strongest business attributes are:
____ 1. Marketing/Sales
____ 2. General management
____ 3. Finance
____ 4. Engineering/Production
____ 5. Other skills

F. My attitude is:
____ 1. Generally optimistic
____ 2. Always optimistic
____ 3. Realistic

G. In dealing with employees and customers I am:
____ 1. Always honest and never lie

_____ 2. Generally honest but lie occasionally

_____ 3. If other people are honest with me I am honest with them

I. The most important business attribute is:

_____ 1. Caring and compassion for others

_____ 2. Being a good manager

_____ 3. Ability to turn a profit

_____ 4. Knowing how to get what I want

How I feel about myself

J. I like who I am:

_____ 1. Always

_____ 2. Most of the time

_____ 3. I would like to be a better person

K. I trust my own judgment:

_____ 1. Always

_____ 2. Most of the time

_____ 3. Only if I can verify it with facts

L. Which of the following describes my health:

_____ 1. I am physically fit and healthy most of the time

_____ 2. I have frequent colds, the flu or other minor illnesses

_____ 3. I have frequent headaches or back problems

_____ 4. I am overweight

_____ 5. I am very nervous and/or tense when I am excited

M. Which of the following describes my fears:

_____ 1. I have little fear but I am concerned

_____ 2. The future is frightening

_____ 3. I am afraid to be without income

_____ 4. The thought of failure frightens me

N. Moral conduct and the practice of ethical principles means:

_____ 1. A great deal and gives me strength

_____ 2. At times such things seem important but at other times such principles just get in the way. I don't put a lot of faith in such matters

_____ 3. There is no such thing as morality in business

_____ 4. I keep my religion in church

Generally, based on the line numbers, the lower the total score, the higher the probability of success in starting a business. With certain exceptions, however—notably Items I, M, and N, which stay constant—the interpretation of the answers must be weighted in conjunction with the particular circumstances involved.

FINANCIAL RISK

Financial risk is the single greatest disadvantage to starting a business. If you cannot or will not risk everything you own, now and in the future, you should not start your own business. Find some other way to earn a living. Hundreds of thousands of businesses file bankruptcy each year, and the number is growing geometrically. I have seen too many would-be entrepreneurs lose everything—their business, personal savings accounts, cars, even their homes—to recommend in good conscience that anyone start a business without being fully cognizant of the financial risk entailed.

The greatest hazard is the use of personal guarantees. Bank debt to buy equipment or facilities, or for working capital, nearly always requires personal guarantees. The assets of your business as well as your personal assets—such as your home, car, and investments—will normally be pledged as collateral to the loan. Clearly, if the business fails, your loss could be monumental. You could lose everything of value and be forced to start all over again to build a new life. Even in the event of your death, most personal guarantees are passed on to the estate, and your spouse, children, and other beneficiaries must settle the loans.

Bankers, consultants, and, yes, even authors who advocate starting (or buying) a business with extraordinarily high levels of borrowed money are doing the potential entrepreneur a disservice. Seldom is consideration given to the personal assets used to secure this debt. And even more seldom do these experts recognize and explain the painful, soul-wrenching experience that inevitably befalls the entrepreneur if the business fails. Surprisingly, with annual business failures almost equal in number to new business starts, the subject of small business bankruptcy has received little press in today's business media. Because failure lacks glamour and because our society as a whole regards business failure as a stigma approaching leprosy, small business bankruptcies are probably not newsworthy—unless, of course, the failure involves a noted celebrity taking a fall in which case we gloat with self-righteous glee. Double standards continue to prevail.

Recovering corporate codependents may have difficulty dealing with this high risk. The fear of failure is hard enough to overcome all by itself, without adding the fear of financial ruin on top of it. To help alleviate this worry, sit down with a good lawyer and work out a plan to protect your personal assets. There are a number of ways to do this, including the transfer of all assets to your spouse—whether they are held jointly or in your name alone. Another is to utilize special trusts to hold the assets for the benefit of your children. Each state has different laws applying to creditor/debtor relations, and a lawyer experienced in this specialty can advise which methods are best for you.

SUPPORT OF FAMILY AND FRIENDS

Chapter 3 stressed the importance of support groups—both family and nonfamily—to the recovering executive. Now as you start up a business, in addition to providing psychological support, your family and friends can be of enormous practical help. For example, if you are starting a video store, open 10 hours a day, seven days a week, sales assistance from a spouse or children would be welcome. After the store catches on outside help can be hired, but in the beginning family members often make the difference between success and failure. Also, if friends will make an effort to patronize the store there will be a ready market the moment the doors are opened.

Psychologically, support groups can be equally helpful to the would-be entrepreneur. Starting a new business is lonely and filled with doubt and uncertainty. Sitting in a store day after day with no customers, mailing thousands of advertising fliers with no response, and watching the bills pile up with little if any income can be disheartening. To be able to share those fears and concerns with a "safe" person can be enormously healing. When I started my first tax practice 25 years ago, and waited patiently for the first client to walk in the door, I could not have made it without the unbounded optimism and support of my wife and friends. Whenever I felt low and near defeat, there was always someone to phone or have lunch with to pick me up.

HOW TO START A BUSINESS

If you're psychologically ready and have mustered support from family and friends, let's proceed with starting a business. There are seven ingredients to a successful start-up:

1. Timing and type of business.
2. Market research.
3. Location.
4. Financing.
5. Training.
6. Advertising.
7. Start-up management.

Timing and Type of Business

Timing is to business start-ups what food is to good health. Without practicing the right diet, a person may still live, but won't be healthy very long. If a business is started at the wrong time, it may survive, but won't be very healthy in the competitive market place. Often overlooked in the zealous desire to get going, timing can be such a critical factor and so often the cause of business failures that it is placed first in the start-up success formula.

Timing has an impact on the type of business chosen. Some businesses thrive in times of economic turmoil (armament companies, home remodeling businesses, the home entertainment industry). Others do well in good times (real estate sales and development, the resort industry, and farm equipment). When considering what type of business to start, watch the economic cycle and then either wait until your cycle comes around or change to a market currently appropriate.

Many experts in business start-ups ignore the element of timing, which makes me wonder if any of them have ever started a business themselves. The prevalent opinion seems to be that any time is all right as long as the would-be entrepreneur is ready, willing, and able. Nothing could be further from the truth. Desire is only one part of the equation; interest rates, the state of the national and regional economies, industry curves, the political climate, and the health of the banking industry all have significant positive or negative effects on starting any business.

Three timing factors have a direct bearing on a person's potential success:

1. Macroeconomic conditions such as interest rates, the inflation rate, and unemployment rates reflected in stock market prices and in government fiscal policies.
2. Industry business cycles and product maturation in the start-up company's market.
3. Banking regulations and bankers' perceived state of the economy in the bank's region and in the company's market.

The following case describing a client's attempt to start a new home construction business is a classic example of poor timing relative to macroeconomic conditions.

Tom and Joel, two ex-GE engineers terminated in a massive cost-cutting move some years ago, decided to start a general contracting company to develop tracts of residential homes. Nine months and $20,000 of their own money later, they filed for protection under the Federal Bankruptcy Code. They had started a business demanding low interest rates, high personal disposable income, and public confidence in the economy at a time of double-digit interest rates, a national inflation rate of over 10 percent, and unemployment in their area topping 13 percent. Clearly, there were few home buyers under these conditions. Debt service was astronomical and the trade unions demanded raises every three months. The partners couldn't have picked a worse time for this type of business.

It should be equally plain that to start a business on the down side of an industry business cycle is asking for trouble. For years, the domestic machine tool industry suffered in the doldrums of low capital expenditures. Prices dropped through the floor, customers demanded delivery of small "just in time" quantities, and machine shop failures outnumbered start-ups nearly four to one. To start up a machine shop in such an environment meant facing abnormally stiff competition from existing shops trying to gain their share of a diminishing market.

Excessive foreign competition can also have an impact on the choice of a business. During the 70s and early 80s, the Japanese cornered the American market for motorcycles. Harley–Davidson, the major American producer, was practically driven out of business by foreign imports. Only the enactment of federal legislation to protect Harley–Davidson at the last minute saved the company from failing. To start up a company servicing the domestic motorcycle industry during this period would have been suicidal.

Finally, to start a business with a high level of borrowed money requires cooperation from a bank. Contrary to TV commercials about the hungry banker wearing out shoe leather trying to locate businesses to loan money to, the economic health of the banking industry determines to a large extent whether such funds are available—at any cost. Since 1984, the Texas banking industry has been suffering an enormous rate of failures. Money supplies have dwindled, collateral requirements are restrictive, and, assuming one could even find a bank willing to make a loan for a small business start-up, payback terms would be prohibitively short.

So, regardless of your background and specific talents, before you venture into the new business marketplace ask yourself three questions:

1. Are market forces conducive to selling this product or service at this time?
2. Will competition put an undue burden on pricing?
3. Can I obtain required debt financing at a reasonable cost?

If the answers are not positive to each question, then either delay starting a business or find another industry more conducive to success now.

Market Research

Know who the customers are, where they are, and how to get them to buy your product or service. Such advice sounds childish. Of course you'd know the answers before starting out. It would be foolish not to do so. Yet over and over again clients have sought my help to resolve financial difficulties created by ignoring basic market research.

Eric wanted to retire to the U.S. Virgin Islands but needed a stream of income to supplement his monthly pension and Social Security checks. Upon visiting the islands on a two-week vacation, he decided an automatic car wash would be just the right business to start. There were none on the island, and because of the salt air and high humidity, residents and local taxi drivers could be seen having their cars washed by local teenagers on the roadside, in parking lots, or wherever space was available. While still in the States, Eric arranged financing with the manufacturer of car wash equipment and scheduled delivery to the islands six months later. He returned to the islands, acquired a piece of land near a busy shopping center, and within nine months had installed his equipment and was ready for business.

He waited patiently, but so few cars entered the turnstile, it seemed his car wash was invisible to the throngs of passing motorists. Advertisements in the local paper, special discounts for volume washes, contests, giveaway programs, and other promotions all failed to generate even a fraction of the volume he had forecast. Eventually, in less than 18 months after opening its doors, the car wash was out of business and Eric filed for bankruptcy.

While there were several reasons for Eric's failure, two circumstances stand out. First, the location he chose was far removed from his two markets: taxicab stands and affluent local residents. People were not willing to make the extra effort to drive 15 minutes out of their way to get their cars washed. Second, to cover the cost of water, debt service, and payroll, Eric priced his washes at between $7.00 to $12.00 – 15 percent below similar businesses in his home state of New Jersey. The teenagers, however, washing cars by hand in parking lots or on the roadside, charged

$4.00. The largest market, taxicab drivers, refused to pay the increased prices for the convenience of an automatic wash. If Eric had performed the most basic market research before buying his equipment and land, he would have learned that income was so scarce on the island that $7.00 to $12.00 was out of range for 90 percent of the population. Eric violated two basic rules: (1) He did not perform market research to be certain that what he planned would actually work, and (2) he chose a location that did not meet the demographics of competition and market demand.

After you decide what business to get into, the temptation will be strong to jump right in. However, doing enough research to be sure you have chosen the right market and the appropriate location can pay big dividends later on. Choosing the wrong market or location can lead to financial ruin.

Getting Going

Roger Johnson engaged me to help him start up a computer services business. Five months of market research and testing led Roger to lease a small storefront office in a new shopping center adjacent to a large commercial and industrial development. There was plenty of parking, and the number of small and mid-sized businesses in the office building complex appeared to offer an ample market for his services. But now he was stuck. He needed to raise financing for equipment and working capital, and somehow he needed to assure the financial institutions that he was capable of running his own business.

Roger wanted to open the doors as soon after the Christmas holidays as possible, which meant six months to get the financing, acquire the equipment, develop creditable management credentials, and implement an advertising program. Together we laid out the following sequence of events:

1. Structure the business organization.
2. Develop a strategic business plan.
3. Source financing alternatives.
4. Implement a training program.
5. Devise a marketing and advertising schedule.
6. Test the marketing hypotheses for four months after the doors open.

Roger did not envision bringing in a partner but did plan to have his wife and eldest daughter work full-time. The first step was to form a corporation—with Roger, his wife, and his daughter as shareholders—to own the assets of the business. This afforded Roger and his family at least some protection against potential lawsuits and other liabilities as the business grew. Also, most banks prefer to loan money to a corporation rather than a sole proprietor; it gives them a sense of security. Although lawyers will jump at the opportunity to perform the incorporating work, fees ranging from $400 to $2,000 seem a bit unreasonable. I have used The Company Corporation; 725 Market Street; Wilmington, DE 19801, to set up 11 Delaware corporations for my own businesses and many more for clients without ever consulting a lawyer; the cost for each was about $165. Roger followed this tack and incorporated RSJ Computer Services, Inc. Services performed by The Company Corporation included a formal incorporation filing in the state of Delaware, a minute book, a corporate seal, and stock certificates. Annual Delaware agent fees totaled $35.00.

Next we developed a strategic business plan. Without such a document, no financial institution will entertain a financing proposal. Additionally, its preparation forced Roger to articulate his detailed plans for starting and growing the business. The following outline of a strategic business plan has been used repeatedly with good success in arranging start-up financing:

Outline of Strategic Business Plan

I. The Business
   A. Background of Products and Services
   B. Objectives and Goals
   C. Capitalization and Business Structure
      1. Corporation, Partnership, or Proprietorship
   D. Organization Structure: Start-up and Future Plans
   E. Personal Resumes and Background of Owner/Spouse
   F. Current Personal Financial Statement
II. Economic/Market Conditions/Timing Analysis
   A. Macro Factors
      1. What are the Department of Commerce, Trade Association, and other economic authorities predicting for the key indicators affecting this industry and location?

2. Interest rate trends
3. Inflation factors
4. Impact of foreign competition
5. Projected changes in distribution patterns
   B. Micro Factors
1. Projection of the annual growth rate of the specific market
2. Competition, customer loyalty, and competitive pricing
3. Entering the market, why customers buy from a specific vendor
4. Pricing policies
III. Proposed Costs and Financing
   A. Getting Started Costs
1. The cost of each of the following before the doors are opened:
   a. Space: land, building, office
   b. Furniture and fixtures
   c. Production equipment and vehicles
   d. Inventory
   e. Market research
   f. Advertising
   g. Office supplies and postage
   h. Telephone
   i. Licenses, permits and taxes
   j. Legal, accounting and consulting fees
   k. Travel expense
   l. Other expenses not listed
2. The source of these funds:
   a. Savings and personal investments
   b. Other equity investors
   c. Private borrowings
   d. Bank debt
   e. Other sources
   B. Operating Costs once the doors are open
1. The cost per month of each of the following for the first three years:
   a. Salaries and wages (excluding owner's)
   b. Payroll taxes and group insurance

c. Operating supplies
d. Inventory purchases
e. Utilities: electric, gas, oil, water
f. Telephone
g. Rent or lease payments
h. Maintenance to equipment and space
i. Liability and casualty insurance
j. Vehicle costs
k. Taxes: federal, state, and municipal (excluding income taxes)
l. Licenses and permit fees
m. Security costs
n. Principal payment on debt
o. Interest expense on debt
p. Legal, accounting, and consulting fees
q. Other costs not listed
2. The source of these funds:
a. Revenues (sales) generated from each type of product or service by month for three years
b. Bank loans for working capital
c. Additional equity investment
d. Other sources
3. Additional equipment, vehicles, or space to be purchased during the first three years and the source of these funds
IV. Pro Forma Financial Statements
The getting started costs, operating costs, revenue forecasts, and financing will be formatted in formal balance sheets, statements of income, and cash flow statements. If you do not know how or have difficulty structuring the format ask a CPA for help.
V. Payments to Owner and Spouse
A. Cash draw for the owner and spouse per month for the first three years
B. Noncash benefits from the company: autos, life and health insurance, personal travel expenses, food, furniture, education expenses, etc.
1. During the start-up period
2. During the first three years

VI. Succession
  A. How will the business continue if you become disabled or die?
  B. Key man life insurance
  C. Contractual agreement with company for disability payments
  D. Contractual agreement with spouse in the event of divorce

Everyone has heard of business plans and anyone who envisions starting his own business has probably recognized that banks require such a document for financing purposes, so to dwell on its detailed preparation here would be redundant. However, the above outline has been used many times for my own start-ups as well as for budding entrepreneur clients and is acceptable to most financial institutions. Using this outline, the actual writing of the plan should be easy.

A Financing Scheme

With a completed strategic business plan, we next arranged for the financing needed to get started. The getting started costs in the plan totaled approximately $150,000—excluding office space, which would be leased. Of this amount, $110,000 would be used for furniture, fixtures, and equipment; $20,000 for an initial stock of supplies, parts, and other inventory items; and $20,000 for expenses. Additionally, Roger estimated that he and his family required at least $25,000 a year for personal living expenses and probably another $20,000 for working capital to finance receivables and inventory once he opened for business. He also estimated that over the first three years he would incur total losses from operations of $25,000. This meant $220,000 had to be raised to be reasonably sure of adequate capitalization. The question was, where would he get almost a quarter of a million dollars when his total savings amounted to only $32,000? We worked out the following financing plan:

Contribution from Roger Johnson	$ 25,000
Second mortgage on Roger's house	25,000

Five-year loan from finance company for purchase of hard assets, secured by all furniture and equipment	90,000
Four-year term loan from commercial bank, guaranteed by the SBA, secured by inventory, supplies, Roger's house and car, and a second position on the hard assets	40,000
Line of credit with commercial bank secured by receivables and guaranteed by Roger	40,000
Total funds required	$220,000

Since the appraisal on Roger's house netted equity of nearly $200,000 after an existing mortgage of $45,000, the second mortgage still left Roger with $130,000 to draw on for future emergencies or to pay off the SBA guaranteed loan.

In addition to savings accounts and second mortgages, relatives, friends, and the cash value of a life insurance policy are other possible sources of seed money. Perhaps some unused personal assets could also be sold.

Most commercial banks are not eager to loan money for a start-up business. No matter how well-conceived the strategic business plan is, bankers are always afraid that the entrepreneur will become one of the business failure statistics. That's why the SBA has been active for years in helping new businesses get going. There are two ways the SBA can help with financing: a direct loan and a guarantee against a commercial bank loan. Practices governing direct loans vary by geography and current government policies. If a direct loan isn't possible, try the bank loan guarantee route. The SBA guarantees 90 percent of the loan balance to the bank which means that you only have to satisfy the banker with collateral for 10 percent. Additionally, if you happen to be a designated minority, you can be certain of preferential treatment from SBA loan officers.

Finance companies (or asset-based lenders as they prefer to be called) can be helpful in financing hard assets such as furniture, equipment, or machinery. The rates are high and these lenders are difficult to work with, but most are willing to lend a very high percentage of the auction value of the assets. Therefore, given the right circumstances, they can be helpful in the initial acquisition of these assets. Leasing equipment also works well, although contrary to leasing company advertisements, this is a very expensive way to go.

Another possibility might be to acquire used equipment either at an equipment auction or as a private purchase from a used equipment dealer. Depending on the type of equipment needed, there are a variety of such dealers. Any finance company can provide recommendations of local used equipment dealers (usually auctioneers used in foreclosures). For used computer equipment, the Boston Computer Exchange (BoCoEx) in Boston, MA, is probably the biggest dealer. Used furniture and fixtures can be acquired through local used office furniture outlets listed in the telephone Yellow Pages.

If you are contemplating newly designed high-tech electronic or computer-based products with potentially burgeoning markets, a venture capital firm or an investment banking institution may be the best financing choice. Chapter 10, which deals with buying a business, discusses the advantages and risks of using these sources.

Training

Although Roger had been the manager of a corporate data processing department and was therefore highly qualified in the technical aspects of computers, he did not have any experience in sales, finance, or the myriad of administrative tasks required to run a business. Before the commercial bank would make the $40,000 term loan the loan officer insisted that Roger take some courses in these disciplines as well as general management. Most local SBA offices offer the fastest and cheapest way to pick up training in missing business skills. Almost any large-city SBA office maintains a continuing education program in all skills of business management offered at a very low cost, or none at all. Instructors are either retired executives or current managers from the local business community, so there is very little blue-sky theory. For teaching hard-core business practices, the SBA training programs are hard to beat. Roger did take three courses in accounting and business finance, one course in sales techniques, and attended four lectures covering general management practices. This satisfied the bank and the loan was granted. Next it was necessary to let the market know what Roger had to sell.

Advertising

Although the cost/value trade-off of advertising campaigns for small businesses is at best questionable, it is one way to get to the market in the beginning. Before you open the doors, potential customers must know what you have to sell and why your product or service is better than the competition's. If you have excess cash lying around, hire a large advertising and public relations company to get your name in front of the marketplace. But if you are strapped for cash—and most small businessmen are—try an approach similar to what we devised for Roger, which cost under $6,000. This effort resulted in substantial business during the first three months. The approach consisted of the following:

1. A two-color, glossy product brochure sent to all businesses in the shopping center, in the adjacent commercial development, and within a three-mile radius of Roger's office.
2. In addition to describing Roger's unique approach to computer training and other services, the brochure announced a grand opening celebration with free coffee, drinks, snacks, and shrimp cocktail.
3. To gain admittance, the attendee was required to present his business card at the door.
4. Three days after the celebration, a second mailing went out to all attendees describing a 10 percent discount policy in effect for the first month.
5. Included in this second mailing was a brief vita of Roger's corporate background together with an admission of his corporate codependent experience, why he left the corporate rat race, and a brief description of the recovery program.

At the end of the first month, the campaign was so successful that Roger and his wife were already considering hiring two technicians to help with field service. Although certainly the discount helped, over 90 percent of his new customers revealed that they were trying his service because anyone with enough guts to admit publicly that his distaste for corporate machinations was the reason for starting his business earned their respect and deserved a chance to succeed. Of course, if there had been a blizzard on the day of the grand opening celebration, perhaps $6,000 would have been wasted.

The Doors are Opened

In the euphoric atmosphere of having their own company, many small businessmen ignore one or more of the four basic tenets of entrepreneurship:

1. *Use professional help.* Because the entrepreneur must manage all aspects of the business—from developing the product or service, to selling it, to accounting for the cash, to dealing with human relations problems—the tendency is to try to be an expert in all phases of the business. Everyone has weaknesses as well as strengths, however, and if he doesn't recognize the areas in which skills are lacking, energy and time will be stolen from strong subjects to bolster the weak. This is the "Jack of all trades; master of none" syndrome which can easily lead an otherwise thriving business into financial ruin. It is far better to invest the money in appropriate professional advice to help with the weak spots. It is faster, easier, and, in the long run, cheaper than trying to do everything yourself.

2. *Prepare for restricted freedom.* Another fallacy is that owning a business allows the entrepreneur more freedom of action and permits him to make more money and be less subject to the whims of others than as an employee. *This is not so!* Successful business owners will readily admit that customers are far more demanding than corporate bosses. They will also acknowledge that they work harder, with longer hours and significantly less freedom of choice, than an employee. If honest, they will also admit that at least in the first three years, a lot more money can be made working as a corporate executive.

3. *Handle stress.* A recovering codependent must be constantly aware of and on guard against stressful situations. This

does not mean that he can't handle stress. It does mean he must recognize and deal with it on the spot rather than allow it to fester. Starting a business will be far more stressful than anything he experienced as an employee, if for no other reason than the personal liability for a sizable amount of debt. It can be handled, but to do so requires a high level of self-confidence, faith in your abilities, and a finely tuned ear to instincts and intuition (or conscience if you prefer). Trust your intuition. With continued attention to ethical behavior, you can cope with this added stress.

4. *Plan for succession.* No one lives forever. Every small businessman must be aware of and plan for the continuance or disposal of his business when it's time to leave because of bad health, retirement, or any number of other reasons. Succession should be planned in the beginning. Work closely with a competent attorney to develop a succession program either within the family or with an outsider as soon as it is economically feasible. Don't wait. If you die or become disabled, your spouse will have enough to worry about without trying to dispose of the business. For a more comprehensive description of how to structure a getting out position, take a look at another book I have written, entitled *Getting Out: A Step-by-Step Guide to Selling a Business or Professional Practice.*

A FRANCHISE AS AN ALTERNATIVE

An alternative to starting from scratch is to start a franchise business. Though expensive and restrictive, franchising has become a way of life in small business America. The U.S. Department of Commerce lists well over 1,000 franchisers standing ready, willing, and able to help a person start his own business—for a fee. Franchising has grown rapidly over the past two decades as a way for inexperienced entrepreneurs to own a business. It has become especially popular in the small retail and service industries from fast food, to laundries, to hotels, to employment agencies, to real estate firms. Franchising has become an American way of life for the small businessman, and with good reason. Assuming a willingness to pay the franchise fee and with the minimum required personal net worth, anyone can become a business owner; no experience is necessary. But beware: the same seven ingredients to a successful start-up from scratch are also present with a franchise:

1. Timing and type of business.
2. Market research.
3. Location.
4. Financing.
5. Training.
6. Advertising.
7. Start-up management.

The big difference is that a franchiser will help with nearly all of these items. In fact, most franchisers dictate location, training, advertising, and start-up management procedures. They all perform their own market research and some will even provide financing.

The two big disadvantages in starting up a franchise are cost:

- You must buy all the equipment, furniture, and fixtures as specified by the franchiser, thus eliminating the possibility of shopping for the best deal.
- There is always a franchise fee up front for the privilege of using the franchise name. The amount can range from $5,000 to $500,000 or more.
- Once you are in operation, the franchiser will take a percentage of gross receipts as additional fees. Although the rate varies widely, many charge between 5 percent and 10 percent of gross sales.

and independence:

- A person owns his own business, and yet he doesn't. He has responsibility for all its debts and its success or failure. However, most franchisers dictate what location to choose, what and how much advertising to do, systems and procedures to be followed, and in general how the business will be run. The owner has the responsibility, but the franchiser has the authority.

If this sounds like the corporate life-style you just left that's because it is, only worse. With most franchises the potential owner must be interviewed and accepted as a franchisee, take all the risk, conform to all the addictive rules and policies of the franchiser, and still pay a large up-front fee and an average of 8 percent of the sales dollar for the privilege of being beaten over the head.

That's not to say that all franchises are a bad deal. Many have become a mainstay of American life: McDonald's, Holiday Inn, H & R Block, and Century 21 Real Estate, to mention a few. Small businessmen who were fortunate to get into one of these systems early in the game have done very well financially. But for every "name" franchise there are 10 "no-name" operations which can be as big or bigger a risk than starting from scratch.

In addition to hotels, fast food, and real estate, the printing industry has become heavily involved in franchising. One example of how a franchiser works in this industry is Sir Speedy, Inc., which has over 750 individual franchised prints shops worldwide. The following information was taken from the material furnished by the company in mid-1988 to anyone interested in exploring the possibility of joining their network. Further information can be obtained from: Sir Speedy, Inc.; Corporate Offices; 23131 Verdugo Drive; Laguna Hills, CA 92653-1342.

The cost to own a Sir Speedy franchise printing center is as follows:

- Franchise fee $ 17,500
  for which you get the use of their name, logos, and
  trademarks
  $5,000 is payable with application for the franchise
  and the balance payable prior to attendance at the
  required training program

- Start-up Costs   22,500
  covers the cost of the training program, travel and
  lodging while in training, market research, site
  location study, lease negotiation assistance, applied
  window and wall graphics, initial fixtures, furniture, and inventory. Payable prior to attendance at
  required training program

- Equipment   71,000
  includes equipment, cabinets, counters, shelving,
  and furniture. Though not required to buy this
  equipment from Sir Speedy, a person must use this
  specific equipment (How can you use it if you don't
  get it from them?)

- Signage   1,750
  must meet the specifications set forth by Sir
  Speedy. Cost will vary with local ordinances.

- Working Capital
  pre-opening expenses   8,000

- Operating capital for first few months   37,000

- Total cash required to start $157,750

   In addition to this, Sir Speedy recommends that new owners
have additional funds available to cover their personal living
expenses for a minimum of eight months. In other words, the
franchiser estimates that for eight months there will be no cash
available from the business for the owner's draw. And of course
there are royalty payments:

- For the first year   4% of gross sales
- Each subsequent year   6% of gross sales

An incentive program offers a descending sliding scale of royal-
ties based on attaining specific levels of sales volume.
   In addition to the name, logos, and trademarks, Sir Speedy
provides the following support to its printing center owner-
operators:

- Training: two weeks at their National Training School in
  Laguna Hills, CA.
- Equipment: offset printing, laser graphic, computer and fax
  equipment, fixtures, and furniture.
- Supplies: optional centralized national purchasing agreements.
- Market Survey and Site Selection: will determine appropriate site location and assist in negotiating lease arrange-
  ments.

- Opening Promotion: opening marketing program and advertising.
- National Advertising: nationwide advertising campaign to promote Sir Speedy as "The Business Printers."
- Continuing Field Support: Qualified representatives will give assistance with the growth and development of the printing center.

The franchiser will, at the option of the new owner, provide a leasing arrangement for the equipment totaling $71,000 from its affiliated leasing company with monthly lease payments of approximately $1,400 plus sales tax, for seven years. Additionally, the franchiser will assist in arranging SBA guaranteed financing for up to $40,000 on a 10-year amortization schedule through Allied Credit, providing the owner has adequate outside collateral to secure the loan.

Sir Speedy is used as an example of how a typical franchise arrangement works. I neither recommend nor disparage Sir Speedy as a possible start-up opportunity. The above description is merely one example of how a franchise is structured. It is by no means inclusive. Every franchiser has slightly different conditions. In nearly all cases, however, the franchise agreement calls for an up-front cash down payment; working capital; pre-opening and living expense requirements; and strict compliance with the format, advertising, and operating systems defined by the franchiser. Many franchisers prefer the owner/operator to be untainted by prior experience in the specific trade or business so he can be more easily trained in the designated system.

Starting a franchise business can be the best way for a neophyte entrepreneur to get started in his own business. However, for the recovering executive, having suffered through corporate addictive behavior, a franchise business is probably a bigger psychological risk than he should take. A franchisee is always subject to the behavioral patterns of the parent company and the owner/operator can never really be in charge of his own destiny. The recovering executive is probably better off starting or buying his own business rather than getting involved in a franchise operation.

If a restrictive franchise or a high risk start-up is not for you, perhaps buying a going business will be a better choice. As a minimum, it provides a salary faster than beginning at the bottom. The next chapter explores how to buy a business and the advantages and risks of moving your career in this direction.

CHAPTER 10

FAST ACTION, QUICK CASH: BUYING A GOING BUSINESS

Rick was laid off after 10 years with MARYCORE. Having worked his way up the corporate ladder, Rick believed he had played the game to perfection; his recently won title of Manager of Human Relations proved the claim. Loyal to the company, adept at political maneuvering, technically competent, and an efficient manager, Rick believed he was the perfect company man. He knew who to cater to and how to win approval for his programs. Avoiding controversy, he never took a stand against his boss. Nevertheless, Rick was now out of a job. Beleaguered and frightened, he felt betrayed by the one constant in his life. Guilt, anger, fear, and a host of other unsavory feelings churned in his head. To make matters worse, his bank balance showed a meager $24,000, his eldest daughter was entering college in the fall, and his wife was pregnant with their fourth child. A frightened wife, mortified kids (their dad had been fired!), and empty pockets created a family crisis of catastrophic proportions.

Still coping with what he perceived as a personal failure, Rick resurrected his old resume and started the job search. No longer a young man, he soon realized that getting another job with comparable salary and benefits would not be easy. As weeks passed without leads, it became painfully clear that at age 49 he was considered "over the hill" by most employers. Rick started thinking about owning his own business.

He had always dreamed of being his own boss. There were any number of businesses he felt qualified to operate: an employment agency, a real estate sales office, a hardware store, or a plumbing supplies distribution company. He realized, however, that starting a business from scratch would take time and cash— both scarce commodities. No, Rick needed a way to earn cash quickly and yet be his own boss. "I've always wanted to have my own business. Now is my chance to buy a company and make some real money. All I have to do is find the right company and I can double what I made at MARYCORE," he thought. Optimism reigned supreme.

It is true that buying a going business with an existing cash flow provides cash income faster than starting a business from scratch—and a much larger company can be acquired for the same amount of equity. For the recovering executive with a broad management background, excess ambition and drive, and a risk-taking philosophy, buying a going business can be an excellent choice.

One chapter cannot do justice to the broad subject of business acquisitions. Neither space nor the intent of this book permit a full exploration of techniques to be employed in buying a company. Therefore, for those genuinely interested in exploring this possibility in depth, I suggest reading the book *Buying In: A Complete Guide to Acquiring a Business or Professional Practice*, in which you'll find a complete analysis and techniques for finding, financing, and closing your first business acquisition. The balance of this chapter covers only the highlights of buying a business but perhaps will pique enough interest for you to explore the possibility further.

Buying a company can be a difficult undertaking. The mechanics of locating a viable target, negotiating an equitable price and terms, financing the deal, and coping with the myriad of legal issues make an acquisition even more risky than starting a business from scratch. Even though he can follow these acquisition steps through a clearly defined set of procedures applicable to every deal, a recovering corporate codependent must also cope with several psychological barriers. The high level of stress engendered during the acquisition process can be the most difficult barrier to get over and many times aborts an otherwise doable deal. A second and equally treacherous hurdle for the recovering executive is his tendency to become addicted to the enormous amount of power that comes with the immediate control over a great many people. Though there isn't any sure-fire remedy for avoiding these psychological hazards, if a buyer knows at the beginning that they exist and recognizes the danger signals early enough, he can usually find ways to manage them effectively.

THE STRESS FACTOR

Money, power, and freedom—the triumvirate of entrepreneurship —sound wonderful, but is anything worth risking further damage to one's health? For one who is already emotionally fractured from corporate dependency, another bout with stress and tension could easily end in further emotional turmoil. Although having avoided damage to physical well-being the first time around, a person might not be as fortunate a second time. Stress and anxiety during the acquisition process, as well as after closing the deal, can be substantial. Hypertension, fear, and desperation can, and frequently do, cause physical ailments. Ulcers, a stroke or heart attack, and even cancer are often derivatives of severe emotional stress, as pointed out by Dr. Bernie Siegel in his book, *Love, Medicine & Miracles.* Even if physical disorders can be avoided, mental and emotional stress often prevent a person from making the intelligent decisions necessary to run a company, and business failure may then loom on the horizon.

Rick, the ex-manager from MARYCORE, started down the acquisition trail and soon realized he could buy a much larger company with significantly greater cash flow if he could find two or three partners to ante up $200,000 of equity capital— and it would certainly help him to have partners with backgrounds in sales and finance. Several phone calls to other ex-employees of MARYCORE netted two interested parties; Maury, a super salesman who had chosen retirement when laid off, and Craig, who had been a division Controller with MARYCORE. Within a month the three formed a new corporation—Atcohe, Inc.—with capitalization of $210,000, and off they went to buy an industrial valve manufacturing company.

Seven months later the group was no closer to finding the right company than when it started. Maury became discouraged with the search, took his $100,000 equity, and retreated to his retirement home in Florida. Craig, although discouraged, agreed to stick it out a while longer. Rick, having seen his dream fall apart and his bank account shrink to less than $10,000, began waking up in the middle of the night in a cold sweat. Fear was overpowering him. Pressure from his wife to find some source of income was unrelenting. Even though they had come a long way in identifying sources of potential candidates—and certainly knew the valve industry better than ever before—they couldn't come up with the right target. Rick was ready to throw in the towel.

When he began this escapade, no one had cautioned him it would be so difficult. No one had warned him of the psychological pressures, tension, and fear that went along with an acquisition search. And no one had even intimated how much money would be needed just to find a company.

This story does not have a happy ending. Rick and Craig eventually found a company to buy, but it was losing money and nothing they did could turn it around. Within two years, Craig had a nervous breakdown and Rick turned to alcohol. With Craig in the hospital, Rick couldn't manage the stress any more. He took the company into bankruptcy under Chapter XI and turned his stock holdings over to the bank. The two partners lost everything, including their health.

Stress and anxiety are very real factors, particularly when trouble hits (as it always does). Invariably, both during the search and for the first two years after the closing, Murphy's Law will prevail: if anything can go wrong, it will go wrong. Be prepared for it mentally and physically. Be certain you can stand the heat before joining the battle. And don't be ashamed to back out once you learn how difficult buying a business can be.

THE HAZARDS OF POWER

Remember the addictive power circle from Chapter 2: greed leads to the desire for power, which leads to fear of losing it, which leads to other addictions to support it, which leads to greed to feed these addictions, which leads to the desire for more power.

The same thing can happen with owning a company, only in spades. At least in a corporation the board of directors has some influence over top management. A business owner reports to no one but himself.

If used wisely, this omnipotent power can bring happiness and well-being to employees, customers, and the owner himself. But the peril of power addiction is great. Of all the career choices examined in this book, buying a business presents the greatest risk to the recovering codependent because of the ease of misusing the immediate onslaught of pure power. Control is absolute: to hire or fire, praise or condemn, elevate or humble, promote divisiveness or encourage community.

The neurotic abuse of excessive power by corporate bosses contributed to the recovering executive's emotional problems in the first place, so it should be clear to him that he must act differently or lives of others who are entrusted to his care can be undone just as easily. Whether starting from scratch or buying a going concern (and power comes much faster with a company already functioning), the executive will have enormous power over other people and events. He must understand clearly the responsibility such power carries with it and the damage it can bring if misused. In the long run, hurting others will be far more damaging to the personal psyche than any previous feelings of anger, fear, or depression.

As shown in the priority listing of responsibilities in Chapter 3, the first responsibility of a recovering codependent is to himself. This means he must be continually aware of the insidious nature of power and of how easily he can become addicted to it. It means that the twin columns supporting the power circle—greed and fear—must be recognized and guarded against. The temptation to use power for self-gratification or to cover up a fearful situation must be resisted. By being constantly on guard against the enticement to use domination as a means of satisfying personal lust for more money or material possessions, the entrepreneur can prevent greed from satiating his thirst for even more power. And this precludes addiction.

The next three responsibilities have to do with family members. The lure of power as a means of controlling the family is easy to counteract. A spouse or child can readily spot such behavior and, unless already meekly subordinated to the new business owner's domination, will prevent him from inflicting pain on the home front. It's a built-in safeguard, and he should listen carefully when told that his actions will not be accepted.

The fifth responsibility is to friends, but can just as easily refer to employees. Excessive power leads to other addictive behavior traits: denial, dishonesty, obsessive control, self-centeredness, and perfectionism. The easiest way to avoid such behavior is to remember what it felt like in the corporation when you were subjected to these by your boss, and then to follow the Golden Rule: "Do unto others as you would have them do unto you" characterizes merciful management. The allure of power can be overwhelming, but remembering what it feels like to be on the other side of the fence—assuming you really do want to continue down the road to recovery—obviates the compulsion to abuse such power.

Along with the power to build or destroy human lives comes the responsibility to wield this power for the good of employees, customers, and others influenced by one's actions as a business owner. This does *not* mean one must concern oneself with the well-being of all employees on the job and off. Obviously, this leads to obsessive control. But it does mean that actions and policies in the work environment should be directed toward the good of the group, not toward the self-aggrandizement of the business owner alone.

Mary suffered the angry, obsessive, addicted behavior of her boss at Arthur Andersen & Co. for eight years. Feeling betrayed and helpless, she finally mustered the courage to resign. Searching for a career change as part of her recovery program, but still wanting to remain in public accounting, she sought and found a small CPA practice to purchase. The firm had seven employees. Recognizing her responsibility for the welfare of these workers, Mary concentrated on getting to know each of them and their families personally during the first six months of ownership.

The next two years proved a trying experience for Mary. Several clients dropped off the rolls, and she had difficulty maintaining a positive cash flow. Payments on funds borrowed to make the purchase soaked up all available cash, but Mary scrimped and somehow made it through. In the third year she landed four large audit jobs necessitating the hiring of two more staff auditors. The practice began to blossom and Mary was indeed off to the races. By the fifth year, however, two of these four big clients had been sold and Mary lost the accounts. A third filed bankruptcy, and the fourth, after losing a major Government contract, delayed paying its account for six months. Mary's cash flow dried up. She had no choice but to lay off not only the two new staff auditors, but also three people from her original payroll. But she couldn't bring herself to make the move.

Remembering her experience with Arthur Andersen and how much pain the firm had inflicted in its annual layoffs after the tax season, Mary cut her own draw to virtually nothing rather than hurt the employees. She became too enmeshed in their personal lives. Knowing their families, recognizing how each of them was also struggling to make ends meet, and feeling responsible for their personal well-being, she became obsessed with protecting everyone but herself.

Obviously, such an extreme can only lead to failure. Mary's authority as owner and boss clouded her thinking process. Rather than making rational decisions for the good of the business—and concurrently for the well-being of the group of employees in total —she succumbed to the reverse form of power addiction. After finally finding a buyer for her practice, Mary left public accounting and withdrew to a small town in Iowa to try to regain her emotional stability.

Mary forgot two important lessons: She neglected to place responsibility for survival of herself first, and she misunderstood that obsessive use of power to protect others can be just as devastating as its unbridled application for personal gain. As Mary learned, the abrogation of the responsibility to employ power for the good of oneself as well as the group can, and usually does, lead to the eventual demise of the business.

Are you capable of wielding power benevolently without destroying the company, or, when the pressure becomes severe, will you abdicate your position as Mary did? Or will you become addicted to power and run the company as your old corporate leaders did? Be honest with yourself. If you really are not sure what kind of an owner–manager you will be, then try some other career. Don't buy a business! The risk is too great. Failure will only cause heartache and suffering for yourself and others.

THE RULES OF ACQUISITION

Over the years many would-be entrepreneurial clients have followed my eight Rules of Acquisition. They have proven workable and have resulted in many successful acquisitions.

Rules of Acquisition

1. *Know yourself.* As a recovering codependent you should know yourself pretty well by this time: strengths, weaknesses, what can be done and what can't be done, which friends are true and which are best avoided, what attitudes you have toward other people, your level of moral strength, and the degree of honesty with yourself and others. The importance of caring and compassionate management relationships should have hit home by this time as well.

2. *Trust your conscience.* Have faith in intuitive perceptions. Weigh unconscious feelings against intellectually rational decisions. Do what is right. Instinctively you know what it is. Don't be afraid to show feelings—it's healthy. Emotional highs and lows occur throughout the process. Let go, be yourself, trust yourself.

3. *Establish a support group.* Outside support is extremely important because of the high stress and many anxieties in buying a business. Family and friends should be completely supportive. Let them know how you are progressing. Confide in them. Let them know when you are disappointed or elated. Listen to their suggestions.

4. *Match goals and objectives.* It's crucial to search out a target candidate with goals common to yours. To go after a company with dishonest management, dictatorial owners, contemptuous employees, and malevolent customers can be deadly. Establish search criteria to produce targets with benevolent management,

---

caring employees, morally strong ownership, and satisfied customers.

5. *Deal with the psychology of defeat.* The fear of failure always permeates the acquisition search. The further along you go, the greater the emotional and monetary commitments, and the higher the loss if the deal doesn't close. To cope with defeat you must have a personal contingency plan, deep faith in yourself, moral commitment, abiding and loving care from support groups, and, above all, confidence in the knowledge that if one deal falls through there is always another. You will be successful in the end.

6. *Hire professional assistance.* No one is a marketing, legal, technical, and financial genius. In those areas where you feel inadequate, spend the money to hire competent professional advisors: lawyers, accountants, consultants, even financing specialists. Don't try to do everything yourself. It can't be done.

7. *Go for the "little" victories.* During the long acquisition process, there will be a multitude of little defeats and little victories. Ignore the defeats but savor the victories. Remember the war is won by winning battles. Each little victory is a battle won: finding the target, negotiating a price, locating the financing, agreeing on the contract language. And each victory brings you that much closer to your goal. Even if the deal collapses, these little victories will have been emotionally therapeutic.

8. *Adhere strictly to the Acquisition Steps (see following).* Believe in yourself, believe in your goals, but follow the steps! Don't try to cut corners or go out of sequence. You may win the war but it will be much more costly and time-consuming than if you follow the proven sequence of acquisition steps.

The Acquisition Steps

What are these acquisition steps? A series of 12 procedures, sequentially ordered to ensure a thorough, efficient, and comprehensive method for buying a business. By following these steps in the sequence listed, a prospective business buyer should be able to close a deal in the shortest possible time at the least cost. Any other combination of methods and procedures takes longer, costs more, and increases the risk of failure.

The Acquisition Steps

1. Define realistic acquisition criteria.
2. Lay out a strategic plan.
3. Evaluate the proper timing.
4. Develop a detailed plan for sourcing potential targets.
5. Perform a preliminary due diligence investigation.
6. Negotiate price and terms based on realistic valuation of the target.
7. Perform a thorough due diligence investigation.
8. Prepare a complete business plan.
9. Develop at least three alternative financing structures.
10. Arrange for final updated due diligence investigation.
11. Write a buy/sell agreement and negotiate final language and terms of sale.
12. Plan how to operate the company after the closing.

There are five critical questions to deal with in Step 1:

1. How much income do you need to live on?
2. Do you want or need a partner?
3. Where should the business be located?
4. In what industries do you have experience?
5. What cash investment can you make?

How Much Income

One of the most obvious and yet consistently ignored questions is "How much cash draw do I need to survive for the next three years?" Do you really need $70,000 a year or can you get by with $30,000? If it is $70,000, then don't waste time and money searching for a video store which can only yield $30,000. Granted, $30,000 might not be enough to live on for very long, but having a realistic minimum requirement determines how big the business must be, whether it must be profitable now or in a turnaround situation, and how much of the company's earnings can be used for debt service.

Obviously, to determine a minimum earnings requirement you need to evaluate all other sources of income, including whether or not your family can contribute an income stream and which expenditures can be delayed for several years. Do you really need that new car now? Or that new addition to the house? Is there some way the kids can earn part or all of their college tuition, or can they borrow it? But be realistic. No matter how much you may want to buy a company, if your standard of living dictates an acquisition size beyond your current equity means then stop now, get that resume out, and forget about buying a company until your personal conditions change.

A good friend of mine ignored this rule and let his ego get the better of him. Claude purchased a business that generated $2 million in sales with profits of 20 percent before taxes, and expected to draw $100,000 in salary. Being a super salesman, he convinced the bank holding his operating line that rapid growth was just around the corner. Although the company continued to generate about the same level of sales, Claude couldn't wait. Instead of drawing a salary commensurate with company earnings, for two years he drew down on the company's operating line to pay himself. Debt mounted. The company's sales level remained stable, but because of his high salary, there wasn't enough cash to pay short-term trade payables. In the third year, after failing to meet debt service obligations and extending trade payables to 180 days, Claude filed for protection from creditors under the Bankruptcy Code. Greed had sapped the life blood from his company and, in the end, Claude lost everything.

What About a Partner?

Earnings requirements also influence the decision about structuring the acquisition as a partnership. Do you want to go it alone or would you be more comfortable operating a business with partners? Will the acquisition be a one-family business, a two-family business, or more? Are you willing to give up a piece of the action for an additional equity contribution from a partner? There are some definite advantages to having partners: more equity and therefore a lower debt load; continuity of the business in the event of illness, disability, or death; and varied backgrounds, providing a much broader and sounder management base. The catch is that the business must be big enough to support these other equity owners.

The biggest risk in an equal partnership—which most work ing partners insist on—is that of having continually differing opinions about how to solve a particular problem or handle a specific operating decision. This can lead to pure misery. Employees know there can be only one boss. When two people try to direct a company, nothing gets done.

What About Location?

Unfortunately the most viable target may not be in a buyer's home town—especially if it is a larger company or one offering specialty products or services. A winter sports equipment manufacturer might not be found in Phoenix, Arizona, or a supplier of yachting accessories in Casper, Wyoming, or a swimming pool distributor in International Falls, Minnesota. But there might also be very real reasons for staying close to home. Family considerations or health conditions may prohibit the acquisition of a company hundreds of miles away. Therefore, deciding location goals early in the planning stage can be important. There's no sense in pursuing deals that aren't doable because of location; that only wastes time and money. Of course, absentee ownership is always a possibility, but from a management perspective difficult to handle, and bankers frown on it.

Experience

A practicing CPA came to my office one day armed with a brief-case of pro forma financial statements, company brochures, and industry statistics for a company he wanted to acquire. "A client of mine told me about this wire and cable manufacturing business for sale at a very reasonable price. What do you think?" he asked me. Although cash flow projections seemed to support his minimum living requirements and the business was within commuting distance of his residence, I was stunned. He was seriously planning to give up his accounting practice of 15 years. "How certain are you that this is really what you want?" I asked. For a man with a reputation as an outstanding CPA with a clear head, his answer shocked me even more: "I've had enough of accounting. I want to try something new; so I just decided to sell my share of the practice to Bill and go do it!"

"But why wire and cable manufacturing? You know nothing about that business."

"I know, but the company is available, the price looks about right, I can get there in 35 minutes, and I'm a quick learner."

I spent the next four hours trying to convince him that even though the deal seemed to match his goals fairly well, he had missed the most important consideration of all: choosing an industry or market you have some experience in. Don't under any circumstance tackle a business you know nothing about. That's a sure road to defeat.

Bart ignored my advice, acquired the company with nearly all his life savings, incurred a significant amount of debt, and then found out that making wire and cable was much more difficult than he imagined. The industry began a prolonged retraction and, coupled with Bart's lack of technical background, the possibility of growing the company became remote. Within 14 months he had sold the business at a substantial loss and is now back practicing accounting, much wiser but also much poorer.

Buying a business without synergistic market and industry background has led more than one optimistic entrepreneur astray. It might sound simple to make and sell chemicals, but if one's background is in computer system analysis, a lengthy learning curve can easily spell defeat—no matter how intelligent and savvy one may be.

How Much to Invest?

The biggest and most important question of all is "How much can you afford to invest in an acquisition?" Buying a business may be just a dream unless you have the personal cash to handle the deal. In determining how much you can afford to put into a business, bear in mind that a financial institution expects a buyer to be fully committed financially, including valuable personal assets.

The more equity you have, the larger the target can be and the easier it is to raise debt or investor capital. Under current financial market conditions, a ratio of 1:3 is generally safe. That is, a dollar of equity will command three dollars of debt. If you have $100,000 to contribute as an equity investment, a financial institution should be willing to lend $300,000, everything else being equal.

A few commercial banks, most asset-based lenders, and nearly all investment banks encourage buying with a lower ratio. Since leverage financing became popular 20 years ago, these financing institutions have thrived because people continue to want something for nothing, without realizing the terrible risk involved.

It is possible to buy a business with very little personal equity. Given the right circumstances, a buyer with $25,000 equity can conceivably leverage it up to almost any price—$3 million, $4 million, or more. But high leveraging, whether through an asset-based lender or an investment bank is always very risky. The money has to be paid back and always, without exception, at exorbitant rates. Cash used to make these payments could otherwise be used to buy new equipment, finance research and development efforts, or pay higher wages—or it could even go to the owner in the form of increased draws. Instead, it must be paid to the financial institution and everyone loses. The ultimate loss occurs during an economic downturn, when, without sufficient cash to meet these obligations, the business owner either concedes the company to the investors and creditors or files for bankruptcy. Either way he loses. High leveraged deals, whether done with debt or outside equity, continue to be the bane of the entrepreneur.

THE STRATEGIC PLAN

Once basic criteria are established, the next step is to construct a strategic plan—a sequential outline of major steps in the acquisition process—with go-no-go decision points and estimated costs to be incurred at each step. Search, investigation, and closing expenditures can thus be budgeted and controlled according to the progression of the plan. Here is a typical outline:

Action	Start Date	Finish Date	Estimate Cost
A. Survey Industry/Product Market	1/1	3/1	$ 1,000
1. Economic growth curves (historical and future)			
2. Market dominance (competition and pricing)			
3. Foreign competition			
4. Economics of user applications			
5. List of companies			
6. Sales literature and financial data of companies in industry			
7. Trade association interviews			
B. Target Search	3/1	6/1	$ 2,000
1. Brokers, consultants, lawyers, accountants			
2. Investment bankers, venture capital firms, commercial banks			
3. *Wall Street Journal*, trade journals			
4. Unsolicited mailings			
5. Personal contacts			
C. Preliminary Due Diligence for Each Viable Target	6/1	7/15	$ 2,400
1. Meet with seller			
2. Facilities tour			
3. Obtain financials and sales literature			
D. Negotiate Price and Payment Terms for the Best of the Three Targets	7/15	8/15	$ 800
1. Valuation of the business			
2. Earn outs, contingencies, hold backs			
3. Buyer paper			

Action	Start Date	Finish Date	Estimate Cost
E. Perform Detailed Due Diligence	8/15	10/15	$ 2,000
1. Financial: three years historical audit reports and monthly internal reports			
2. Prepare pro formas			
3. Organization chart			
4. Meet management and second plant tour			
5. Customer data: competitors, pricing, market size and share			
6. Outstanding lawsuits or claims: government, employees, customers, etc.			
7. Contracts in force: union, vendor, customer, employee, leases			
F. Source Financing	8/15	11/15	$ 2,000
1. Prepare comprehensive business plan			
2. Investment banks and venture capital firms			
3. Commercial banks			
4. Finance companies: commercial and asset-based lenders			
5. Others			
G. Final Due Diligence	11/1	11/25	$15,000
1. Update pro formas			
2. Appraisal of equipment and real estate			
3. Audit review by CPA firm			
H. Write Buy/Sell Agreement and Other Closing Documents	11/15	12/15	$ 5,000
1. Engage legal counsel			
2. Negotiate final language and terms of sale			
3. Coordinate with financing parties			

A total of 12 months and $30,000 may seem a bit steep, but it's difficult to close an acquisition in less than 9 months and the extra time in the plan won't hurt. There's also a pretty good chance something will go wrong along the way. Far better to be conservative and plan for the worst— remember Murphy's Law. Twelve months and expenditures of approximately $30,000 are reasonable expectations for a mid-sized business, six months and $15,000 for a small retail or service company. To this budget, of course, one must add personal living expenses during this period when no income will be generated.

TIMING

The same timing factors that influence starting up a business are relevant to buying. The bigger the target, the more crucial timing becomes. Valuation and pricing of any company generating more than $2 million sales will be significantly influenced by current performance in the stock market, especially a bull market. Published price/earnings ratios exert strong upward pressure on company valuations whether privately or publicly held. Additionally, if the target is a subsidiary of a listed parent, performance of the parent's stock determines pricing of the subsidiary. Macroeconomic indicators, foreign competition, current government regulations, tax laws, and industry business cycles all bear on the timing of when to start, negotiate, and close a deal.

THE TARGET SEARCH

Jerry wanted to buy a company, but he also needed an annual salary of about $100,000 to maintain his standard of living. A small retail or service business just wouldn't do the trick. He needed something in distribution or manufacturing with enough volume to provide this salary. But answering ads in the local newspaper wasn't getting him anywhere. A mutual friend suggested he talk to me about helping in the search. Because of who the referral came from, I agreed to accept the engagement on a contingency fee schedule. Jerry was shocked. "I though all consultants charged enormous retainers and then stretched the project out as long as possible," he said.

"Some do, unfortunately," I answered. "But the good ones are willing to gamble right along with you—providing they are convinced you are serious, financially viable, and come well recommended."

"Well, I guess I could have done it myself if I had too."

"Don't be too sure, Jerry, unless you have excess cash and plenty of time. A merger and acquisition (M&A) consultant is just like any other professional. If you're sick, see a doctor. If you're sued, use a lawyer. A CPA does your tax planning. The reason for using professionals is to shorten the time in getting something done, and getting it done better than you could do it yourself."

Outside assistance is almost mandatory in locating the right target. There are too many variables, too many combinations and too many creative opportunities to do the job all by yourself. Shortly, we'll examine where you can get this assistance.

The ideal target should have the following characteristics:

1. A company profile fitting your personal goals.
2. A product, service, or industry you know something about.
3. Key management or critical employees in place.
4. Proprietary products or services.
5. A market composed of several small suppliers.
6. A long-term industry growth trend.
7. A purchase price commensurate with your equity.

Prior to a detailed target search, research the specific market characteristics of those industries of interest to you. A local Department of Commerce office can provide valuable information as can library resources. Trade journals and other business publications are also good sources of data. It's also necessary to determine what companies are in this industry, who controls the submarkets, which companies are divisions of larger parent companies and, of course, which companies are available for purchase. But how to get all this done with limited resources and time is the key question. That's where professional advisors can be helpful.

If you are going after a small business–such as a retail store, print shop, insurance agency, auto repair shop, or other small service or retail business–try a local business broker. They are listed in the Yellow Pages and generally advertise in local newspapers. Business brokers list companies for sale in much the same way as real estate firms do, but have little knowledge of the actual business they are selling other than what the owner tells them. The seller usually pays the broker's fee.

For a larger company, with sales over $2 million, a qualified M&A consultant can do a better and faster job. His fee is borne by the buyer, frequently with a monthly retainer deductible from the total fee at closing. M&A consultants have access to broad markets of available companies and can even search out targets that may not be actively on the market. They also know of large corporations planning to divest divisions or subsidiaries. Neither brokers nor consultants are usually licensed, however, so beware of charlatans, who abound in these businesses.

Investment bankers and venture capital firms can be an excellent source for larger candidates. Although difficult to approach, they are generally more than happy to turn over leads abandoned from their own searches. Lawyers and public accountants may also be of assistance in a given situation, although they're usually unwilling to risk a conflict of interest by recommending a specific client as a target. Bankers are in the same boat. Occasionally bankers may help with leads, but in most cases they won't understand what you are talking about when you approach them for help in a search.

Another source of targets currently on the market (mostly for smaller companies) is the Business Opportunity section of the Thursday issue of the *Wall Street Journal*. Unfortunately, many of these companies are losers and are not worth pursuing. Don't overlook all those personal contacts made over the years while you worked as an employee. Old customers, vendors, other employees, or perhaps an ex-boss are all valuable contacts with a combined source of knowledge that may surprise you. Most will be thrilled to help. But don't ask for money; ask for advice.

A final method for locating target candidates is through unsolicited mailings. At times this can be useful to uncover available businesses not yet on the market. In other cases it is a time-consuming, wasted endeavor. Locating a target business is really a matter of luck and perseverance. There are a number of sources of data bases with company names and addresses (check your library and the Yellow Pages), some of which provide names of the chairman, president, and other officers. Additionally, hundreds of mailing list companies will customize listings to any specification. However, purchased data bases, either on computer disc or with hard copy mailing labels, can be quite expensive. A small listing might run $1,000, and a large one upwards of $5,000. It all depends on the number of companies listed, number of sorts required, and other special services offered.

DUE DILIGENCE INVESTIGATION AND NEGOTIATIONS

Once a target has been identified, preliminary investigations begin. A tour of the facility, examination of historical financial statements, and meetings with the seller lead to the negotiation of purchase price and terms of payment. During this preliminary investigation, the seller may be unwilling to release sufficient financial or other information for you to make a judgment about valuation and negotiating strategy. If that happens, try sending him a level of interest letter. This letter should indicate a desire to proceed with negotiations within a broad price range (including the seller's asking price) but contingent on the satisfactory completion of due diligence investigations. A sample of such a letter can be found in the Appendix. Also execute a confidentiality agreement (also found in the Appendix) promising to keep all the seller's confidential information private. Most sellers accept these documents as evidence of a genuine desire to proceed and will cooperate with financial statements. Some will not, however, and that's where an M&A consultant can help.

A fair price for the business can be based on the value of the assets, cash flow, profitability, or any combination therefore, but must recognize current economic conditions in the industry. Once you determine how much you are willing to pay, negotiations of final price and terms follow. Each negotiation is different and there are no rules to go by; however, three principles should make the job easier:

1. *Know the people against whom you will negotiate.* If the seller does his own negotiations, it's much easier to resolve issues. Many times, however, a seller elects to be in the background and delegates negotiating responsibility to his legal counsel, accountant, or an outside consultant. To plan the appropriate strategy, it's important to know who will be across the table. Negotiating with an accountant requires a thorough understanding of the target's financial condition. Bringing your own CPA to explain calculations can be enormously helpful. If his lawyer handles negotiations, bring along your legal counsel. Lawyers love to outfox naive laymen and, with their persuasive abilities, can very easily outmaneuver an unwary buyer without him ever knowing it. But regardless of who the opponent is, strategy based on kindness and compassion will gain more than one founded on hardnosed bullying.

2. *Plan a strategy in advance of negotiations.* Good planning pays off at negotiations. Before getting to the table, have a strategy worked out. Know what the numbers are and what your top price is. Try to estimate how the seller will proceed with negotiations. Judge his degree of aggressiveness and how low he will go for a cash price. A starting figure can then be established to allow room for bargaining. Also try to determine what the seller is really after. Does he want or need a lump sum cash payment? Does he have tax or other liens pending against the assets of the business which must be liquidated? Are there family members employed by the company he wants to protect? Always do the research and construct a planned strategy before entering negotiations.

3. *Exercise perceptive judgments and don't be afraid to trust your intuition.* Trust your instincts. By now you should have a good feel for the people and the business. Many facts will be missing, but first impressions are usually accurate and you probably know more about the company than you realize. Subconsciously, you know the right price and terms. Trust your instincts and rely on that new code of moral ethics. Honesty, integrity, and caring are a pretty tough combination for any seller to beat.

FINANCING THE DEAL

There are three sources of acquisition financing: (1) the buyer, (2) a financial institution or outside investors, and (3) the seller. Most deals are financed by a combination of the three. A buyer must put up some of his own equity, borrow some from a bank, and try to get the seller to finance part of the deal.

Borrowing money from a bank can be a confusing and wearying pursuit. If not done properly, it can also be the most time-consuming and frustrating phase of the acquisition program. Those so-called friendly bankers turn out to be anything but friendly when you try to borrow money. All the advertisements about competitive interest rates, loan closings in three days, and excess funds to invest turn out to be just so many come-ons. In the real world of finance, bankers are stubborn and cautious, and generally don't understand your business. That's why a business plan must be prepared before you approach any financial institution.

The Business Plan

A business plan pulls together all of the data gathered during the due diligence investigation, incorporates the plans of the buyer for the ensuing five years, and presents an overall picture of the target company and its prospects for the future. Its primary purpose is to give a banker a quick overview of the company—including products, facilities, markets, competition, personnel, and financial performance. It is also a fast, easy way for the buyer to get a grasp of at least the salient features of the target. By being forced to articulate his plans and how they correlate with the company's history, he reduces dreams and wish lists to quantifiable terms. Along the way, a buyer should uncover any major skeletons that have potential for causing future problems. By this time, you are probably thinking, "Why make such a big production out of just a written description of the business and some financial projections?" Take a look at the outline of a typical business plan in the Appendix and you may change your mind.

Too many times, a would-be business buyer spends significant out-of-pocket funds for travel and telephone expenses, data bases, mailings, and consulting fees only to see the deal fall through because he can't convince a bank to handle the financing. The reason is usually a poorly prepared or sloppily presented business plan. A well-prepared plan presents hard facts about the company but also casts light on the ability of the buyer to analyze and make intelligent decisions about markets, products, and financial results. Even when a plan is well-documented, if the presentation is sloppy, incomplete, or hard to follow, the reader will probably assume that the buyer either doesn't have all the facts or doesn't care enough to do a good job. Either way, a lending officer will probably back away. After all, a banker places at least as much importance on the buyer's ability to manage the company effectively as he does on the underlying assets and historical financial performance.

If there is any question about how to prepare and present a well-documented and carefully written business plan read *Buying In* (mentioned earlier). If you are hesitant to put pen to paper, hire a qualified M&A consultant, CPA, or even a professional writer to do the writing for you.

Sources of Funds

There are four major sources of outside financing for acquisitions available to the private entrepreneur: (1) finance companies, (2) investment banks, (3) venture capital firms, and (4) commercial banks. Commercial finance companies (or asset-based lenders as they prefer to be called) are in business to make loans to companies that a commercial bank is unwilling to take. For an existing business, a finance company loans on inventory and receivables that a commercial bank wouldn't touch because of aging, unique industry requirements, or qualification of account. For acquisition funding, long term loans of five to seven years are common, using hard assets (real estate and equipment) as collateral. Small equity contributions are acceptable because an asset-based lender is ready, willing, and able to force liquidation of the business to collect his debt. He calculates that nearly as much profit can be made through liquidation sales as from interest income. As further consideration, asset-based lenders normally charge interest of three to five points above the prime rate, and substantial placement fees; they also require a first position on all assets not already pledged, and of course, personal guarantees from the borrower. The greatest drawback in borrowing from an asset-based lender—aside from the high cost—is that the first signs of financial trouble frequently lead to interference in the operating decisions of the business, as Richard Clear learned the hard way.

Richard Clear was the Manager of Contract Administration for a major East Coast aerospace manufacturer. After becoming disgruntled with his new boss and increasingly upset by corrupt dealings with government officials, Richard finally quit. Having always dreamed of running his own business, he purchased a small manufacturing company in the government contracting business, which had undergone several years of widely fluctuating profits. With only $30,000 to put into a deal, he felt fortunate to locate a company with substantial machinery and equipment, and negotiated a financing package with an asset-based lender recently merged into a major commercial bank. The price seemed reasonable and even though the deal was highly leveraged Richard was confident he could stabilize the company and make it grow.

During Richard's first year of ownership, the company lost two follow-on contracts for the space shuttle, and Richard began to panic. The pressure of trying to keep his company afloat led to severe headaches and high blood pressure, but Richard hung on, knowing that if he could land a contract during the next bidding phase he would be saved. Electing not to lay off any employees, he missed two monthly interest payments to the lender, which immediately sent a representative to camp in Richard's office. He tried to follow this banker's direction but personality clashes prohibited congenial relations. Soon they were at each other's throats and Richard booted him out the door.

To Richard's horror, when he missed another interest payment the next month, the lender notified him that if he missed one more payment it would foreclose on the loan. There was nothing Richard could do, since the bidding date was still three months off. The following month, the bank foreclosed and forced an auction to liquidate the loan. Richard was out of business, out his investment, and still owed the lender $800,000 on a personal guarantee.

Investment Banking Houses

During the 80s, investment banks became a prime source of acquisition funding. They mastered a number of financing schemes for corporate takeovers and have become the principal suppliers of funds for many smaller deals as well. Typically an investment banker acts as the lead player and recruits other participants as required in putting together a complete financing package. Under the investment banker's auspices, commercial banks and asset-based lenders are more than willing to take a piece of the action as long as the investment banker also puts up some of his own funds as equity. As consideration for this effort and in exchange for an equity contribution, he normally wants between 15 percent and 75 percent of the company—plus board membership or control. An investment banker sitting on the board can provide invaluable professional advice in those specialized areas of the industry where he has considerably more expertise than the owner/manager.

Additionally, there are literally hundreds of small investment banking firms called "boutique houses," which specialize in one industry or in a unique products or services. Expert advice from these bankers can be invaluable to the business owner.

There is, however, one major disadvantage in using an investment banking firm. In addition to a share in the ownership of the company—maybe even controlling interest—the return on investment demanded in lieu of interest ranges from 30 percent to 45 percent. There are not many businesses around capable of generating sufficient cash to pay this amount of debt service and still have much left over for expansion or improvements. And, except in unusual circumstances, the owner always gets shortchanged. On the other hand, without hard assets or adequate personal equity, the business buyer may not have any choice if he still wants to make the deal.

Venture Capital Firms

Venture capital firms are normally not a good source of financing for acquisitions. Their primary niche is with small, start-up companies in high-tech, glamour-type industries. Providing equity seed capital for start-ups, and first and second stage financing for initial growth spurts, these financial institutions serve a special need in the financial market. Many times, a small company with little or no collateral to secure a loan and an earnings history insufficient to support substantial cash flow projections cannot raise funds anywhere else. This type of investment creates the greatest risk for the financier. Therefore, his reward for taking the risk must be substantial. Interested primarily in rapid investment appreciation realized through an initial public stock issue (IPO), a venture capitalist will inevitably want controlling interest in the company or at least controlling interest on the board to safeguard his investment. Venture capital is not predominant in acquisitions unless the company happens to be one of these relatively new high-tech start-ups.

The Appendix includes names and addresses of many of the most reputable investment bankers, venture capital firms, and asset-based lenders currently active in acquisition financing.

Commercial Banks

Commercial banks aren't worth the effort for a deal in excess of $2 million in sales. They usually consider the risk too great, and without extremely unusual circumstances—such as being related to the CEO or board chairman—an individual buyer won't have the clout to interest a commercial bank. On the other hand, for small deals— such as a deli, jewelry store, hardware store, or office supplies house—a commercial bank may be the only way to go. But don't expect to do a high leverage deal: regardless of the size of the company, it just doesn't happen.

A commercial bank is the primary source of working capital funding, however, and good personal contacts might encourage consideration for acquisition financing as well. Don't spend a lot of time trying to convince a commercial banker what a great deal you have, though. Depending on the structure of the deal, an investment banker, venture capitalist, or reputable finance company will yield much better results.

In addition to outside financing, try to get the seller to carry a portion of the purchase price. His willingness to help shows confidence both in you as a buyer and in the business as a viable entity. This can be extremely helpful in attracting bank financing. There are three common forms of seller financing:

1. Buyer paper, generally in the form of a promissory note.
2. Earn outs, where part of the company's profits over a fixed time period are paid back to the seller.
3. Contingency payments, which are specified payments made over time only if certain conditions occur.

Each of these schemes defers part of the purchase price to a later time and as such can have beneficial tax consequences to the seller. Obviously, a buyer can save cash by prolonging payments as long as possible. With both parties as winners, deferred payments (at least for part of the purchase price) are quite common and should be used wherever possible. Remember the general rule of thumb is: seller's price but buyer's terms. If you can't get your price, at least make sure the terms include deferred payments.

THE LEGAL SIDE

Unfortunately, there is also a legal side to buying a business. A myriad of closing documents must be prepared by a lawyer, in language not readily intelligible to the layperson. The most important of these is the buy/sell agreement which consists of four parts:

1. Price, terms, and conditions of sale.
2. Representations and warranties of seller and buyer.
3. Conditions precedent to closing for both seller and buyer.
4. General statements of law.

Retain a competent lawyer with specific expertise and experience in drafting and negotiating buy/sell agreements for deals similar to yours. Do *not* use a lawyer without such credentials.

Be especially careful that language in the seller's representations and warranties section provides recourse at a later date, if or when it becomes necessary to sue for breach of contract—for example, if the data furnished during the due diligence phase turns out to be inaccurate or misleading.

That's all there is to it. Follow the 12 acquisition steps and you should be well on the way to a new life as an entrepreneur. You can buy a business and you can structure it to meet your specific psychological needs and wants. It won't be easy, but then nothing in the recovery process ever is. Stick with it and, in the end, persistent efforts can bring a mentally challenging, financially rewarding, and emotionally fulfilling life-style.

We have now seen four possibilities for joining the ranks of entrepreneurs: consulting, starting a business from scratch, starting a franchise, and buying a going business. But each of these alternatives requires some personal capital, a lot of stress, and high risk. Maybe you've had enough of the business rat race and want to slow down. The next chapter explores some ideas for structuring a life-style in semi-retirement.

CHAPTER 11

OUT OF THE MAINSTREAM: ENJOYING A PRODUCTIVE RETIREMENT

"You Are *Always* Too Young to Retire, But *Never* Too Old to Learn" was the topic of a luncheon speech I gave to a group of Rotarians. In the middle of the speech, a hand raised from the audience. I acknowledged the question and a stoop-shouldered gentleman with an aluminum walker arose and barked, "I'm pushing 90, and I've always liked golf. Do you think I'm too old to learn to play?" I thanked him for the question and answered with the following story.

Brad Forestreet was 28 years old when he lost both legs during World War II. Four years of therapy at the VA Hospital left him disillusioned, angry, and without hope. But time is a great healer and last year, on his 70th birthday, Brad won the championship at White Willow Golf Club. At the banquet that night, when asked his secret to success he replied, "No secret. I learned to believe in my mind and trust my heart. When the doctors gave up, a greater power stepped in and wouldn't let me retire from life."

Two months later I received a note in the mail from the old Rotarian: "Took your advice. Managed three holes today. Aiming for six by August. Keep the faith."

In spite of federal age discrimination laws, executives over 50 are frequently passed over for promotions in favor of younger managers. In many cases, they are the first to go in cost-cutting moves, and once on the street they find it difficult, if not impossible, to get another job. Years of experience, company loyalty, and job performance mean little in the youth-conscious business world. When queried, corporate personnel managers—careful to avoid charges of age discrimination—come up with all kinds of excuses: we need someone who will be with us for many years, the job is strenuous and requires physical stamina, the company is floundering and needs new ideas and new blood, we need people who are not set in their ways, and so on. The truth is, with baby boomers assuming ever higher posts in the corporation, the age of top executives is declining rapidly, and youthful leaders want even younger subordinates. They fear competition from older executives who have more experience in solving the company's problems than they do. Personnel policies are structured to further the job security of young corporate leaders. Hiring and firing, advancement, and organization planning policies, while keeping to the letter of the law, are often skewed in favor of youth; the older executive is left to fend for himself.

In her book, *Forced Out*, Juliet F. Brudney describes her conclusions from attending a 1985 conference on aging:

> I came to the conclusion that the problem of older job-seekers was simply not being addressed. About that time articles started to appear, not about how hard it was for experienced older workers to find jobs, but about how many older people in the professional, managerial, and technical category were being thrown out of work. Companies had been making use of early retirement programs as a cost-cutting measure for years, offering special severance or pension benefits to older executives to persuade them to leave before pension age.[1]

If age discrimination does, in fact, pervade executive ranks and, assuming that we either do not want or cannot afford to line a lawyer's pockets by taking the corporation to court, what choices remain for those of us past the age of 50? We've looked at a couple of possibilities--starting up a new business or buying a going concern. But the financial community is even more discriminatory in granting loans to older executives than the corporation is in promoting them. Starting a management consulting practice can be a viable alternative, as seen in Chapter 8. However, the difficulty for a recovering codependent in dealing with other people's problems may preclude this option. There is another alternative: retirement. This does not mean sedentary retirement spent watching TV or playing solitaire, but dynamic retirement with income-producing activities coupled with personal and moral growth. There are a host of options available; this chapter will introduce some ideas that should start you thinking in the right direction.

A physically and mentally healthy executive never retires completely. His psyche won't let him. He continues to have the urge to do something constructive—maybe not another full-time job or the strenuous exercise of starting or buying a business, but something to add to the well-being of other people and to his own personal growth. An interesting phenomenon in older executives being forced out of corporate life is that either they turn inward with bittersweet memories and focus their remaining days on themselves, or they recognize the value of kindness and caring for others and make an honest effort to make a positive contribution to society. There doesn't seem to be any middle ground.

In discussing the cultural concept of work as it relates to the emotional well-being of the individual, Robert N. Bellah, in *Habits of the Heart* makes the point that in searching for meaning through what he calls "expressive individualism," a person generally strives to structure his retirement years with the same rules, competition, and orderly environment as he experienced on the job—golf and bridge being the most popular pursuits. This leads to a continuation of the me-ism inculcated throughout years of corporate obedience. The implication is that little attempt is made to find the true meaning of life in what he terms the "moral community of the calling."[2]

A continuation of self-gratification might work for some who choose the retirement route, but it certainly will not suffice for the recovering corporate codependent. On the contrary, to progress on the road to recovery, he must dispense with his former despondency-breeding ethical nihilism and conscientiously seek solutions through moral self-consciousness. He must continue to strive for enhancement of true community and must direct at least part of his life toward others.

A recovering executive has learned to live one day at a time, to experience feelings and events as if each day were his last. With this attitude, life after 50 and beyond the corporation can and will be a glorious time to begin new activities, broaden interests, and help others. Semi-retirement best describes this paradigm. As Dr. Siegel states:

> The person suffering in an unsatisfying career (or unsatisfying retirement) often argues that there aren't enough interesting, creative jobs to go around. This may be true, but so few people exercise their creativity that the opportunities exist for those who seek them. Nothing can be gained without effort and, as William James noted, most people live too far within self-imposed limits.[3]

But there are hazards to semi-retirement and, before exploring ideas for productive income-producing activities, an understanding of psychological disorientation would be helpful.

PSYCHOLOGICAL DISORIENTATION

I use the phrase psychological disorientation to describe those mental and emotional conditions that arise from lack of constructive physical and mental exertion commonly experienced by a person living a highly pressured life and suddenly retiring from active pursuits. They can be categorized as follows:

1. Boredom and loss of interest.
2. Changing relations within the family.
3. Fear of financial catastrophe.
4. Psychosomatic health problems.
5. Lack of self discipline and structure.

Kim Wu Rhie earned his medical degree in Korea and, after several years of private practice in Seoul, came to the United States to practice internal medicine. Disenchanted with the American medical system—particularly with the influence of the AMA on new medical procedures—Kim took a position with a hospital in Puerto Rico. Four years later, he recognized that Puerto Rico was no better than the States and decided to retire. He was tired, confused, and burned out. He wanted nothing to do with the medical profession. He purchased a small house with a garden overlooking the bay. In the beginning, tending his garden, catching up on his reading, and practicing the English language kept Kim busy. Eventually, however, this was not enough. He was still a healthy, young 52. Isolating himself in his cottage led to a loss of interest in any outside activities. The longer Kim stayed by himself, the less interest he had in anything or anyone else. Longing for his homeland but financially unable to go back, he started to become depressed. Then came the headaches and eventually cancer. On his deathbed two years later, a broken, unhappy man, Kim confessed to his closest friend that retirement had killed him. Without people, without new interests, and without hope for a better tomorrow he was ready to die—and he did.

Inactive retirement causes boredom, and boredom can be deadly. Psychologists, psychiatrists, and social workers who work with older people have recognized this for a long time. Retirement communities have sprung up throughout the country in an attempt to provide retirees a way to meet new people and develop new interests. Discounts offered to senior citizens by airlines, hotels, auto rental companies, movie theaters, golf courses, and almost every other leisure or travel business can also help retirees keep active. However, though physical activity is important, travel or golf do not require much mental exertion. Without an active mind, the body will soon lose its energy, and for executives who have spent years performing mental gymnastics in corporate meetings, planning sessions, boardrooms, and political confrontations, the need to stay mentally challenged remains paramount. Additionally, retirement communities and discount policies usually apply to people past the age of 62 or 65. What about the executive retiree who leaves the business world at age 50, 55, or 60? According to society's standards, he is too young to retire and there are few, if any, programs designed to offer assistance or challenges.

This is the same problem a codependent confronts in trying to locate a support group. There are plenty of formal support groups for people with special afflictions: Alcoholics Anonymous, Narcotics Anonymous, Overeaters Anonymous, Children of Alcoholics, Al-Anon. There are also support groups for people recently divorced, people whose child committed suicide, spouses whose husbands are MIA's, battered women, and so on. But what about the person who needs support but does not fit into any of these categories? The disenchanted executive whose only malady is that he is emotionally dysfunctional? More often than not he must form his own "community" support group as described in Chapter 3.

The 50-year-old retiree faces the same dilemma. He is not supposed to retire in his 50s, so there are no social programs designed to help him. That is precisely why, even without the inclination, such a maverick retiree must force himself to become active in his own way, just to keep his sanity. Boredom must be avoided at all costs. A lifetime of business activities points the executive to some form of income-producing agenda as a logical choice.

In addition to the obvious physical activities, some other ways to broaden your interests while laying the groundwork for a stream of income might include the following:

1. *Expand an existing hobby.* With a little creativity, woodworking, ham radios, auto mechanics, or personal computer programming can generate income. Hidden talents for painting, sculpting, or performing in a musical group may be the ticket. Horticulture, animal husbandry, or farming can provide opportunities. Collecting rare stamps, coins, jewelry, or antiques might fill the bill. Furniture refinishing, reupholstering, and tailoring are always in high demand, as are creative drawing or writing, counseling Boy Scouts or Girl Scouts, and hospital auxiliary work. Most of us have at least one hobby we have enjoyed over the years, and whatever it may be, chances are good it can be expanded into a productive endeavor to broaden interests and provide either mental or physical exertion, or both.

2. *Take an extended trip.* Fly or take a boat trip around the world. Cruise the Caribbean or the Great Lakes on a sailboat or a freighter. Tour Europe or the United States by train or bicycle. Take an expedition to the Himalayas or Antarctica. Hike the Appalachian Trail or the Grand Canyon. Join an Outward Bound school. After years of sedentary life with the corporation, a change of scenery offering new experiences will breathe fresh energy into your life and activate those little gray cells to further creativity.

3. *Relocate: move your household.* At first glance a drastic step, relocating a household poses new problems and opportunities to awaken dormant interests. Sell the house and buy a condo on the shore, or sell the condo and buy a house. Spend a year or two in a foreign country. Move to an island in the Pacific or the Caribbean or to a village in Mexico or Venezuela. If you live on the East Coast, move to the West Coast; if you live in the North, try the South; or if you are a city dweller, move to the country or a small town. Although expensive, such a new living environment forces you to find new friends, challenges, and opportunities for a changed life-style.

4. *Develop an investment portfolio.* Expand your investments to corporate bonds or municipal funds. Research investments in precious metals such as platinum, gold, or silver. Research penny stocks and IPOs. Try the commodity markets in grain, corn, wheat, or copper. How about standing lumber, oil exploration or ocean shipping fleets? Real estate investments, limited partnerships, and venture capital projects all offer opportunities. Whatever avenue you choose, dive into extensive research; learn to chart trends; project economic vicissitudes; and gather annual reports, proxy statements, and 10-Ks. Attend annual shareholder meetings, challenge board decisions, or write letters of commendation or criticism to board chairmen. An active investment program broadens horizons while permitting continued participation in the business world.

5. *Invent a new product, process, or practice.* Not everyone can be a Thomas Edison, but you don't need an engineering degree from MIT to come up with a new recipe for a meat sauce, a unique shelf to store paint, or a way to raise charitable funds. If you do have an ingenious idea for a new product or process, try it out and maybe it will be marketable. Even if you can't sell it, the creative process alone will broaden your horizons.

The local elementary school PTA was having difficulty finding new ways to raise funds for the school library and asked me for ideas. "Why not put on a play for the children and their parents?" I suggested. Before I knew what happened, my wife and I had started a theater group of teachers and parents to produce, act, make the sets, design and sew costumes, and handle business affairs for the first school district production of *Alice in Wonderland*. Over 100 parents and teachers struggling to make the production as professional as possible created a new togetherness in the neighborhood. We also raised several hundred dollars for the school, and best of all, provided both of us with a whole new spectrum of interests in the theater. Twenty years later, the annual productions are still going strong.

CHANGING FAMILY RELATIONSHIPS

After you leave active employment and start to spend days at home rather than in the office, relationships with your spouse and children will never be the same. For a recovering codependent this will probably be a big help, as it can provide constant family support not otherwise available. However, the immediate reaction to being unemployed—sitting around the house—will certainly drive your spouse nuts. So get out. Do something. Play golf, go to the library, or work on the car—do anything but stay at home. The added free time can be therapeutic for a while, but not forever. Get to know your spouse and kids again. Chances are that as an active executive you haven't spent much time with your family for many years. Do it now. Cultivate their interests and in so doing your own interests will broaden.

But don't do it too long or the reverse can happen; instead of becoming strengthened the family unit can be destroyed. Remember that your spouse and kids have developed their own lives while you've been busy with the corporation. By inserting yourself in the middle of their routines now, there's a good chance stress and anxiety will build for them, which you obviously don't want. It's difficult, but by being careful, by practicing those new ethical standards and recognizing the rights of family members to live their own lives, you should be able to garner significant benefits from being at home—at least for a time.

FEAR OF FINANCIAL CATASTROPHE

For many retirees the greatest cause of psychological disorientation is an overriding fear of losing financial independence. An employee seldom pays much attention to the luxury of a monthly paycheck but when it suddenly stops, and those monthly bills have to be paid out of savings, the knot of fear begins to form. It doesn't seem to matter how much the executive has saved over the years, how big his investment portfolio may be, or what assets he possesses: the realization that there will no longer be a regular stream of income is staggering. The fear of not having income can, and usually does, provide the impetus for the executive to start looking for some way to earn money. The best intentions of religiously following a recovery program can be forgotten with the onslaught of financial disjunction.

But you can prevent such disorientation very easily by planning for retirement activities and financial requirements *before* you leave the corporation. Since it's unlikely you will know when the next round of layoffs might come, if you still have a job the time to begin retirement planning is right now. Company pension plans, IRAs, retirement annuities, and "paid-up-at-65" life insurance policies are certainly worth having, but they only kick in when you reach 60 or 65. What about retiring before then? What financial insurance can you plan for in the event of early retirement? What vehicles are available to provide ready cash when the paycheck stops unexpectedly? Part of a retirement plan must be defining where the cash will come from and whether it will be sufficient to cover living expenses. If you know income will exceed expenses, you can rest a lot easier. On the other hand, a cash shortfall should prod you into action to devise some type of income-generating activity.

Constructing personal financial statements and updating them every six months can help in such planning. The Appendix includes a format for such financial statements which I have found easy to follow and also helpful for estate planning. When calculating income and expenses it's important to *exclude* your current salary from the corporation because once you retire, that will be gone. And clearly, any expected "golden handshake" should be added to available cash income. With such an updated personal financial statement, your financial situation can be seen any time. If there isn't enough cash to live on by combining the liquidation proceeds of assets with annual net income, then *now* is the time to do something about it.

PSYCHOSOMATIC HEALTH PROBLEMS

Mental and emotional disorders can and generally do cause very real physical ailments. As Dr. Bernie S. Siegel points out in *Love, Medicine & Miracles*:

> If a person deals with anger or despair when they first appear, illness need not occur. When we don't deal with our emotional needs, we set ourselves up for physical illness.... The simple truth is, happy people generally don't get sick. One's attitude toward oneself is the single most important factor in healing or staying well.[4]

A middle-aged executive terminated suddenly from his corporate imitation family will inevitably feel angry. No matter how well he has prepared a personal financial plan, he will experience self-doubt, despair, and fear. These feelings can be dealt with as we saw in Chapters 1 and 2. In fact, they must be dealt with—and fast.

As the recovering executive travels the road to recovery and begins the search for a new life-style, periods of doubt and remorse do occur. For the older executive who is unable or unwilling to take another job and for whom consulting or his own business are not viable alternatives, a sense of defeat and feelings of depression and despair can easily lead to a desire to give up. These are the people who quickly contract cancer, strokes, or other physical disorders soon after leaving the corporation.

But even illness need not interfere with a productive retirement, unless, of course, its seriousness completely incapacitates a person. Though medical authorities dispute experiential evidence with scientific zeal, many people stricken with incurable or terminal illnesses do not die when doctors tell them they should, do not suffer rapidly deteriorating conditions, but do, in fact, recover sufficiently to live many additional useful years. Though inexplicable by rational argument, over 8 million reported cases of near-death experiences have been documented—many involving terminal illness—where people declared dead by physicians and surgeons miraculously come back to life. Contrary to all medical and scientific evidence, people do live productive lives carrying the remnants of cancer, severe strokes, or heart attacks. I certainly don't have a rational answer, but I do know it happens.

I've seen it. Whatever the reason, if you retire and then fall seriously ill, there is enough experiential evidence on the books to at least provide a ray of hope for an extended life—or perhaps even recovery.

On a less controversial level, physical or mental inactivity that comes after a lifetime of challenges can easily cause illnesses that are mainly psychosomatic. The surest way to avoid or recover from such maladies is to substitute new mental challenges and intellectual stimulation and to stick with the Nine-Step Program to recovery. Don't lose faith. Don't give up. You can make retirement as productive and enjoyable as you want. Approach life holistically. Stick with the recovery program and search out activities that offer intellectual, spiritual, and physical stimulation. This does take self-discipline, however, and a certain structure to one's life.

SELF-DISCIPLINE AND STRUCTURE

The recovering executive has already proven to himself that he has self-discipline. He couldn't be moving down the recovery trail without it. It's hard to be without the warm corporate womb for comfort. It's difficult and at times frustrating to strike out on your own. There are many roadblocks along the way. This is where self-discipline comes in. Whenever you start to slip back, stop, take a breather, don't be afraid to ask for advice, and discipline yourself to keep moving.

To maintain this high level of discipline, it's helpful to structure the day. Plan each day, one at a time. What comes first, second, third, or so on. Force yourself to eat, go to bed, and get up at the same time every day—including Saturday and Sunday. It's very tempting to sleep in on the weekends or after a bad night, but don't do it. Get up at the regular time and start your planned schedule. This can be crucial for the retiree. It is easy with excess time on one's hands to procrastinate and ignore what one knows should be done. Structuring each day with set times for key events will force the development of self-discipline.

Mary left the corporation at age 57 with a plan to open a small sewing center in her neighborhood. After two false starts, she gave up and decided to retire on her abbreviated pension and Social Security. After a lifetime of catching the 6:05 A.M. commuter train, Mary started sleeping in. Risings at 9:00, 10:00, and even 11:00 became common. She wasn't happy doing nothing, but couldn't muster enough energy to get going on a new project. Mary had lost her structure and with it her self-discipline. Within a year, Mary suffered a stroke and became bedridden.

It's naive to believe that structuring your day will prevent all illnesses from occurring, and I'm certainly not implying that. However, I have known many retirees who have forced discipline into their lives and gone on to experience new, productive life-styles after leaving the corporation. I have also known a number of executives who have acquiesced to the temptations of inactivity and unstructured lives once they leave their corporate jobs, have subsequently become morose and unhappy and, eventually, in effect, give up on life. Though an active, structured life in semi-retirement may not prevent serious physical illness, it will probably at least help keep you interested in daily challenges.

The following is a summary of the ways to avoid psychological disorientation in retirement:

1. Plan for retirement *before* leaving the corporation.
2. Keep busy; search out productive activities.
3. Broaden interests.
4. Stay out of the way of your spouse—absolutely crucial!
5. Prepare and update personal financial statements.
6. Approach life holistically.
7. Practice loving yourself and other people.
8. Structure a daily routine.
9. Stick with the Nine-Step Program.

One question remains: how to generate a stream of income to pay the bills.

INCOME-PRODUCING RETIREMENT VOCATIONS

There are so many possibilities for creating a stream of income in semi-retirement it would be a Herculean task to try to list even a small percentage. There are four vocations, however, which have met the needs of my clients and friends over the years and which one might at least consider: (1) Part-time teaching, (2) investing in small privately owned companies, (3) directorships, and (4) writing your memoirs.

Part-Time Teaching

In Chapter 7, full-time teaching was considered as a career change. The psychological, social, and philosophical criteria examined then are equally applicable to part-time teaching— with one major difference. As a part-time instructor, with no illusions of becoming full-time tenured faculty, a person presents no job security challenges to other professors. By not competing for political, financial, or social status, one shouldn't feel the stress and anxiety associated with a full-time position. One can safely enter the world of academia without fear of being influenced by addictive behavior or codependency hazards.

Financially, don't expect too much. A recent survey of small state universities and community colleges in eastern Pennsylvania revealed that salaries for part-time instructors in business subjects range between $1,000 and $4,000 per class. This may not be enough to build a fortune, but a least it results in steady income and, coupled with other sources, can ease the financial burden.

With a reasonably good academic background and expert knowledge in at least one of the college-oriented business subjects (accounting, marketing, production management, computer sciences, corporate finance, and so on), an ex-executive should be warmly received by most small local colleges. As with a full-time teaching career, the better one's credentials are, the easier it is to get a position.

Investment in a Small Private Company

Small companies—especially start-ups—are always looking for sources of money. Some can be terrific opportunities for the investor to realize not only dividend income but substantial appreciation of invested dollars. Many retired executives never investigate this opportunity because of the substantial risk. Such an investment will certainly not yield a steady stream of income right away. It might be several years before there is any cash throw-off. On the other hand, by judicious investigation an investor can locate good opportunities at minimum risk. A good example of such an investment occurred in the early 80s when two partners started a company from scratch without sufficient seed money.

Joe and Vernon planned to design, build, and distribute temperature control sensors to the hospitality trade and were searching for seed money to get their company off the ground. An interested venture capital firm wrote me a letter asking if I knew of any investors for this type of business. The financial institution was ready and willing to invest $2 million in first-phase financing but wanted the partners to bring in one or two minority shareholders with solid business backgrounds to provide stability to the company. From the venture capitalist's perspective, the problem wasn't seed money as much as good management experience. I contacted a friend, Bill Walker, who had just been terminated after many years of running an electronics division of a NYSE corporation. He was 59, ready to retire, and looking for an opportunity to keep his finger in the business pie without working full-time at it. Making a few dollars on the side would also help. Bill was thrilled at the opportunity, met with the venture capitalist and the two entrepreneurs, and within three months found himself owning 15 percent of the new venture. Today, he still sits on the board, has recouped his investment many times over, and found a satisfying, low-stress way to put his business experience to good use. Everyone was a winner.

If you're interested in this kind of investment, write some letters to venture capital firms, investment bankers, lawyers, and public accountants in your area and let them know your investment criteria, background, and availability. Chances are high you will get at least a couple of good leads and that's all it takes to be off and running.

Directorships

Investment bankers and venture capital firms are always on the lookout for experienced executives to sit on the board of directors of small companies they have financed. No investment on the part of the executive is required and director's fees are usually paid for each meeting attended. Many times, the company needs help on a particular problem matching the executive's background, and a consulting fee can be charged for the time spent working with management.

A good friend of mine entered semi-retirement several years ago after serving as CEO and Chairman of a listed company. Although most of his time was spent managing his investment portfolio, he also held several directorships of small companies. His background in organization planning enabled him to spend six to eight days each month as a "consulting" director to these companies. The fees from this consulting work, plus director's fees, provided a small but comfortable source of income over and above his other investments.

There is one caveat about directorships, however. Over the last 15 years, a number of lawsuits charging mismanagement have been brought against company officers and board members. In the past, officers' and directors' liability insurance would protect against such an occurrence. Since 1984, however, the cost of such insurance has skyrocketed to the point where few small companies can afford to carry it. This makes holding a board seat too risky for many otherwise qualified executives.

An alternative to a straight directorship, board advisor positions have grown in popularity. Board advisors sit at director's meetings and, although equally influential in setting company policy, do not vote on corporate board matters. For board advisors most of the legal liability goes away.

If this activity holds any appeal, the best way to get started is to develop a public image as an expert in your field. Speeches, articles in local newspapers, or even writing a book can provide credentials sought after by financiers. It also wouldn't hurt to write to the same investment bankers and venture capitalists recommended previously for investment opportunities.

Writing Memoirs

Don't place a lot of hope in writing your memoirs as an income-producing activity. Few people are interested in reading about the exploits of the average executive, no matter how interesting they may seem to the writer. However, if you have a good public image, experience in a very unusual or unique business career, or something specific and useful to say, then go ahead and write. If you have no writing abilities, there are literally thousands of starving writers who would be only too happy to ghostwrite the story. Names and addresses are readily available in any of the writing trade journals or through the English departments of colleges and universities. Few people get rich writing memoirs but it can be a lot of fun and will certainly clear the cobwebs from retirement inactivity.

CANTANKEROUS CHARLIE AND THE CORMORANT

For the benefit of landlubbers, a cormorant is a sea bird with graceful features who likes to roost on pilings or other obstacles in shallow waters, principally in warm climates. This is a true story about a disenchanted executive who found more than he bargained for after retiring to an island in the Caribbean. It is such an unusual story with such a positive ending that it may lend courage and hope to the disgruntled, angry, and lost retiree.

Fired from his position with a major NYSE corporation after 25 years of service, Charles (Charlie to his friends) and his wife Margaret decided to retire to an island in the Caribbean. Using a sizable percentage of their life savings and investment funds from several friends, the couple purchased a run-down, bankrupt, and abandoned resort property on the beach.

Charlie's feelings toward his old company had gone beyond surprise and disappointment at his dismissal. He was furious at his old boss, the President of the corporation, for daring to fire him after all Charlie had done to cover up the President's mistakes, take the blame for several indiscretions, and pick up the pieces every time his boss screwed up. Charlies' fury carried over to innocent outsiders and was the main reason Margaret had insisted that they get away from New England before Charlie physically hurt someone.

Charlie was no less ill-tempered after arriving in the Islands. He dove into the reconstruction of their newly acquired resort with vengeance, berating construction workers, rebuking suppliers, severely chiding local government officials, and using abusive language with everyone. Margaret, fearing for their safety, tried to get Charlie to calm down.

Reconstruction was finally completed, the doors opened for their first guests, and Margaret and Charlie were at last able to breathe easily in their new retirement home. The first season was spectacular, with full occupancy for three months running. The resort quickly developed a reputation as one of the best and most exclusive retreats in the Caribbean. The million dollars Charlie and his investors had poured into the project looked secure, and to all outward appearances the future seemed bright. But Charlie's attitude toward people hadn't changed. If anything, it worsened. His days were filled with anger, nothing seemed to satisfy him, and depression and despair were only a step away.

One morning while strolling the beach in morbid solitude, Charlie noticed a cormorant sitting on a piling nearby. He gathered up a handful of stones ready to pummel the fowl and wound up for his first barrage. Suddenly his throwing arm froze. Charlie couldn't move it forward. It was as if an invisible hand had grabbed his arm and forced the stones to the ground. Charlie turned, startled, and standing under a palm tree 20 feet away was a little native boy no more than seven years old. The boy spoke, "Hey mahn, we wishes you not hurt da big birds no more. Dey don do you no harm. You keep dis up we gong have to stop you."

"What do you mean *we*? I don't see anyone else here. And how did you manage that 'holding my arm' trick?"

"Da *we* is me and God. He don like you be so angry and hurt tings. He say stop 'fore you really do some harm. God, he gettin mad at you and say eider get good or go home!" With that the little boy turned and ran. Charlie stood aghast, wondering what had happened, when suddenly he heard, or rather felt, a quiet voice from within telling him to be kind and loving and to stop his hating. When he returned home, Margaret couldn't believe the change in Charlie. His face was glowing and his smile was warm.

Within the year, the resort was sold for twice their investment, and Charlie and Margaret moved back to New England. Charlie had begun his recovery program and was well on his way to becoming a new man. Back in the States, the couple became active in support groups and neighborhood environmental projects. Today, Charlie is attempting to translate his experiences to the written word in the hope that others may learn from his mistakes.

SUPPORT GROUPS

I keep reiterating the desirability of searching out and participating in support groups because I know of no better way to receive constant reassurance that you are an OK person. Older executives choosing semi-retirement are probably in greater need of reassurance than younger codependents. Disenchanted executives in their 30s and 40s are still young enough to start over and build new long-term relationships and life-styles. Our society applauds youth and stresses the acceptability of looking, acting, and feeling young. Corporate offices are staffed by young executives exuding confidence in the future and in their own abilities to deal with whatever may arise. But an executive in his 50s or 60s finds, too often, that he is excluded from group activities and banished to the far reaches of unwanted solitude.

Beyond the corporation is no different. Society's standards continue to be structured toward the youth movement. Social gatherings, sporting events, and civic happenings all seem to emphasize me-ism and the wants of youth. So, not only does the older executive need to deal with his own corporate disenchantment, but he must also come to grips with his elder stature. The young do not understand the saying "you are only as old as you feel," but the older person understands the concept completely. He realizes that if he is to continue in life's journey—learn new concepts, experience new events, promote changes for himself and others—he must not only think young but he must also act young. Too many so-called retirement communities are populated with retirees who do *not* think or act young and this only makes a person feel older than he really is. Obviously, this is not the kind of group to get involved with.

There are, however, a number of "community" support groups that can be very helpful. Some must be formed by yourself with friends and neighbors; others are already in existence and can be joined simply by appearing at a meeting. The best source of either existing groups or information on how to form a new group can be obtained from The Foundation for Community Encouragement, mentioned in Chapter 3. Write the foundation or call for guidance. The staff members are very helpful.

Being an older ex-executive myself, I have learned to avoid all of the organizations formed by and for retired people. Some do provide assistance in a number of areas—such as the American Association of Retired Persons,[5] which offers travel, insurance, and other discounts—and lobbies for older people in Washington. However, the AARP is not a formal support group and it does not provide psychological support to the older recovering codependent or anyone else. I have found "community" support groups the best answer, even though they are not restricted to any one age group.

Contrary to how you may feel when shunted aside by the corporation, life does not end at 50, or 60, or 70—it just begins. For the first time in a person's life he has the time and freedom to do those things that really matter. He is unrestricted by corporate schedules or office guidelines. He can think and act as he pleases without interference. At least for myself, life began at 55. It certainly can for anyone else as well—if they want it badly enough.

ENDNOTES

1. Hilda Scott and Juliet F. Brudney, *Forced Out* (New York: Simon & Schuster, Inc., 1987), p. 15.
2. Robert Bellah, et al., *Habits of the Heart* (New York: Harper & Row, 1986), p. 71.
3. Bernie S. Siegel, *Love, Medicine & Miracles* (New York: Harper & Row, 1988), p. 169.
4. *Ibid.*, p. 76.
5. American Association of Retired Persons, 3200 E. Carson St., Lakewood, CA 90712.

CHAPTER 12

ENTREPRENEURIAL BETRAYAL: A RECOVERY PROGRAM FOR THE BUSINESS OWNER

The ideas, suggestions, and most of the case studies examined so far have been directed toward the corporate employee, or ex-corporate employee, who feels betrayed by the corporation. But what about the private business owner, running his own company, who is in many respects the epitome of a corporate CEO? Is he immune to feelings of disenchantment and disappointment simply because he is the boss? Or is it possible that an entrepreneur can also feel betrayed by the very system he has created? Are there business owners who recognize their addiction to power, become dissatisfied with their life-styles, and long to make a change?

Robert Cornell began his career in computer systems design right out of college with a well-known West Coast software developer. By age 30 he had advanced to the vice president level and was earning a six-figure compensation package. He was pleased with his progress, loved the work, and was loyal to his company. Robert could certainly not be accused of harboring any disenchantment or feelings of betrayal. He expected to make a life-long career with the company.

Soon after Robert's 31st birthday, his brother Jerome died suddenly in a car accident. Much to his surprise, Robert learned from the estate lawyer that Jerome had named him executor and sole beneficiary of his small robotic electronics business. With no way to dispose of the company quickly, Robert was forced to leave his comfortable corporate job and become an entrepreneur.

Angry at this turn of fate, Robert nevertheless threw himself into the task of running Q-X-R Automated Electronics, Inc. Over a period of four years, he employed the same tactics that had brought him success in his previous employment. With the introduction of two state-of-the-art robotic machines for the defense industry, Q-X-R prospered and sales climbed 10-fold, to the $20 million level. Greed began to overtake this intrepid entrepreneur. At 36, well on his way to becoming a millionaire, Robert wanted more. The power circle became fully activated, and he purchased an oil field supplies company in Texas. With the addition of a third company, a computer service company in New England, Robert's power addiction became full-blown.

Much later, Robert would mark the beginning of the great Texas oil bust as the beginning of his demise. On the heels of the death of his oil field supplies venture came a disastrous drop in sales at the New England operation. Frustrated and bewildered at the rapid decline in his fortunes, Robert disposed of his two acquisitions and, in the throes of emotional dysfunction, withdrew to a hermetic existence at his seaside home south of San Francisco. Management employees at Q-X-R managed to keep that company going, but customers became more and more disillusioned with the owner's lack of response to quality and delivery problems.

Suffering all the anger, fear, and disillusionment of a corporate codependent, Robert eventually sought professional help. In six months, emerging from concentrated therapy, Robert returned to Q-X-R a new man. Determined to follow his recovery program, he began to put the broken pieces of his company back together again.

Clearly, Robert Cornell, entrepreneur, was beleaguered by the same emotional dysfunction that corporate employees experience. Addictive behavior patterns can, and frequently do, afflict the private business owner just as easily as a corporate executive. However, there are two fundamental variations: (1) Events or conditions which trigger the problem emanate from different sources, and (2) options available for changes in life-style are more limited and more complex to attain.

THE TRIGGER

For an employee, the stimulus for emotional dysfunction is fairly clear. The corporation (or other organization) and its addicted leaders create rules, procedures, policies, and attitudes in the workplace that are conducive to codependency. Even though addictive behavior traits by the employee actually cause the bad feelings, emotional dysfunction would not occur if the corporation and its leaders did not foster an environment to encourage such comportment—and then do everything possible to convince the employee that addictive behavior patterns enhance his position, security, and general well-being. The corporation and its leaders act as the trigger that unleashes compliant behavior patterns from the employee.

With a business owner, the shoe is on the other foot. He exercises absolute authority over his own actions and is accountable to no one except himself. Thus, if the entrepreneur succumbs to power addiction, the blame must be laid squarely on his doorstep. No one forces him to make decisions under threat of termination. No one demands that he take specific actions to get a promotion, satisfy a boss's ego, or retain the respect of his peers. No one insists that he abandon his family and friends to join a fictitious imitation family. And no one exerts obsessive control over him by exacting compliance with predetermined Rules of the Game. Or do they?

As illustrated in Chapters 9 and 10, freedom of choice by a business owner is really just a myth. Pragmatically, while he does have absolute authority to do whatever he desires, if his actions and decisions do not meet with the approval of the three cornerstones of any company—employees, customers, and banks —he will be out of business very quickly. For example, if he violates loan covenants he soon learns that the bank is ready, willing, and able to replace him as CEO of his own company.

External controls over the owner's decisions create the same stress and anxiety as a boss's control over a corporate executive:

Freedom is every bit as limited, repercussions from violating proclaimed standards are just as severe, and opportunities for failure and consequent loss of income are used as tools to control the business owner even more effectively than a corporate executive. To the extent that major customers, employee groups, and financial institutions can determine the success or failure of the business enterprise, they demand the same type of unwavering compliance to addictive norms as corporate leaders do. A union that demands changes in work rules or higher wages under the threat of shutting down the business with a strike; a bank that threatens to enforce unmanageable loan provisions; and customers who threaten not to buy the goods or services without unreasonable price, service, or delivery concessions are just as effective as a corporate boss in coercing the business owner to act in a specified manner. In fact, they are even more effective because the loss of one's company causes far greater pain, anguish, and financial strain than losing one's job. In addition, subsequent options are far more limited, as we'll see a little later.

In the normal, closely-held business environment, one expects performance demands from employees, customers, and banks. That's part of the penalty for being an entrepreneur. These conditions are not particularly harmful in and of themselves. Many business owners cope with this type of stressful decision making on an hourly basis every day of the year without suffering emotional dysfunction. But a different result occurs when either of two conditions are present: (1) The business owner himself is addicted to his power and authority, or (2) employee groups, banks, or major customers are themselves power addicts. In the case of Robert Cornell, power addiction had clearly overtaken his thinking processes. Buoyed by the initial success of Q-X-R, he felt godlike and invincible: nothing could deter him from building an empire. Dishonest with himself, he denied that key employees and a burgeoning defense market for robotics were major determinants of his success. Attributing the growth to his own cleverness and skills, he became so self-centered that he would not listen to warnings from key managers that the Department of Defense could withdraw a contract as easily as grant one. Devising his own expansion plan for a mini-conglomerate, he insisted that others comply with his wishes, which he believed were infallible. He became a perfectionist. Obsessed with controlling events, he forced managements at the New England operation and Q-X-R to funnel all available cash to the faltering Texas business.

Robert exhibited all the symptoms of a confirmed power addict. Even as his empire was collapsing around him, he refused to admit that anything was seriously wrong or that he could possibly have made a mistake. No codependency here, Robert was fully addicted to the entrepreneurial process. Disillusionment didn't come until events beyond his immediate control forced emotional dysfunction on him. Both new acquisitions may have failed regardless of any actions Robert took, but certainly his addictive behavior patterns prevented any possibility of saving them.

Fueled by the remarkable growth of Q-X-R, Robert's addictive affections were unleashed through greed for more power and non-synergistic acquisitions contrary to the stated mission of Q-X-R. Self-centered goals prevented Robert from acknowledging judgment errors as matters went from bad to worse. The breakup of his empire, in turn, stimulated further fears and anxieties until finally Robert's emotions waxed totally out of control. Instead of corporate rules and corporate leaders, external events interacted with embedded addictive behavior patterns to trip the switch for his eventual emotional collapse.

A second condition that stimulates emotional dysfunction occurs when one of the three cornerstones of a business—employees, customers, or banks—behaves addictively. The most common situation arises in dealing with a powerful union business agent or shop steward. Attempting to deal rationally with authoritative, power-addicted union bosses who exert absolute control over membership ranks usually ends in futile frustration. Given the right circumstances—such as when a business owner is unwilling or unable to risk a strike—acquiescing to union demands that are totally without economic merit for the business enterprise can trigger dishonesty, denial, self-serving actions, and attempted obsessive control. Over time, the owner becomes as much a codependent of the union's addictive behavior as any employee working in a corporation.

Major customers who exert the same type of addictive compulsion through price, delivery, and quality demands can also trigger codependency. Industries characterized by a few giant corporations that dominate thousands of smaller suppliers promote the most flagrant abuse of customer power. Such is the case in the aerospace industry, especially the segment that provides products for the Department of Defense (DOD). The DOD, itself a powerfully addicted organization, forces major contractors such as Boeing, Lockheed, United Technologies, and so on to play by dictated Rules of the Game under threats of decertification, withholding of future contracts, disqualification of products and congressional pressure. This obsessive control is in turn passed on to subcontractors—many of which are privately owned businesses—with promises of favored treatment for new contracts or threats of termination. It doesn't take long under such coercion for the business owner to succumb. Faced with pressures from employees for better working conditions, higher pay, and a more sympathetic ear, and from banks for compliance with loan provisions, many business owners resort either to similar addictive behavior themselves or become distraught and suffer emotional dysfunction.

Financial institutions that hold mortgages, promissory notes from the owner, or liens against the business are probably the most devious of external addicts. Under the guise of helping the business owner, a bank officer's insidious demands for obeying unreasonable loan provisions are very often contrary to good business judgment. At the mercy of the money lender, a business owner quickly adopts addictive behavior characteristics: dishonesty, repression of feelings, and denial are the most common. After he recognizes the harm that policies enacted under such behavior patterns have on his business, it isn't long before frustration, fear, and despair overtake him. Emotional dysfunction has occurred.

THE RECOVERY PROGRAM

Here again is the recovery program for corporate codependency that was outlined in Chapters 2 and 3:

1. The First Stage: Transition
   a. *Admission* that disappointment, frustration and disenchantment with a specific life style result from the distortion of one's own beliefs and moral values.

b. *Recognition* that definable behavior characteristics cause corporate leaders to maintain control and dependency of the individual.

c. *Identification* of those bad feelings and emotions—through a self-evaluation—which must be dispelled to open the heart and mind to a new code of ethics.

d. *Redefinition* of a personal code of ethics based on moral beliefs and behavior and acceptance of the Nine-Step Program.

2. The Second Stage: Personal Changes

a. Dispel codependent behavior traits: dishonesty, denial, obsessive control, perfectionism, and self-centeredness.

b. Develop a new behavior pattern: honesty, acceptance of personal responsibility for one's own actions, admittance of errors, acceptance of people and events for what they are, caring and compassion for others, altruistic love.

c. Reorder responsibility priorities with self, family, and friends above the corporation.

d. Develop warm family relationships.

e. Build a true community of friends.

f. Broaden horizons and learn new interests.

g. Establish a new set of personal goals based on moral values.

3. The Third Stage: A New Life-Style

a. New priorities and behavior while staying with the corporation.

b. A search for nonaddictive organizations.

c. Opportunities for self-employment: management consulting, starting a business, buying a going business.

d. A productive program for semi-retirement.

The recovery program for the small business owner, whether he is a confirmed power addict or a codependent of external power addiction, is similar to that used by corporate employees, but with slightly different emphasis.

A corporate codependent must begin by admitting that the corporation controls his life and that he has no control over the corporation or its leaders. A business owner must make a similar admission. He must first acknowledge that he is, in fact, a power addict, and that greed for more money and thirst for more power influence and overshadow all his decisions and actions. Without such an honest admission he can go no further. If an alcoholic cannot acknowledge openly that he is an alcoholic, he can never find a cure. A business owner who refuses to acknowledge that his unbridled power has become addictive cannot hope to resolve the issue. If he can't admit his own affliction, he doesn't really want to change.

He must also identify what has caused the addiction. If it's merely being the boss of his own business, this must be conceded. If it's a result of demands placed on him by external parties— unions, banks, or customers—he must identify what actions or threatened actions produced his responsive addictive behavior. Furthermore, he must openly admit that he has no control over the behavior of these external parties. He cannot change how they behave. He cannot influence their policies or programs. He must learn to live with what is, not what he would like to be.

Along with such open admission of vulnerability, the business owner must recognize why banks, customers, or union leaders act as they do. To deal with external addictive behavior one must first recognize why it exists. Following definitions of such behavior from Chapter 2, one should quickly spot obsession, repression, dishonesty, and all the rest of the characteristics.

Third, just as with the corporate codependent, the business owner must identify his own bad feelings, attach names and reasons to them, and then begin actions to alleviate pent-up emotions. The self-evaluation questionnaire for employees from Chapter 2 works equally well for a business owner.

Finally, one's personal code of ethics must be examined and probably redefined. For a corporate employee, moral determination is important to recovery. For the business owner, who has authority over and responsibility for his employees—not to mention moral responsibility to customers—a firm foundation of beliefs based on moral self-consciousness is necessary. Without it he will never survive the wars of entrepreneurship. Soft feelings of kindness, caring, and compassion for others may bring derisive comments from addicted outsiders, but they will be welcomed and supported by employees, customers, vendors, and others who recognize that personal benefits can be derived from moral community. It may surprise many entrepreneurs, but most people do react more favorably to soft feelings than to dictatorial behavior.

The Nine-Step Program proposed in Chapter 2 must be adhered to if recovery is genuinely desired. No one has yet found a substitute for the nine steps. Some national support groups such as Alcoholics Anonymous and Narcotics Anonymous go further and make it a twelve-step program, but if religiously followed, the nine steps work well enough for most people.

THE SECOND STAGE

When Robert Cornell returned to Q-X-R after undergoing psychotherapy, a reevaluation of his personal code of ethics permitted him to achieve a number of important milestones. The key employees at Q-X-R, who held the company together while Robert was convalescing, were astonished at the changes in his demeanor. In place of a self-centered, perfectionist, dictatorial boss, they saw a leader cloaked in soft feelings, willing and eager to listen to their suggestions. He was concerned with the welfare of employees in the lowest echelon, actively solicitous of ideas for improving customer relations, and altogether a different person. Substantial layoffs were required to bring the cost structure in line with sales volume, but rather than delegating this unpleasant chore to a subordinate, Robert handled each layoff himself. He tried to explain to each employee the errors he had made in the past, accepted full responsibility for the current straits of the business, and promised to offer reemployment as soon as, and if, conditions improved.

A few months later, as the company was gradually being rebuilt, the Vice President of Engineering asked Robert point blank what had come over him and why he had changed so much. He answered, "Nothing very complicated, Jerry. One morning, after I abdicated my responsibility for the company and took that sabbatical, something inside made me realize that if I didn't change my ways I would soon be dead. All I had ever thought about was myself and how I could get more of everything. I realized how many people I had hurt along the way. It dawned on me that if I was going to fold up my tent, the least I could do was try to make amends to as many people as possible first. And that's what I'm trying to do."

For the first time in his life, Robert heeded his conscience. As we saw in Chapter 3, this is the essence of the second stage to recovery. A business owner on the road to recovery must realign his behavior patterns just as a corporate executive must do. For the business owner, however, it is a much easier step. With the authority to act as he pleases, there are no artificial barriers to hold him back—such as corporate policies or addictive bosses to please. Only his ego can get in the way of open admission of error. Only his pride can prevent him from becoming honest and caring. Only narcissism holds him from reaching out to others in kindness and compassion. Substituting moral traits for addictive behavior can be done quickly and smoothly without fear of harmful reverberations.

New goals that incorporate reverence of the family unit, observance of the human dignity of employees, consideration for the needs of customers, and the extension of a caring hand to a not-so-friendly banker will inevitably produce surprise and in some cases disbelief. But it's important to push forward and implement these changes as soon as possible. Procrastination at this point in the recovery process will only lead to reversals. By incorporating his new goals both in dealing with people and in decisions affecting the operation of the business, an owner proves to himself that his desire for change is genuine. And this is crucial. Too often, having tasted the bitter fruit of potential failure in his own business, an enthusiastic entrepreneur decides to start over, but never gets off the ground. The daily press of crises and potential catastrophes ends up taking precedence over the Nine-Step Program. As we've seen before, aborting the program means relapse to emotional dysfunction almost overnight. So once you make up your mind to make the change, implement *all* your new goals as soon as possible. Even with resistance from certain employees, an occasional customer, or even a banker beginning immediately is the only way to go.

The other key step to accomplish right up front is to change your priorities. It is no longer acceptable to put the business before family and friends. You must recognize that even though employees, customers, vendors and bankers are important nothing comes before your own emotional health and that of your family. Martha was well on her way to recovery until she forgot this important lesson.

After her husband died of cancer, Martha struggled for years to build her plumbing distributorship business in the face of sex discrimination from customers, suppliers, employees, and bankers. She learned that to survive in the plumbing business she had to be just as tough and ruthless as everyone else. In her late 40s, Martha spent long hours, six days a week, dealing with recalcitrant customers and defiant employees. Eventually, for no apparent reason, her friendly banker called the operating loan of $400,000. Devastated, Martha found another bank by lying about the current state of the business and projecting totally fictitious estimates of future growth and profitability. Denying the existence of major cracks in the business, Martha continued to rule with an iron hand. When the building boom in South Florida collapsed, major customers dropped from the fold, Martha's new bank demanded performance incompatible with her abilities, and suppliers started insisting on COD terms. The combination of events was too much and Martha became confused, frustrated, and eventually despondent.

Jimmy Gonzalez, who had been a tough competitor for years, saw what was happening to Martha and asked her one day to meet with him. Over the luncheon table Jimmy explained how he had suffered the same business setbacks and concomitant disenchantment five years earlier. He offered to help direct her to the recovery path he had used. Recognizing her need for help, Martha readily accepted and thus she began the recovery program.

Within six months, although the business was still floundering, Martha had become a new woman—softer, kinder, and less dictatorial in her management practices. Two of her key employees returned to the shop. Soon a few lost customers began buying from her again, and the bank started backing off. It looked like Martha would make it. But then something unforeseen happened: Her youngest daughter was expelled from college for plagiarizing a course paper. When she returned home, the daughter desperately needed Martha's guidance and comfort, but Martha was too busy at the shop. She knew she was turning the business around and making good progress in her personal recovery program. She just didn't have time to take off and spend with her daughter.

Martha's story does not have a happy ending. During the ensuing 12 months four things happened: (1) her daughter was picked up by the police for using drugs, (2) the bank reverted to a hard line and called the loan, (3) customers who had come back started slacking off, and (4) Martha abandoned her recovery program and reverted to her previous hard-line management practices.

She eventually liquidated the business and moved with her daughter to an island in the Caribbean where both women took jobs in a resort. When I met Martha again two years later, she had aged 20 years. As she related her unfortunate story she finally recognized that her major mistake was putting the business ahead of her family. She did not take the time to help her daughter when help was really needed. According to Martha, it was this and this alone that led her to revert to previous addictive behavior and eventually caused the demise of the plumbing distributorship.

THE FINAL STAGE: CHANGING LIFE-STYLES

As mentioned in the beginning of this chapter, there are two major differences between a recovery program for the power-addicted or codependent business owner and a disenchanted corporate executive: (1) the event or person that triggers emotional dysfunction differs, and (2) options available for a new life-style are more complex. Changing his life-style, though difficult and at times confusing, at least offers the corporate executive many options: remaining employed, changing jobs, defining a new career, becoming a professional consultant, starting or buying a business, or retirement. Each has attendant risks but all are clearly definable paths of action.

For the business owner, however, choices of alternative life-styles are considerably more limited. He can't just walk away from his business. The mere fact that he has personal investment tied up in the company precludes abandonment. He also has responsibility to employees and customers, not to mention outstanding loans and other liabilities to settle. It is not only morally impossible to abandon a business, but also financially impossible. So what can the business owner who is beset with emotional dysfunction, but proceeding down the road to recovery, do to effect the final stage of the recovery program? How can he implement those changes in his life-style demanded by the third stage of the program without increasing the stress and anxiety of potential failure? Although there are other less desirable avenues, most recovering entrepreneurs seek changes through one or a combination of three actions:

1. Selling the business and changing careers similar to the corporate executive.
2. Bringing in a co-owner (partner) to handle part of the management.
3. Remaining in command of the business but restructuring the organization.

Getting Out

The initial reaction of business owners who suffer severe cases of emotional dysfunction is to get out: sell the business, merge, liquidate, do anything to escape from the environment that triggers bad feelings. If anger has turned to hate, mild depression to despair, normal fear of failure to terror at the thought of financial ruin, getting out is really the only choice. In less severe cases, disposing of the business might not be the preferential choice. But with few viable alternatives, the business owner should at least consider selling the business and going after a new life-style in a different environment. Very small retail or service businesses generally do not lend themselves to any other option. Unless very profitable a one-family business is not large enough to support a partner. With few, if any, employees, restructuring the organization is not a viable alternative. Unless the events or people that stimulated the dysfunction can be dispelled, the owner's best chance at a new life-style is to get away from the business.

The big question is: How do you get rid of it as fast as possible at the best price? Speed is crucial to the recovering business owner. Since a new life-style is mandatory to complete the recovery program, stagnation along the way can only diminish the likelihood of recovery. Depending on the type of business and its size, it could take from six months to two years to find the right buyer. But a recovering business addict doesn't have this long.

Normally, a sale should be planned years ahead of actually placing the business on the market. Estate planning, tax laws, and personal financial planning should be carefully weighed against the need to get out now. The time it takes to clean up the company, locate a buyer, negotiate a deal, arrange financing, and negotiate and write a buy/sell agreement can be protracted. None of these steps are easy and to cope with the myriad of details involved in a sale may be more than an emotionally weak person can tolerate. There are steps to take, however, which can mitigate the problem as much as possible. My recent book, *Getting Out: A Step-by-Step Guide to Selling a Business or Professional Practice*, should be of immeasurable help for any business owner who is thinking of selling or otherwise disposing of his company.

It would be impossible to encapsulate all the steps in selling a business in a few short paragraphs but the following are five broad suggestions to get you going.

Hire Professionals

The biggest mistake a business owner can make is to try to sell his company on his own, no matter how small it is. There are just too many complications for one person to be an expert in all areas and too many legal, tax, and financing pitfalls for the unwary entrepreneur. The following professionals, at least, should be hired as needed throughout the selling process:

1. An M & A consultant (for companies over $2 million in sales) to locate a buyer and assist in negotiations.

2. A business broker (for businesses under $2 million) to source buyers.

3. A CPA for tax and perhaps estate advice.

4. An experienced attorney for drafting the closing documents, other legal contracts, and hopefully, estate planning advice.

Clean Up the Company

Nobody wants to buy someone else's dirty laundry. To get the maximum price for a residence, the owner paints, fixes the roof and plumbing, cleans the carpets, and generally makes the house attractive. It should be the same with a business. There are three areas that need to be put in order:

1. Facilities: Clean up the equipment; fix the roof; paint the walls and floor; replace worn furniture, carpets, and drapes; and so on.

2. Outstanding contingent liabilities: Settle disputes with employees, customers, suppliers, government agencies, and tax authorities. If these don't get resolved prior to the sale, the price will be reduced – and the reduction will be generally more than it would cost to settle the claim.

3. Accounting records: You might get by with sloppy records for the IRS but not with an intelligent buyer. Get the books in order. Write off bad accounts, take a physical inventory, clean up any accruals, reconcile pension or retirement programs with the actuary, and understand what is in each of the asset accounts.

Prepare an Offering Prospectus

No, this is not just for big companies. A sales document must be prepared to give potential buyers a bird's-eye view of the business regardless of the company's size. Many sellers have a great deal of trouble finding the right buyer simply because they don't have an offering prospectus to hand out. It's really just a selling tool: a document describing the business; the future market, product, and people plans of the present owner; and summary financial data for the past three years. Many sellers also prefer to include projected pro forma financial statements showing how great the company will be in the future. Photos of the facility, products, and people are also important. Finally, the document should be professionally typed and bound to indicate that you really do care about your company.

Learn the Financing Options

While it is true that the buyer must put together his own financing package, if you really want to sell in the shortest time possible, you'll probably need to help him. This means (1) suggesting financial institutions that might be interested, (2) introducing existing banking affiliations, or (3) agreeing to some form of deferred payment (buyer paper, earn out, or contingency). Too many sellers make the mistake of thinking a buyer either has his own cash to cover the entire purchase price or has good banking connections to raise the required debt or equity financing. Both assumptions are usually wrong, unless, of course, the buyer is a large corporation. Familiarization with current acquisition financing sources, and openness and honesty in existing banking relationships about intentions to sell can only strengthen a seller's position. A willingness to defer part of the selling price shows the banking community, customers, and employees that you are confident the buyer is competent and right for the business.

Protect Personal Assets

No one is immune from the current wave of personal lawsuits. Inequitable courts and unscrupulous lawyers encourage frivolous lawsuits against anyone with visible signs of money. A seller who garners substantial cash from the sale of his business and perhaps continued significant chunks of cash over ensuing years is a prime target for these greedy distorters of the legal system. The surest way to keep what you have so laboriously earned is to implement procedures *before* the sale to immunize this cash from usurpation. Personal assets can be protected in a number of ways, as any competent lawyer can advise. Three of the most common are: (1) establishing an irrevocable trust in favor of your spouse or children to hold the proceeds of the sale, (2) forming a holding corporation to own the company and receive the proceeds from its sale, and (3) transferring all personal assets—ownership of the business, residence, autos, bank accounts, investments, and so on—to your spouse, including all assets held jointly.

Once the business is sold, the recovering entrepreneur is free to examine and pursue any of the new career paths explored in previous chapters. Cash received for his business and possible income from deferred payments over a period of years, provide a financial foundation to serve as a buffer while developing a new life-style. Free from financial survival pressures, the ex-business owner can learn new vocations, experiment with alternative possibilities, and even test out the desirability of semi-retirement.

A Co-Owner or Partner

Selling the business might not be practical or even necessary to effect a new life-style. Especially in personal service businesses or professional practices, immediate disposal of the business can be extremely difficult. Clients (or customers or patients) buy the service because of the identity of the practitioner, and if a new owner takes over, many clients will be lost. There are exceptions, of course, but in most cases a person hires a lawyer or a physician because of his or her experience, credentials, and reputation. A recovering addict or codependent who tries to dispose of such a business would probably meet with great resistance, and not finding an immediate buyer could jeopardize his recovery program.

A better solution might be to relieve business pressures by bringing in a partner to share the load. Even if it is really a one-family business now, the practitioner who takes a cut in income can preserve his practice and still have time to develop outside interests. Depending on a person's age, eventual retirement can be anticipated by structuring the partnership as a planned succession. By purchasing the business over a period of years while actively engaged in the practice, the new partner can provide a smooth transition of ownership with few, if any, clients lost. My book *Getting Out* also includes a detailed description of how to locate such a successor and structure a succession partnership.

Even if eventual disposal of a professional practice or personal service business does not rank as a prime requisite for your recovery program, simply having a partner to share the load can generate a completely new outlook.

Janice had built her bookkeeping and tax service over the years by active promotion and solicitation of business at her golf club, college alumni functions, participation in civic and community organizations, and constantly catering to the wishes of her clients. At 44, Janice felt she had finally made it as a successful businesswoman. Then catastrophe hit her family. Her mother suffered a paralyzing stroke, a brother was killed while serving in the Marine Corps, and her unmarried sister brought her three children to live with Janice in her two-bedroom condo. Constant family demands on her time forced Janice to redistribute her priorities. Her business could no longer command preferential time and effort. Marginal clients who had succumbed to Janice's super sales pitches began to drop by the wayside. Pressures from her family on one side and clients on the other eventually led to emotional dysfunction.

Not wanting to give up her practice but recognizing the need to change her behavior, Janice brought in a partner—a friend of her brother's who had recently received a medical discharge from the Marine Corps. Young, ambitious, and eager to learn the business, Ted rapidly became well-liked by many of Janice's clients. This allowed Janice to begin pursuing a second career while she cared for her invalid mother. She had always wanted to write poetry; through this second vocation, Janice reshaped her life style to conform to her new moral commitments. Today, still actively involved in the bookkeeping and tax service but allowing her partner to handle the majority of clients, Janice has published two small books of poetry, continues to care for her mother, assists her sister in raising the children, and is altogether the happiest she has ever been. Furthermore, she is well on her way to emotional recovery.

Restructure the Organization

Certain types of larger businesses require a management staff or a group of key employees. The mark of a power addict is that he tries to be all things to all people. Unwilling to delegate decision-making authority to others for fear of losing his power base, he robs employees—and especially management employees—of personal initiative. This fortifies his control, feeds his insatiable appetite for more power, and continues to repress the personal growth and development of other managers. With no intention of retiring or of disposing of the business to solve his distorted emotional feelings, the business owner has only one choice: He must transfer the decision making process to his key employees and relinquish his obsessive control over other people's lives.

Probably the easiest, and certainly the fastest, way to accomplish a transfer of power is to take a sabbatical. Go on a long vacation or maybe even a cruise around the world. The natural reaction of one who has dictatorially run his company with an iron hand for many years is to answer, "How can I do that? There is no one who has the ability or training to make command decisions without me. The business will fall apart. By the time I get back there will be nothing left." Belief in one's own invincibility and denial of the abilities of others are characteristics of addictive behavior. To break the power circle and practice the Nine-Step Program, you must let go. You must find out who does have the ability to manage. To practice moral determination you must begin to value human dignity and have faith in others. By taking an extended leave of absence you force key personnel to make decisions and take responsibility for their actions; this encourages the development of your entire management team.

A slightly less dramatic approach, which works in smaller companies, is to entrust certain employees with financial responsibility. For example, if a business owner has always insisted on signing checks or making bank deposits himself, he could delegate this authority to someone else and then back off and see what happens. If the employee steals, he loses. If not, he's a winner. He could also inform the bank liaison officer and major customers that new personal commitments makes it impossible for him to deal with them directly and any problem arising will be handled by Mr. So-and-So. If this is done diplomatically, neither the banker nor the customer will be too upset.

All the arguments against making these restructuring changes notwithstanding, you really don't have any choice. The power circle must be broken immediately. There is no time to gradually evaluate individual talents because such a course will inevitably impede and probably disable the recovery process. The risk must be taken. Regardless of the method used, control must be lessened, objectives redirected, and dictatorial authority replaced by a caring management philosophy—and the sooner the better.

With the transfer of power, a business owner has the time and wherewithal to broaden his horizons outside the business. Several business owners have successfully passed through the labyrinth of emotional dysfunction and gone on to become active in community social welfare, volunteer work, and even second careers in politics while still owning and managing their business. To effectively activate the full recovery program, this third stage—developing a new life-style—cannot be ignored, even if it must be done within the confines of an existing business environment.

By following the Nine-Step Program and completing all three stages of the recovery process, a business owner can overcome emotional dysfunction just as well as the corporate executive, although it might be more difficult and may require greater dedication and effort. In the end, the sacrifice of power, prestige, and even income is a small price to pay to regain your sanity.

EPILOGUE

A NEW TOMORROW

Regardless of one's social position, income level, or occupation, emotional dysfunction can interrupt an otherwise satisfying and apparently complete life. Whether one is a CEO, executive, manager, secretary, or other corporate employee; whether a social worker, politician, government employee, teacher, or minister; whether serving in the armed forces, the CIA, or a local police force; whether the owner of a mid-sized manufacturing company, a small retail or service business, or a professional practice, one can manage disenchantment with the rules of living that are forced upon all of us by our work environment, bosses, or external events. Anyone, in any vocation, can rejuvenate his spirit and make appropriate personal changes to live a fulfilling life. It takes courage. It takes determination and effort. It takes support. But above all, it takes a redefinition of how we want to live the rest of our lives.

This book has defined the disease and recommended solutions in the context of a business environment. But the same disease, caused by the same distortion of personal moral values, applies to people in all vocations. It is not the job or the profession that causes the malady of emotional dysfunction. It is the person himself. If his personal code of ethics, his behavior, and his goals preclude a moral commitment to others, emotional distress nearly always follows. Once the executive resolves the moral issues affecting his personal life, the next logical step to a new tomorrow is to transfer individual moral values and standards to the work environment.

A well-defined step that can be taken by leaders in all walks of life is to introduce the concepts and practice of moral community. Chapter 3 examined how the codependent executive can utilize a formal community of friends as a support group to encourage and foster his recovery from emotional dysfunction. True community groups can also be started in companies, churches, neighborhoods, civic organizations, political and social organizations–anywhere people are brought together. Communities of peers fill a void in the emptiness of individualism. The inherent, yet often ignored need of the human species to learn from, love, and interact with each other can only be achieved when people are honest one with the other. As stated in *Habits of the Heart*:

> We find ourselves not independently of other people and institutions but through them. We never get to the bottom of ourselves on our own. We discover who we are face to face and side by side with others in work, love and learning.[1]

Such is the basis of community: a gathering of people who work together for the common good and who are interdependent, one on the other, for achieving results. Individual self-gratification must be subjugated to the social ecology that supports the very foundation of community. Just think how wonderful it would be to work in a company where from the chairman on down, policies were enacted not to enhance the wealth or protect the power of any one individual but for the general betterment of employees, customers, and society. Where honesty and integrity are valued assets. Where caring for and helping employees or customers in trouble takes precedence over increased quarterly earnings or meeting irrational forecasts. Where achievement is measured by benefits contributed to others rather than political acumen. A dream? A fantasy? An ideal? Perhaps. But some companies are already beginning to practice moral community with just such results.

SOME UNANSWERED QUESTIONS

During a recent symposium, questions arose about how to create a desire on the part of bosses, peers, and subordinates to work toward moral community. Generalizations pointed the direction, but what practical actions on the part of the individual could foster such community feelings? Was there a way to translate community concepts to everyday living, without formal group meetings or gatherings?

A second, corollary question emerged when a participant commented that the Nine-Step Program made a lot of sense and certainly proved helpful in mastering the recovery process but the steps were difficult to implement regularly in his office environment. Discussion followed about what set of easily applied rules could be advanced as a supplement to the program. Was there a way to practice the Nine-Step Program on a daily or even hourly basis in the workplace? If so, could a set of guidelines be constructed that could immediately become concrete standards to assist in this endeavor?

In an attempt to address both points of concern, five guidelines for daily living evolved and are included in the Appendix. These guidelines can be practiced by everyone, not just those suffering recognizable emotional dysfunction. In fact, adherence to them on a daily basis should prevent emotional dysfunction from ever occurring. Preventive maintenance goes a long way toward turning hard feelings to soft feelings before they ever get out of control. There's nothing very profound about these guidelines. They present no magic formula for curing the ills of our culture, and they certainly are not unique.

But therein lies the strength of community. Living in community with others is not a new paradigm. All it really means is that each of us, every day, takes the time and makes the effort to consider the effect of our words and actions on others. Whether the group is one other person or 100, if we match our thoughts and actions to the needs and wants of others, harmony in the family, workplace, and society result. On the other hand, it takes two (or more) to form true community. One person cannot do it alone. If there is no interest on the part of bosses, peers, and subordinates in the workplace, how can community be practiced? Easy, pragmatic answers are not forthcoming. Although an individual can encourage community, he cannot force it on an unwilling group.

Even in community, however, emotional dysfunction remains a personal phenomenon resolvable only by the individual, not the group. Full and continuous admission of vulnerability and adherence to the Nine-Step Program is the only reasonable method for breaking the barrier.

Social change is an evolutionary process, but it must begin somewhere. Individual regeneration of moral standards is as good a place to begin as any.

ENDNOTE

1. Robert Bellah, et al., *Habits of the Heart* (New York: Harper & Row, 1986), p. 84.

BIBLIOGRAPHY

Chapter 1

Geneen, Harold, with Alvin Moscow. *Managing*. New York: Avon Books, 1984.

Hyatt, Carole, and Linda Gottlieb. *When Smart People Fail*. New York: Simon & Schuster, 1987.

Jenks, James M., and Brian L.P. Zeunik. *Managers Caught in the Crunch*. New York: Franklin Watts, 1988.

Levinson, Harry. *Executive Stress*. New York: New American Library, 1975.

Morrow, Alfred J., ed. *The Failure of Success*. New York: AMACON, 1972.

Schaef, Anne Wilson, and Diane Fassel, *The Addictive Organization*. San Francisco: Harper & Row, 1988.

Siegel, Bernie S. *Love, Medicine & Miracles*. New York: Harper & Row, 1988.

Chapter 2

Beattie, Melody. *Codependent No More*. New York: Harper & Row, 1987.

Bellah, Robert, et al. *Habits of the Heart*. New York: Harper & Row, 1986.

Colson, Charles. *Loving God*. Grand Rapids, MI: Zondervan Publishing House, 1987.

Gaylin, Willard. *Feelings*. New York: Harper & Row, 1988.

Jung, C.G. "On Synchronicity," in *The Portable Jung*. Joseph Campbell, ed. New York: The Viking Press, Inc. 1971.

Lewis, C.S. *Mere Christianity*. New York: Macmillan Publishing Co., 1952.

Peale, Norman Vincent. *Enthusiasm Makes the Difference*. New York: Prentice–Hall, Inc., 1967.

Tavris, Carol. *Anger: The Misunderstood Emotion.* New York: Simon & Schuster, 1984.

Chapter 3

Anderson, Walter. *The Greatest Risk of All.* Boston, MA: Houghton–Mifflin, 1988.
Burns, David D. *Feeling Good: The New Mood Therapy.* New York: William Morrow & Co., 1980.
Buscaglia, Leo F. *Living, Loving & Learning.* New York: Random House, Inc., 1983.
Gaylin, Willard. *Rediscovering Love.* New York: The Viking Press, Inc., 1986.
Peck, M. Scott. *People of the Lie.* New York: Simon & Schuster, 1985.
Peck, M. Scott. *The Different Drum.* New York: Simon & Schuster, 1988.
Peck, M. Scott. *The Road Less Traveled.* New York: Simon & Schuster, 1985.
Woodward, Harry, and Steve Buchholz. *Aftershock: Helping People Through Corporate Change.* New York: John Wiley & Sons, Inc., 1987.

Chapter 4

Buscaglia, Leo. *Bus 9 to Paradise.* New York: Ballantine Books, Random House, Inc., 1986.
Simon, Sidney B. *Getting Unstuck.* New York: Warner Books, 1988.

Chapter 6

Scott, Hilda, and Juliet F. Brudney. *Forced Out.* New York: Simon & Schuster, Inc., 1987.
The Professional Job Hunting System. Verona, NJ: Performance Dynamics, Inc., 1970.

Chapter 7

George, Susan. *How the Other Half Dies.* Totowa, NJ: Powman & Allanheld, 1980.
Voices For Freedom. London, England: Amnesty International Publications, 1986.
Vogeler, Ingol, and Anthony De Souza. *Dialectics of Third World Development.* Totowa, NJ: Powman & Allanheld, 1980.
Woods, Donald. *BIKO.* New York: Henry Holt & Co., 1987.

Chapter 8

Bermont, Hubert, *The Complete Consultant.* Washington, DC: The Consultant's Library, Bermont Books, Inc., 1982.
Hameroff, Eugene J., and Sandra S. Nichols. *How to Guarantee Professional Success.* Washington, DC: The Consultant's Library, Bermont Books, Inc. 1982.
Rich, Andrew M., *How to Survive & Succeed in a Small Financial Planning Practice.* New York: Reston Division of Simon & Schuster, 1984.
Schiffman, Stephan, *The Consultant's Handbook.* Boston, MA: Bob Adams, Inc., 1988.

Chapter 9

Comiskey, James C. *How to Start, Expand and Sell a Business.* New York: Venture Prospectives Press, 1985.
Corder, Gene L. *The Five Deadly Mistakes that Lead to Bankruptcy! A Successful Business Handbook for Today's Men & Women.* New York: Redcor Book Publishing Co., 1981.
Goldstein, Arnold S. *Starting on a Shoestring.* New York: Wiley & Sons, Inc., 1984.
Gustafson, Ray L. *Buying, Selling, Starting a Business.* New York: GHC Press, 1982.
Mancuso, Joseph R. *Small Busines Survival Guide.* New York: Prentice-Hall, 1980.
Mucciolo, Louis. *Make It Yours: How to Own Your Own Business.* New York: Wiley & Sons, Inc., 1987.
Nichols, Ted. *Where the Money Is and How to Get It.* Wilmington, DE: Enterprise Publishing, 1980.
O'Brien, Robert. *Marriott: The J. Willard Marriott Story.* Salt Lake City, UT: Deseret Book Company, 1987.
Stevens, Mark. *Leveraged Finance: How to Raise and Invest Capital.* New York: Prentice-Hall, 1980.
Tuller, Lawrence W. *Getting Out: A Step-by-Step Guide to Selling a Business or Professional Practice.* Blue Ridge Summit, PA: TAB Books, Inc., 1990.

Chapter 10

Bunn, Verne A. *Buying and Selling a Small Business.* New York: Arno Press, 1979.

Comisky, James C. *Negotiating the Purchase or Sale of a Business.* New York: PSI Research, 1986.

Douglas, F. Gordon. *How to Profitably Sell or Buy a Company or Business.* New York: Van Nostrand Reinhold Co., 1981.

Editors of *Venture Magazine, Guide to International Venture Capital.* New York: Simon & Schuster, 1985.

Goldstein, Arnold S. *The Complete Guide to Buying and Selling a Business.* New York: New American Library, 1986.

Klueger, Robert F. *Buying and Selling a Business.* New York: Wiley & Sons, 1988.

Marren, Joseph H. *Mergers & Acquisitions: Will You Overpay?* Homewood, IL: Dow Jones-Irwin, 1985.

Michel, Allen, and Israel Shaked. *The Complete Guide to a Successful Leveraged Buyout.* Homewood, IL: Dow Jones-Irwin, 1987.

Pratt, Stanley E., ed. *Guide to Venture Capital Sources.* Washington, DC: Capital Publishing Corp., 1982.

Sharf, Charles A., et al. *Acquisitions, Mergers, Sales, Buyouts & Takeovers: A Handbook With Forms.* New York: Prentice-Hall, 1985.

Spurga, Ronald C. *Anatomy of a Bankruptcy: A Lending Primer for Commercial Bankers.* New York: Ballinger Publications, 1987.

Tuller, Lawrence W. *Buying In: A Complete Guide to Acquiring a Business or Professional Practice,* in press.

Weschsberg, Joseph, The Merchant Bankers. New York: Pocket Books, 1966.

Chapter 11

Crumbly, Larry D. *Handbook of Estate Planning,* Homewood, IL: Dow Jones-Irwin, 1988.

Lipper, Arthur III, with George Ryan. *Guide to Investing in Private Companies.* Homewood, IL: Dow Jones-Irwin, 1984.

Petterle, Elmo A. *Legacy of Love: How to Make Life Easier for Those You Leave Behind.* New York: Shelter Publications, Inc., 1986.

Plotnick, Charles, and Stephan Leimberg. *Get Rich—Stay Rich: Making It, Keeping It, Passing It Along Under the New Tax Laws.* New York: Stein & Day, 1984.

Starr, Herbert F. *Estate Planning Made Easy.* Blue Ridge Summit, PA: TAB Books, Inc., 1984.

Weinstock, Harold. *Planning An Estate: A Guidebook of Principles and Techniques.* New York: Shepards-McGraw Hill, 1982.

APPENDIXES

APPENDIX A

ACQUISITION BUSINESS PLAN

Table of Contents

C. Market and Product Analysis
   1. Market Economics
   2. Competition and Market Share Analysis
   3. Product Applications and Product Life Cycles
   4. Pricing Policies
   5. Distribution Channels
   6. Marketing/Sales Organization
       i. Current
       ii. Future Plans
D. Manufacturing Analysis
   1. Plant Layout and Material Flow
   2. Manufacturing and Cost Systems
   3. Manufacturing Organization Chart
   4. Capital Expenditures – Historical, Projected
   5. Utilization and Capacity Analysis
E. Personnel
   1. Total Company Organization Chart
   2. Personal Resumes of Key Management
   3. Historical, Current, Projected Manpower Head-
      counts
   4. Labor Relations/Union Contract
   5. Pension Plan and Other Benefit Programs
F. Facilities
   1. Real Estate Description
   2. Listing of Equipment
   3. Outstanding Liens
   4. Real Estate and/or Equipment Lease Arrange-
      ments
   5. Current Appraisals – Real Estate and Equipment
G. Financial
   1. Three Years Historical P & L's, Balance Sheets
      and Statements of Cash Flow
   2. Three Years Corporate Income Tax Returns
   3. Listing of Assumptions Made for Pro Formas
   4. Five Year Pro Forma P & L's, Balance Sheets and
      Statements of Cash Flow – with and without pro-
      posed Acquisition Financing
   5. Calculation of Debt and Equity Return and Pay-
      back

APPENDIX B

INVESTMENT BANKS AND VENTURE CAPITAL FIRMS

ACQUIVEST GROUP, INC.
1 Newtown Executive Park
Suite 204
Newton, MA 01262

ADVEST INCORPORATED
6 Central Row
Hartford, CT 06103

**ALLIED CAPITAL
CORPORATION**
1625 I Street, NW., Suite 603
Washington, DC 20006

ALLSTATE INSURANCE CO.
Allstate Plaza E-2
Northbrook, IL 60062

AMERVEST CORPORATION
10 Commercial Wharf West
Boston, MA 02110

AMEV CAPITAL CORP.
1 World Trade Center, 50th Floor
New York, NY 10048

**ATLANTIC AMERICAN
CAPITAL, LTD.**
Lincoln Center. Suite 851
5401 W. Kennedy Blvd.
Tampa, FL 33609

**ATLANTIC VENTURE
PARTNERS**
P.O. Box 1493
Richmond, VA 23212

**BANCBOSTON CAPITAL
CORP.**
100 Federal Street
Boston, MA 02110

**BANKAMERICA CAPITAL
CORPORATION**
555 California Street, 42nd Floor
San Francisco, CA 94104

BEAR STERNS & COMPANY
Investment Banking Division
55 Water St.
New York, NY 10041

**BLAKE INVESTMENT
  GROUP**
1101–30th Street, NW, Suite 101
Washington, DC 20007

BNE ASSOCIATES
Bank of New England
60 State Street
Boston, MA 02109

BRADFORD ASSOCIATES
22 Chambers Street
Princeton, NJ 08540

BUTLER CAPITAL CORP.
767 Fifth Avenue, Sixth Floor
New York, NY 10153

**CAPITAL CORPORATION
  OF AMERICA**
225 So. 15th Street, Suite 920
Philadelphia, PA 19102

CARL MARKS & CO., INC.
77 Water Street
New York, NY 10005

CHARLES DeTHAN GROUP
51 E. 67th Street
New York, NY 10021

**CHARTERHOUSE GROUP
  INTERNATIONAL**
535 Madison Avenue,
New York, NY 10022

**CHASE MANHATTAN
  CAPITAL MARKETS**
1 Chase Manhattan Plaza–
  3rd Flr
New York, NY 10081

**CITICORP VENTURE
  CAPITAL, LTD.**
Citicorp Center
153 E. 53rd Street, 28th Floor
New York, NY 10043

**CONNECTICUT NATIONAL
  BANK**
Investment Banking Division
1604 Walnut Street
Philadelphia, PA 19103

**CONTINENTAL ILLINOIS
  VENTURE CORP.**
231 So. LaSalle Street
Chicago, IL 60697

DAIN BOSWORTH, INC.
100 Dain Tower
Minneapolis, MN 55402

**DILLON REED &
  COMPANY, INC.**
535 Madison Avenue
New York, NY 10022

DJS GROUP
745 Park Avenue, 21st Floor
New York, NY 10155

**DREXEL BURNHAM
  LAMBERT, INC.**
55 Broad Street
New York, NY 10004

E.F. HUTTON LBO, INC.
1 Battery Park Plaza
New York, NY 10004

**EAB VENTURE
  CORPORATION**
90 Park Avenue
New York, NY 10016

FIDELITY BANK
Investment Banking Division
Broad & Walnut, Sixth Floor
Philadelphia, PA 19109

**FIRST CHICAGO VENTURE
  CAPITAL**
1 First National Plaza
Suite 2628
Chicago, IL 60670

FIRST CONNECTICUT SBIC
177 State Street
Bridgeport, CT 06604

**FIRST INTERSTATE
  CAPITAL CORP.**
515 So. Figueroa Street
Los Angeles, CA 90071

**FLEET GROWTH
  INDUSTRIES, INC.**
111 Westminster St.
Providence, RI 02903

**FOOTHILL CAPITAL
  CORPORATION**
2049 Century Park East
Los Angeles, CA 90067

**FOUNDERS VENTURES,
  INC.**
477 Madison Avenue
New York, NY 10022

**FRONTENAC CAPITAL
  CORP.**
208 So. LaSalle Street
Suite 1900
Chicago, IL 60604

**GENERAL ELECTRIC
  VENTURE CAPITAL**
3135 Easton Turnpike
Fairfield, CT 06431

**GOLDER, THOMA &
  CRESSEY**
120 So. LaSalle Street
Chicago, IL 60603

HAMBRECHT & QUIST
235 Montgomery Street
San Francisco, CA 94104

**HAMBRO INTERNATIONAL
  VENTURE FUND**
17 E. 71st Street
New York, NY 10021

HILLMAN VENTURES, INC.
2000 Grant Bldg.
Pittsburgh, PA 15219

**HOWARD, LAWSON & CO.,
  INC.**
2 Penn Center Plaza
Philadelphia, PA 19102

**INTERFIRST VENTURE
  CORPORATION**
P.O. Box 83644
Dallas, TX 75283

**ITC CAPITAL
CORPORATION**
1290 Avenue of the Americas
New York, NY 10104

**JAMES RIVER CAPITAL
ASSOCIATES**
9 So. 12th Street
Richmond, VA 23219

**JOHN HANCOCK VENTURE
CAPITAL MANAGEMENT,
INC.**
John Hancock Place, 57th Floor
Boston, MA 02117

**KEELEY MANAGEMENT
COMPANY**
2 Radnor Corporate Center
Radnor, PA 19087

**KIDDER PEABODY &
COMPANY**
Investment Banking Division
Mellon Bank Center
Philadelphia, PA 19102

**LEPERQ de NEUFLIZE &
COMPANY**
345 Park Avenue
New York, NY 10154

**MANUFACTURERS
HANOVER VENTURE
CAPITAL CORP.**
140 E. 45th Street
New York, NY 10017

**MARYLAND NATIONAL
BANK**
Investment Banking Group
P.O. Box 987
Baltimore, MD 21203

MELLON BANK
Corporate Finance Group
Mellon Bank Center
Philadelphia, PA 19102

MENLO VENTURE
3000 Sand Hill Road
Menlo Park, CA 94025

**MERIDIAN VENTURE
PARTNERS**
259 Radnor-Chester Rd.
Radnor, PA 19087

**MIDLAND CAPITAL
CORPORATION**
950 Third Avenue
New York, NY 10022

NARRAGANSETT CAPITAL
40 Westminster Street
Providence, RI 02903

**NORWEST VENTURE
CAPITAL MANAGEMENT**
1730 Midwest Plaza Bldg.
801 Nicollet Mall
Minneapolis, MN 55402

OXFORD PARTNERS
Soundview Plaza
1266 Main Street
Stamford, CT 06902

**PAINE WEBBER VENTURE
  MANAGEMENT**
100 Federal Street
Boston, MA 02110

**PENNWOOD CAPITAL
  CORPORATION**
645 Madison Avenue
New York, NY 10022

**PHILADELPHIA CAPITAL
  ADVISORS**
Philadelphia National Bank
  Bldg.
Broad & Chestnut Streets
Philadelphia, PA 19107

**PNC VENTURE CAPITAL
  GROUP**
Fifth Avenue & Woods Streets
Pittsburgh, PA 15222

**PRU CAPITAL,
  INCORPORATED**
1 Seaport Plaza, 31st Floor
199 Water Street
New York, NY 10292

QUINCY PARTNERS
P.O. Box 154
Glen Head, NY 11545

ROSENFELD & COMPANY
625 SW Washington Street
Portland, OR 97205

**ROTHSCHILD,
  INCORPORATED**
Rockefeller Plaza
New York, NY 10020

RUST VENTURES LP
114 W. Seventh Street
Suite 1300
Austin, TX 78701

SALOMON BROTHERS, INC.
1 New York Plaza
New York, NY 10004

**SECURITY PACIFIC
  CAPITAL CORP.**
4000 MacArthur Blvd., Suite 950
Newport Beach, CA 92660

**SEIDLER AMDEC
  SECURITIES, INC.**
515 So. Figueroa Street
Los Angeles, CA 90071

**SMITH, BARNEY, HARRIS,
  UPHAM**
1345 Avenue of the Americas
New York, NY 10105

SPROUT CAPITAL GROUP
140 Broadway
New York, NY 10025

SUMMIT VENTURES
1 Boston Place
Boston, MA 02108

TA ASSOCIATES
45 Milk Street
Boston, MA 02109

TDH II LIMITED
c/o K.S. Sweet Associates
P.O. Box 6780
Radnor, PA 19087

TUCKER ANTHONY AND RL DAY, INC.
120 Broadway
New York, NY 10271

UNION VENTURE CORPORATION
445 So. Figueroa Street
Los Angeles, CA 90071

WARBURG, PINCUS VENTURES, INC.
466 Lexington Avenue
New York, NY 10017

WELLS FARGO EQUITY CORPORATION
1 Embarcadero Center
San Francisco, CA 94111

WELSH, CARSON, ANDERSON & STOWE
45 Wall Street, 16th Floor
New York, NY 10005

WILLIAM BLAIR VENTURE PARTNERS
135 So. LaSalle Street, 29th Floor
Chicago, IL 60603

WISSAHICKON PARTNERS
19 Vandeventer Avenue
Princeton, NJ 08542

APPENDIX C

ASSET BASED LENDERS

CONGRESS FINANCIAL CORPORATION
American City Bldg.
Columbia, MD 21044

GENERAL ELECTRIC CREDIT CORPORATION
Eastern Corporate Finance Dept.
3003 Summer Street
Stamford, CT 06905

GLENFED CAPITAL CORPORATION
Carnegie Center
Princeton, NJ 08540

ITT CAPITAL CORPORATION
1400 North Central Life Tower
St. Paul, MN 55101

SECURITY PACIFIC BUSINESS CREDIT, INC.
45 So. Hudson Avenue
Pasadena, CA 91101

TREFOIL CAPITAL
Fidelity Bank Bldg.
Broad & Walnut Streets
Philadelphia, PA 19109

APPENDIX D

LETTER OF INTENT

This letter will confirm the intention of _____ ("Buyer") to proceed to draft an Offer to Purchase all of the assets and/or common stock of _____ ("Company") as soon as negotiations concerning the aggregate purchase price and terms of sale have been negotiated.

Buyer is prepared to proceed promptly to negotiate such price and terms, to draft and present such an Offer to Purchase, to perform the formal investigations and "due diligence," and to negotiate and draft as rapidly as possible a definitive purchase agreement acceptable to both parties. It is understood by both parties that Buyer will make a detailed review and analysis of the business, financial conditions and prospects of the Company and that Buyer must be satisfied in all respects with the results of its review and analysis prior to the execution of any definitive purchase agreement.

Upon acceptance of this letter, Seller agrees to furnish Buyer with sufficient information regarding the condition and affairs of the Company to enable Buyer to proceed with the abovementioned Offer to Purchase and to negotiate to conclusion such price and terms as will be mutually acceptable. Seller further agrees that until such time as negotiations are terminated by either party, Seller will not continue nor begin any negotiations or make any business disclosures with or to any potential buyer other than the Buyer, as defined herein.

Neither party shall have any legal obligation to the other with respect to the transaction contemplated herein unless and until the parties have executed and delivered a definitive purchase agreement, at which point all obligations and rights of the parties hereto shall be governed by such agreement.

SELLER   BUYER

_____   _____

Date_____   Date_____

APPENDIX E

CONFIDENTIALITY AGREEMENT

Dear Mr. ____ :

This letter is written with respect to the furnishing of certain

information to _____ ("Buyer") regarding Buyer's

possible acquisition of _____ ("Company") from

_____ ("Seller").

In consideration of Seller furnishing to Buyer certain information, all of which Seller regards as confidential ("the Confidential Information"), relating to the Company's business, assets, rights, liabilities and obligations, Buyer hereby agrees as follows:

1. The Confidential Information will be used solely for the purpose of evaluating a possible transaction between Buyer and Seller, and such information will be kept confidential by Buyer and its advisors; provided, however, that (i) any of such information may be disclosed to Buyer's employees and representatives who need to know such information for the purpose of evaluating any such possible transaction between Buyer and Seller (it being understood that such employees and representatives shall be informed by Buyer of the confidential nature of such information and shall be directed by Buyer to treat such information confidentially), and (ii) any disclosure of such information may be made to which Seller consents in writing.

2. The restrictions set forth in paragraph 1 shall not apply to any part of the Confidential Information which:

(a) was at the time of disclosure or thereafter becomes generally available to the public other than as a result of a disclosure by Buyer; or

(b) was at the time of the disclosure, as shown by Buyer's records, already in Buyer's possession on a lawful basis; or,

(c) is lawfully acquired after the time of the disclosure by Buyer through a third party under no obligation of confidence to Seller.

3. Buyer will not disclose to any person either the fact that discussions or negotiations are taking place concerning a possible transaction relating to the Confidential Information or any of the terms, conditions or other facts with respect to any such possible transaction, including the status thereof.

4. At any time, upon the request of Seller, Buyer shall return the Confidential Information to Seller and shall not retain any copies or other reproductions or extracts thereof. At such time all documents, memoranda, notes and other writings whatsoever prepared by Buyer relating to the Confidential Information shall be destroyed.

Sincerely,

President

APPENDIX F

MERGER AND ACQUISITION CONSULTANTS AND LARGER BUSINESS BROKERS

A.H. Gruetzmacher and
   Company
39 South LaSalle Street
Chicago, IL 60603

Albert L. Emmons
580 Jackson Avenue
Westwood, NJ 07675

Arnold S. Cohen Company
1290 Avenue of the Americas
Suite 1614
New York, NY 10104

Bollinger/Wells
230 Park Avenue
New York, NY 10169

Charles K. Murray Associates,
   Inc.
P.O. Box 1406
Greenwich, CT 06836

Corporate Development, Inc.
2235 Park Towne Circle
Suite 100
Sacramento, CA 95825

David A. Faries & Associates
67 Central Avenue
Los Gatos, CA 95030

Duff & Phelps, Inc.
55 East Monroe Street
Chicago, IL 60603

First Corporate Group
100 Northcreek—Suite 108
Atlanta, GA 30327

First Manhattan Group
77 Water Street
New York, NY 10005

FirstMain Associates, Inc.
8235 Douglas Avenue, LB 58
Dallas, TX 75225

Geneva Business Services, Inc.
2923 Pullman
Santa Ana, CA 92705

Growth Dynamics, Inc.
595 Madison Avenue
New York, NY 10022

Hammond, Kennedy &
  Company, Inc.
230 Park Avenue
New York, NY 10169

Howard M. Singer, Inc.
280 Madison Avenue
New York, NY 10016

HRK Associates, Inc.
690 Island Way—Suite 206
Clearwater, FL 33515

Irving B. Gruber
2409 Marbury Road
Pittsburgh, PA 15221

James Brown, Inc.
31 North Porchuck Rd.
Greenwich, CT 06830

John DeElorza Associates
1640 Vaux Hall Rd.
Union, NJ 07083

Joseph W. Prane Co.
213 Church Rd.
Elkins Park, PA 19117

Kenroy Associates, Inc.
20 West Ridgewood Avenue
Ridgewood, NJ 07450

Kyle & Hayes-Morrison
234 Fountainville Center
Fountainville, PA 18923

M + A International, Inc.
600 Cherry St., Suite 1125
Denver, CO 80222

M. Michael Cantor
2150 Ibis Isle Rd., Apt. 14
Palm Beach, FL 33480

MacKenzie Associates, Inc.
111 Presidential Blvd.
Bala Cynwyd, PA 19004

Management Services
  Worldwide
2201 Route 38
The Executive Bldg.
Cherry Hill, NJ 08002

Manhattan Venture Company
340 East 57th Street
New York, NY 10022

Merge Master Company
26 Linden Avenue
Springfield, NJ 07081

Morgan Merritt, Inc.
4000 Town Center—Suite 190
Southfield, MI 48075

Norton Stuart Consultants
P.O. Box 250
Lansdowne, PA 19050

Perreault & Co., Inc.
5656 Stetson Ct.
Anaheim Hills, CA 92807

Pierce International, Ltd.
1910 K Street NW
Washington, DC 20006

Ralph K. Heyman
230 Park Avenue—Suite 1518
New York, NY 10169

Richard H. Rabner & Associates
151 So. Warner Rd.
Wayne, PA 19087

Robert H. Perry & Associates
Greensboro, NC

Roy Bonwick Associates, Inc.
5 South Main Street
Suite 522
Branford, CT 06405

Sigma Companies, Inc.
410 North Michigan Avenue
Chicago, IL 60611

Throne & Company
205 East Joppa Rd—Suite 108
Baltimore, MD 21204

William H. Hill Associates, Inc.
3100 University Blvd South
Suite 210
Jacksonville, FL 32216

Wright-Wyman, Inc.
211 Congress Street
Boston, MA 02110

Zunder Company
1100 Alma St.—Suite 204
Menlo Park, CA 94025

APPENDIX G

VOLUNTEER AND OTHER SOCIAL SERVICES ORGANIZATIONS

ACTION
806 Connecticut Ave., NW
Washington, DC 20525
(202) 634-9135

Amnesty International U.S.A.
National Office
322 Eighth Avenue
New York, NY 10001

OR

International Secretariat
Amnesty International
1 Easton Street
London WC1X 8DJ
United Kingdom

Concern
P.O. Box 1790
Santa Ana, CA 92702
(714) 953-8575

Fourth World Movement
172 First Avenue
New York, NY 10009
(212) 228-1339

Greenpeace
1436 U Street N.W.
P.O. Box 3720
Washington, DC 20007

Habitat For Humanity, Inc.
419 West Church Street
Americus, GA 31709
(912) 924-6935

Heifer Project International
  Learning and Livestock Center
Rte. 2, Box 3
Perryville, AR 72126
(501) 889-5124

International Executive Service
  Corps (IESC)
P.O. Box 10005
Stamford, CT 06904-2005
(203) 967-6000

International Voluntary
  Services, Inc. (IVS)
1424 Sixteenth Street, NW—
  Suite 204
Washington, DC 20036
(202) 387-5533

Medical Volunteers
 International (MVI)
1215 Sixth Avenue
San Francisco, CA 94122
(415) 661-8666

Project Hope
Millwood, VA 22646
(703) 837-2100

Simon Community
129 Malden Rd.
London NW5 4HS, England
(01) 485-6639

Technica
2727 College Ave.
Berkeley, CA 94705
(415) 848-0292

United Nations Volunteers
 (UNV)
Palais des Nations
1211 Geneva 10
Switzerland

U.S. Peace Corps
Office of Recruitment
Room P-301
806 Connecticut Avenue, NW
Washington, DC 20526
(800) 424-8580, Ext. 93

Volunteers in Technical
 Assistance, Inc. (VITA)
1815 North Lynn St.,
 Suite 200
Arlington, VA 22309
(703) 276-1800

APPENDIX H

PERSONAL STATEMENTS OF FINANCIAL CONDITION

Prepared (date) _____ Updated _____

Cash in bank–   *Amount*
   List bank account numbers   _____
                                _____
                                _____
                                _____

Stocks, Bonds, Investment Funds
   (including stock options)
Broker Company # of shares   *Value Last Statement*
                                _____
                                _____
                                _____
                                _____
                                _____

IRAs, Company Pension, Trusts
   Custodian   *Value Last Statement*
                                _____
                                _____
                                _____
                                _____
                                _____

Life insurance and annunities
   Company   Face Value   *Cash Value Last Statement*
                                _____
                                _____
                                _____
                                _____

Personal Assets Which Can Be
Converted to Cash   *Current Market Value*
House   _____
Second/third cars   _____
Household items not needed—   _____
furniture, lawn equipment,   _____
office equipment, etc.   _____
Jewelry   _____
Antiques   _____
Collections—stamps, coins, etc.   _____
Boat/airplane   _____
Motorcycle   _____
Other assets not included
above (list)   _____
Other Investment Assets with
Market Value   *Current Market Value*
Vacation home   _____
Land   _____
Trusts   _____
Rental property   _____
Other assets   _____
  TOTAL CASH VALUE OF
  ASSETS   _____
Debts Which Must Be Paid   *Current Balance*
House mortgage   _____
Life insurance loans   _____
Loans from credit union   _____
Loans from banks (list)   _____
      _____
      _____
      _____

All credit card balances   _____
Other debts   _____
  TOTAL DEBTS WHICH
  MUST BE PAID   _____
CURRENT CASH AVAILABLE
IN AN EMERGENCY
(Subtract total Debts from
total Assets)   _____

PERSONAL STATEMENT OF LIVING INCOME AND EXPENSES

Prepared_____   Updated_____

Annual Income
  Dividends   _____
  Interest   _____
  Annuities   _____
  Rent   _____
  Company pension   _____
  Government pension   _____
  Alimony   _____
  Income from spouse   _____
  Other regular income (list)   _____
    TOTAL ANNUAL INCOME   _____

Annual Expenses
  Household—
    Heating oil, Gas   _____
    Electricity   _____
    Water   _____
    Telephone   _____
    Mortgage payment or rent   _____
    Real estate taxes   _____
    Repairs and maintenance   _____
    Redecorating   _____
  Insurance—
    House   _____
    Auto   _____
    Life   _____
    Health   _____
    Other   _____
  Auto—
    Gas and oil   _____
    Repairs and maintenance   _____
    Tires   _____
  Dues and subscriptions   _____
  Clothes—
    Yourself   _____
    Spouse   _____
    Children   _____
  Medical, including eye glasses   _____

Dental   _____

Contributions and gifts, total   _____

Legal and accounting fees   _____

Travel expenses for vacations/
  trips   _____

Entertainment   _____

College and other educational
  expenses   _____

Alimony   _____

Other expenses (list)   _____

                                             _____

                                             _____

TOTAL ANNUAL EXPENSES   _____

EXCESS INCOME OVER
  EXPENSES   _____

APPENDIX I

GUIDELINES FOR DAILY LIVING FROM SYMPOSIUM ON COMMUNITY PRACTICE

1. *Honesty.* No more lies. No more secrets. When the temptation arises to tell a fib, restrain yourself. If a lie or a half truth slips out, correct what you have said immediately. Don't embellish a story to make it sound better. Don't repeat gossip. Take the blame if something is wrong. Pass along the credit if someone does something good or right. Don't take credit for someone else's actions or ideas. Openly admit errors. If you have a problem or don't know how to do a task, or can't complete a project, admit that you are stumped and ask for help.

2. *Responsibility.* Openly acknowledge responsibility for your own actions each day. If you've taken an action harmful to someone else or said something derogatory about someone, openly admit to the person hurt that you are in error. Apologize. Confess the weakness that caused you to take the action or say the words. Never leave the office or home knowing that you have committed a wrong without acknowledging openly that you are at fault.

3. *Self-indulgence.* Do one thing for yourself and by yourself each day. No matter how small or seemingly insignificant, pamper yourself with something. Enjoy a dessert for lunch if you're dieting. Buy a new purse or tie. Treat yourself to an ice cream cone. Pick up a new book you've wanted to read. Go for a walk.

4. *Bad feelings.* Resolve disputes with family and friends as they arise—don't go to bed with anger, shame or frustration in your heart. If a family member or friend does something or says something that makes you angry, tell him how you feel right

away and get the dispute out in the open. If the shoe is on the other foot and you feel ashamed of your actions, confess how you feel. When frustrated by an event or someone else's actions, talk about it, try to resolve the issue and put it to rest. Don't let problems fester overnight.

5. *Kindness.* Say something kind to your boss each day. Say something kind to a subordinate each day. Compliment someone for what they are wearing or how good they look. Offer to help with a problem even if it's only listening. Go out of your way to cooperate in getting something done. Offer to help someone with his job or task. Wear a smile. Spend quality time just listening or talking with someone. Never be too busy to stop and listen carefully to the other person, even if you're bored or don't care about what he is saying. If you can't say something good about somebody, don't say anything.

INDEX